'This ground-breaking book exposes the econo[...] shape our homes and the work that goes on ins[...]

Bridget Anderson, University of Bristol

'In the first large-scale investigation of a largely hidden world, the authors provide an incisive account of the lived experiences of au pairs and their host families, showing how au pairing has become an integral part of austerity Britain.'

Majella Kilkey, University of Sheffield

'This informative and incisive study reveals the relations of care, inter-dependence, affection and exploitation as young women from Europe "help" more affluent women. The authors provide an indisputable case for reform.'

Linda McDowell, Oxford University (Emerita)

'A revelatory study. This is essential reading for anyone who wants to understand the conundrums and inequalities framing the global crisis of work and care.'

Mary Romero, author of *The Maid's Daughter: Living Inside and Outside the American Dream*

'Fills an important lacuna in the area of transnational migrant domestic and care work. A must read for students and scholars of care work in the age of neoliberal care regimes.'

Helma Lutz, author of *The New Maids*

'A very important contribution to understanding current variations of domestic labour. Brilliantly places the phenomenon of au pairing both in a historical context and in the present-day neoliberal reality of the UK.'

Helle Stenum, Roskilde University

'Brimming with insights, this book challenges the stereotype of the au pair as an equal member of a "traditional" English family. The authors expose the problematic nature of au pairing at a time of deregulation and hidden exploitation.'

Helen Jarvis, Newcastle University

'A much needed account of the reality of au pairing, which also poignantly illustrates how intersectional inequalities are produced in today's Europe. An insightful read for all social scientists.'

Sabrina Marchetti, Ca' Foscari University of Venice

'Using the voices of both au pairs and their hosts, the book expertly demonstrates how the historical context and structural inequalities which frame au p[...] [...]e UK.'

[...]k University

ABOUT THE AUTHORS

Rosie Cox is Professor of Geography at Birkbeck, University of London. She has been researching au pairs and other forms of paid domestic labour in the UK for nearly 20 years. She is the author of *The Servant Problem: Domestic Employment in a Global Economy* (2006), co-editor of *Dirt: New Geographies of Cleanliness and Contamination* (2007), co-author of *Reconnecting Consumers, Producers and Food: Exploring Alternatives* (2008), *Dirt: The Filthy Reality of Everyday Life* (2011) and editor of *Au Pairs' Lives in Global Context* (2015).

Nicky Busch is an academic and author with a particular interest in gender, care and domestic work and migration. She lives in London.

AS AN EQUAL?

AU PAIRING IN THE 21ST CENTURY

Rosie Cox and Nicky Busch

ZED

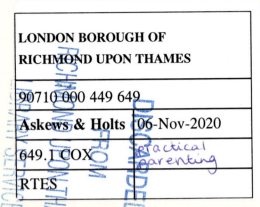
As an Equal? Au Pairing in the 21st Century was first published in 2018 by Zed Books Ltd, The Foundry, 17 Oval Way, London SE11 5RR, UK.

www.zedbooks.net

Typeset in Plantin and Kievit by Swales & Willis Ltd, Exeter, Devon
Index by Rohan Bolton
Cover design by Kika Sroka-Miller
Cover photo © Dmitry Zimin/Shutterstock

A catalogue record for this book is available from the British Library

ISBN 978–1–78360–498–2 hb
ISBN 978–1–78360–497–5 pb
ISBN 978–1–78360–499–9 pdf
ISBN 978–1–78360–500–2 epub
ISBN 978–1–78360–501–9 mobi

Printed and bound in Great Britain by CPI Group (UK) Ltd, Croydon CR0 4YY

MIX
Paper from
responsible sources
FSC® C020471
www.fsc.org

For Ava and Kip Montgomery

CONTENTS

ILLUSTRATIONS

ACKNOWLEDGEMENTS

We would like to thank everyone who participated in our research for giving their time so generously to help us learn about au pairs in contemporary Britain. We would also like to thank Kim Walker at Zed for her patience and encouragement, the anonymous reader for their enthusiasm and helpful comments and Saoirse Cox for her good-humoured and rapid help with reference checking and editing.

This work was funded by ESRC grant ES/J007528/1.

INTRODUCTION

This book examines the experiences of au pairs and 'host families' in the UK during a period of deregulation of the au pair sector and disinvestment in publicly provided childcare. It explores the ways in which inequalities of gender, class, race/ethnicity, nationality and citizenship shape the lives of hosts and au pairs and the organisation of au pairing. As the title suggests, we question how possible it is to live 'as an equal' – the translation of the phrase 'au pair' – in an unequal world.

At the time we carried out the research for this book (2012–2014) au pairing was booming in the UK, particularly in London and southeast England. Various forms of deregulation had created a situation where government exercised no control and made no effective interventions in the sector, entirely unregulated online agencies made finding an au pair or a host cheap and easy, rising costs and limited supply of flexible group childcare fuelled demand for in-home care and, following the global financial crisis of 2008, high rates of youth unemployment in many EU countries fuelled the supply of au pairs.

Au pairing matters, not only to the lives of the thousands of au pairs and host families directly involved in it, but because it is a result of the convergence of historically enduring gender inequalities with a number of global-scale trends which increasingly characterise contemporary social life. Au pairing is an example of what happens in highly unequal, poorly regulated, international labour markets. As Zuzana Uhde (2016 pp683–684) comments:

> [T]he commodification of care in the context of global capitalism reinforces the institution of paid care as a low paid and precarious sector. The negative consequences of this development are distributed along class and 'racial'-ethnic social structures: on one hand market caring services are financially accessible only to higher and middle classes, and on the other hand these jobs with disadvantaged and risk statuses are designed for women from minority groups and lower classes. The processes of marketization and commodification did not turn the private public: it is still private within a private economy.

Like many other low paid migrants in Britain, au pairs are an example of a group of workers who are outside formal labour markets and who lack the protections available to other groups. While Uber drivers and Deliveroo couriers are left without rights through the use of bogus self-employment, and many other workers find themselves on zero-hours contracts, au pairs' work is quite simply defined as not 'work'. This negation of au pairs' labour and the retelling of their efforts as 'help' and cultural exchange is possible because of the gendered nature of domestic work and relations within the private home. The inclusion of particular people – young, white, European women – in the category 'au pair' is possible because of centuries of prejudice about who does and does not do domestic labour and who is welcome within the intimate space of the 'British' family.

Throughout this book we explore how au pairs are produced as highly flexible, low-paid, 'non-workers' without rights. We argue that in the wider context of classed, gendered and ethnicised labour market and employment relations, the equality which is meant to characterise au pairing is rarely on the cards and, unlike most other low-paid migrant workers and their employers, hosts and au pairs have to negotiate this inequality within the intimate space of the home. This location is significant; the private household is a space which preserves and disguises inequality. It makes immediately available the imagining of relations motivated and organised by something other than the market, denying the value of work that is done there. The private location of au pairing means that online spaces matter too. The internet works as a back fence for the sharing of private information about the sector. Au pairs and hosts use online fora for matching and they use social media to compare, evaluate and critique their experiences. With the lack of regulation, this method of data gathering is too often part of a 'race to the bottom' in terms of pay and conditions for au pairs. Au pairing is shaped by structural problems – gender inequalities, racism and national stereotyping, punishing work and childcare cultures – all held together by regulatory neglect.

In this chapter we begin by looking at UK government policy on au pairs (and the lack of it), then explore the trends which have bolstered the growth of au pairing worldwide in recent years, before outlining the empirical research which underpins our arguments and the structure of the rest of the book.

Au pairs in twenty-first-century Britain

The first question to answer in a book on this topic is 'what do we mean by an au pair?' In twenty-first-century Britain, where there is no official definition and little guidance, the answer is not as easy as it might first appear. Broadly speaking, what an au pair is meant to be is perhaps best outlined by the 1969 Strasbourg Agreement, a treaty of the Council of Europe, to which a number of European countries (although not the UK) signed up and which, in the years following, shaped the basic understanding of au pairing worldwide, including in countries outside Europe and those in Europe which were not signatories. The agreement states (Council of Europe 1969 p2):

> 'Au pair' placement is the temporary reception by families, in exchange for certain services, of young foreigners who come to improve their linguistic and possibly professional knowledge as well as their general culture by acquiring a better knowledge of the country where they are received.

The agreement then goes on to detail the arrangement further, setting out a maximum stay of two years, an age range for the au pair of 17–30, that the au pair should be given room and board, including a separate room, remuneration called 'pocket money', at least one free day a week, opportunities to attend language classes and religious observation. In exchange for this, the au pair will help out with the 'day to day' duties of the family for not more than five hours per day. The Strasbourg Agreement reflects the general idea that an au pair is a young person who lives with a family in a foreign country on a temporary basis in order to improve their language skills, and, in exchange for room and board and a small amount of pocket money, helps out with household tasks such as housework and childcare.

The agreement was integrated into national policies in various different ways with various amendments, inclusions and exclusions in a number of countries. In Britain, until 2008, the basic understanding of au pairing expressed in the Strasbourg Agreement shaped the au pair visa. The visa set out that au pairs were to be aged 17–27, should work 25 hours a week plus two evenings of babysitting, be given room and board and opportunities for language learning or cultural exchange and be paid a specified amount of pocket money (£65 per week by 2008). Until 2008 au pairs could come from EEA (European Economic Area) member states, or from a list of other European countries (including Turkey); the list changed over time to reflect EU enlargement and to ensure that enough au pairs were available (in 2002 Bulgaria, Estonia, Latvia, Lithuania, Poland and Romania were added as countries which could send au pairs, see Cox 2006 and Chapter 1). While only those au pairs who were citizens of countries outside the EEA needed a visa, the definition provided by the visa applied to all au pairs and was used by au pairs, hosts, agencies and others to understand what an au pair was and was not.

Since 2008 there has not been an official, binding definition of au pairing in Britain and, as the rest of this book illustrates, that lack of definition has allowed for the mutation of understandings of what an au pair is and an elision of the roles of 'au pair' and 'nanny'. The government now (late 2017) provides some guidance as to what an au pair might be on the gov.uk website (see www.gov.uk/au-pairs-employment-law/au-pairs) and also points readers to the website of the British Au Pairs Agencies Association (BAPAA), a voluntary organisation of au pair agencies who work to promote au pairing and maintain standards in the industry. The guidance provided on the gov. uk website (see Box I.1) now has superficial similarity to the definition provided by the old UK au pair visa or the Strasbourg Agreement.

Despite the superficial similarity to earlier understandings, there are two aspects of this government guidance which prevent it being definitive and, therefore, limit its usefulness. The first is the phrase 'if most of the following apply' before the list of conditions which would be expected of an au pair placement. There are 12 items listed, suggesting that, perhaps, any five of these could be ignored and a person could still be called an 'au pair'. None of the listed characteristics is insisted upon, so it seems, that as far as the UK Government is concerned, an au pair might *not* be given time to attend language classes, be paid reasonable pocket money, be engaged in cultural exchange, eat meals with the host family free of charge or be provided with a room free of charge. The second, less visible, problem with this guidance is that it is not based on primary legislation. While the gov.uk website lists this under 'employment law' it does not, in fact, reflect legislation, other than the statement that au pairs are not entitled to minimum wage or paid holidays, which does reflect National Minimum Wage (NMW) legislation and the Working Time Directive – both of which specifically exclude au pairs from their protections.

Box I.1 UK Government guidance on au pairs as provided on the gov.uk website, December 2017

Au pairs usually live with the family they work for and are unlikely to be classed as a worker or an employee. They aren't entitled to the National Minimum Wage or paid holidays. They're treated as a member of the family they live with and get 'pocket money' instead – usually about £70 to £85 a week.

Au pairs may have to pay Income Tax and National Insurance, depending on how much pocket money they get.

An au pair isn't classed as a worker or an employee if most of the following apply:

- They're an EU citizen or have entered the UK on a Youth Mobility visa or student visa
- They're here on a cultural exchange programme
- They've got a signed letter of invitation from the host family that includes details of their stay, for example accommodation, living conditions, approximate working hour, free time, pocket money
- They learn about British culture from the host family and share their own culture with them
- They have their own private room in the house, provided free of charge
- They eat their main meals with the host family, free of charge
- They help with light housework and childcare for around 30 hours a week, including a couple of evening of babysitting
- They get reasonable pocket money
- They can attend English language classes at a local college in their spare time
- They're allowed time to study and can practise their English with the host family
- They sometimes go on holiday with the host family and help look after the children
- They can travel home to see their family during the year

The guidance provided by BAPAA (2017), and to which the gov.uk website links, is much clearer and more detailed. It sets out a maximum 30-hour working week to include babysitting, mandates paid holiday, own room and full board, emphasises that au pairs should not be left in sole charge of infants or left to care for children overnight, that they should be given opportunities and facilities to study and that host families should make a contribution to the cost of language classes. BAPAA also state that au pairs should spend most of their working hours carrying out childcare rather than housework and, very usefully, provide a list of tasks which it is not acceptable to expect an au pair to do. They also specify what should happen if an au pair arrangement needs to be terminated early (the host family must pay for bed-and-breakfast accommodation or a flight home plus two weeks' pocket money if they do not give sufficient notice) and provide guidance on many other aspects of au pair relationships which are often sources of tension.

Official ambiguity about exactly what is absolutely required for a role to be described as 'au pair' allows unscrupulous or uninformed hosts and agencies to offer 'au pair' posts which are a very long way from the initial intentions and general understandings of the scheme. The expansion of online fora – online au pair agencies and the use of sites such as Gumtree to advertise posts – means that there are now few checks on what is being presented as au pairing. For example, one website, www.startanaupairagency.co.uk, which provides advice to people wanting to set up an au pair agency, has an article titled 'What Is a Live Out Au Pair' (Stratford 2015). This article acknowledges that 'strictly speaking [live-out au pairs] do not adhere to the original intentions of the au pair programme or perhaps the "spirit" of the scheme', but just so long as they are EU nationals 'they do offer a service to families who are looking for this kind of person'. The article goes on to recommend paying a live-out au pair between £4.00 and £6.00 per hour, carefully putting the word 'pay' in inverted commas and providing guidance about how to stay within the law when entering into such an arrangement. This illustrates the ambiguity of government guidance, the lack of clarity about the difference between au pairing and other forms of paid childcare, and the ease with which the 'au pair' label can be applied in order to eliminate the need to pay National Minimum Wage. Someone working as a live-out au pair would be indistinguishable from a nanny or housekeeper, except for their lack of rights. In Chapter 4 we explore in more detail what the effects are of this sort of ambiguity.

Despite, or perhaps because of, this lack of recognition in official channels, au pairing appears to be booming in Britain in the early twenty-first century. As there is no official recognition of au pairs, there are, of course, no official figures on the number of people involved in au pairing, but estimates from the au pair industry and proxy measures such as analysis of advertisements for au pairs, suggest there may be 90,000–100,000 in the country (Smith 2008 and see below for more detail on our analysis of advertisements placed). One online agency, AuPairWorld, had 21,000 applications from people wanting to be au pairs in the UK in 2015 (Parfitt 2017). If these estimates are correct, it suggests that the UK has the largest number of au pairs anywhere in the world; the USA, by contrast, has around 17,500 (Kopplin 2017). Some reports indicate that the numbers of au pairs looking for posts in the UK fell after the vote to leave the EU in June 2017 (Parfitt 2017) but numbers still appear to be higher than for other countries for which figures exist.

The reasons why au pairs are so popular in Britain are not mysterious. Long working hours for parents, high childcare costs, the cultural devaluing of reproductive labour and the availability of a large, low-waged labour force from other EU countries all make au pairs an attractive option. For many British families au pairs are the only workable solution to the 'childcare crisis' as collective forms of care such as nurseries do not offer the hours many working parents need and, even if these are available, they can actually prove more expensive than hosting an au pair. The government's Money Advice Service advised that in 2017 a registered childminder for a child under two years old would cost £212.86 per week (£275.83 in London) and a nursery for one child under two would be £222.36 per week (£277.84 in London). Qualified nannies are prohibitively expensive for all but the most well-off families costing up to £650 per week plus tax, national insurance and room and board, that is £33,800 per year (see www.moneyadviceservice.org. uk/en/articles/childcare-costs) (median household disposable income in 2015/16 was £26,300 according to the ONS 2017). When more than one child needs care, these costs can multiply and other forms of childcare are unlikely to offer the flexibility of an au pair. In Chapters 2 and 3 we explore the trends which have underpinned the growth of au pairing in the UK, highlighting the complex social, political and cultural mix that has made au pairs a particularly practical and desirable solution to the problems families in Britain face with childcare.

Throughout this book we use the term 'au pair' to refer to people performing domestic work in private homes in the UK under conditions that can be seen to reflect varying interpretations by these individuals, their 'hosts' and au pair agencies of the conditions set out in the now-defunct UK au pair visa scheme, which were subsequently adopted by BAPAA. We use the term whilst acknowledging that the 'au pair scheme' no longer exists and the distinction between someone placed as an au pair and someone employed as a nanny is arbitrary. Despite the policy vacuum surrounding au pairing at the time of our research, the term remains in common use. We also use the term 'hosts' to refer to the people au pairs live with and work for, despite arguing that this term obfuscates their role as employers and is part of a discourse within the au pair sector which supports the idea that au pairs are involved in cultural exchange rather than work, or as well as work. We use the term 'hosts' because it is the common parlance within the sector, it also highlights that people who take on an au pair are meant to provide hospitality, rather than just pecuniary rewards.

Au pairing in global context

It is not only in the UK that au pairing has been growing; worldwide it seems that au pairing has grown alongside other forms of paid domestic work but has been relatively invisible in both official statistics and academic research. Au pairs' 'in-between' status – as not workers, students or residents – means that they are missed by almost all official statistics. This is largely because the au pair is imagined as both privileged and temporary (Cox 2015a), a problem in terms of neither welfare nor migration flows. The relaxed attitude towards au pair migration is at odds with broader anti-immigrant sentiment and polices that predominate in many au-pair-receiving countries (Cox 2007) and reflects the conceptualisation of au pairs as something other than labour migrants.

However, despite the lack of official data, there is substantial anecdotal, academic and industry evidence that au pairing has been growing globally in recent years and this growth is part of a broader expansion of migration for domestic work (see for example chapters in Cox 2015b). The International Au Pair Association (IAPA) (an organisation of au pair agencies) claims members in 45 countries worldwide, including China, Peru, Colombia and South Africa. There has also been a recent expansion in academic research on au pairs, revealing the experiences of au pairs in a wide range of situations (see chapters in Cox (2015b) for discussions of the UK, Australia, Ireland, Norway, USA, France; Gullikstad, Kristensen and Ringrose (2016) for UK and Norway; chapters in Isaksen (2010) for the Nordic countries, and articles in the 2016 special issue of *Nordic Journal of Migration Research*, edited by Caterina Rohde-Abuba and Olga Tkach, for discussions of au pairing in Denmark (Dalgas 2016); the UK (Búriková 2016; Cox and Busch 2016a); Russian au pairs in Germany (Rohde-Abuba 2016); au pairs from the Commonwealth of Independent States (CIS) in Norway (Tkach 2016) and German-speaking au pairs in the USA (Geserick 2016)). It is clear that au pairing has spread beyond its traditional European roots and is being adopted as a form of domestic work all around the world.

There is variety in the specific ways in which au pairs are defined in different national contexts; they work only 30 hours a week in Norway, and must be enrolled in language classes paid for by their host families (Gullikstad and Annfelt 2016; Løvdal 2015; Rohde-Abuba and Tkach 2016; see also Calleman 2010 for a description of au pair schemes in four Nordic countries), but in the USA can work 45 hours a week and can be native English speakers. In some countries (for example, the USA) only families with children living at home may host an au pair, in others, such as Australia (Berg 2015), no such restrictions apply. In all situations where the au pair role is officially defined it is as a form of cultural exchange rather than work, it involves living with a host family, and is a temporary status available only to migrants.

Related to their status as participants in cultural exchange, au pairs receive 'pocket money' rather than pay (except in the USA where a 1994 judgement from the Department of Labour determined that au pairs were employees and their remuneration was 'wages' (IRS 2013)) but the amount they are given, its regulation and the other benefits to which they are meant to have access vary considerably between national contexts. In the USA, for example, the stipend is tied to legal minimum wage rates, with au pairs receiving the minimum wage minus a deduction for accommodation (but not paying social security taxes and therefore having no rights to employment benefits). In most other countries, the situation is more like the UK, with au pairs not entitled to minimum wage rates. In Norway, au pairs do not earn minimum wage but pay tax on both their pocket money and an amount which is supposed to represent what their accommodation and food are worth. Their hosts do not pay the taxes that employers normally pay and as a result of this an au pair has only very limited social security rights. In Australia pocket money rates vary substantially and it is agencies rather than government which recommends how much au pairs should be given.

Most au pair schemes specify that au pairs are provided with their own room and given food, but the quantity and quality of these provisions is not defined. The quality of accommodation made available to au pairs can vary immensely from rooms shared with children to whole separate apartments. Food can be an additional expense for au pairs; providing themselves with foods that they like in the quantities they desire as alternatives to those given by the host family which may be unknown, too filling, not filling enough or just served at the wrong time of day can all eat into an au pair's small allowance (Búriková and Miller 2010). For au pairs on very low incomes all of these things matter.

The level of remuneration makes a material difference to au pairs and is an indication of the extent to which they are valued and their labour is respected. The regulation of 'pocket money' rates and other benefits is one of the most important ways in which au pairs' contradictory 'non-worker' position is constructed. Nowhere is there regulatory consistency around au pairs' status; in the USA, where au pairs have legally been deemed employees for tax reasons, they are still considered 'students' for immigration purposes and in Australia au pairs are considered to be working if they fall foul of immigration rules, but not considered to be workers for the purposes of employment laws that would offer them protection (Berg 2015; see also Løvdal 2015 for a similar situation in Norway). These contradictions both reflect and reproduce the idea that the tasks au pairs do are not real 'work' (see chapters in Cox 2015b for international comparison).

International comparison shows that despite no two countries having identical rules, the same ambiguities shape au pairing in all national contexts and they produce conditions which make many au pairs vulnerable to abuse and exploitation, and also make au pairs and many hosts subject to confusion and unnecessary emotional strain. The construction of au pairing as a form of cultural exchange, and the simultaneous denial of it as a form of work, is common around the world; this hides the value of the work that au pairs do, limits their rights and their pay and in the worst cases isolates them in conditions akin to slavery (Smith 2015).

Researching au pairs in contemporary Britain

This book is based on research carried out from 2012 to 2014, with au pairs, hosts and key actors in the sector. We have also analysed secondary data and online sources such as advertisements for au pairs on the website Gumtree.com and discussions on fora such as Mumsnet and Facebook. Given that there are no official sources of information about the numbers of au pairs in the UK, their working arrangements, pay or conditions, nor are there any third sector or other organisations that collect data about au pairs, we used a variety of methods to discover what we could about the au pair sector. In this section, we outline the methods used and some of the difficulties faced in researching au pairs in contemporary Britain.

One of the things that is urgently needed in order to understand au pairing in the UK is basic data about the sorts of work and living conditions which characterise the sector. In the absence of official data, we used advertisements for au pairs on website Gumtree.com to understand the nature of au pair work. Over a three-month period we collected the text of 1,000 advertisements – half placed in London and half in the rest of the country – and coded them into an excel spreadsheet, to capture quantifiable data on hours expected, pay offered, number of children in the family, whether a separate bedroom and/or bathroom were specified, and also things like whether experience was demanded, whether the gender or nationality of the desired au pair was specified and whether a photo was asked for.

These advertisements were an incredibly rich source of information and they provided a picture of an extremely diverse sector, with relatively little standardisation in pay, no clear relationship between the number of hours demanded, or the number of children to be cared for and the pay offered, and a great deal of focus on the 'lovely' home of the hosts. We explore these findings in detail in Chapter 4, where we discuss 'what is an au pair?' While this analysis could not give us the sort of comprehensive coverage of the sector that official data would, we were able to gain a sense of the buoyancy of the au pair job market and the very large number of posts that were being advertised, and presumably filled, each week. We had no trouble finding the 1,000 ads in the time we were looking and in fact could have collected many more. We also noted that it was rare for an advertisement to stay up for more than a few days and we rarely saw the same advertisement twice. This suggested that during the period we were looking at Gumtree, many thousands of au pairs were placed through these ads. Gumtree is just one platform that potential hosts might use to locate an au pair; AuPairWorld is perhaps the largest site (mentioned by many of our interviewees), and they claim to have had 21,000 applications from people wanting to work in the UK (not the same as posts) in 2015. There are also hundreds of au pair agencies and other online matching services, as well as word of mouth, cards in shop windows and advertisements in local papers or neighbourhood noticeboards. Taking these together it is easy to imagine that over 50,000 au pairs are placed each year, and while some of these may change job after a very short period of time, or leave au pairing, many more will remain in their post for more than a year, meaning the total number of au pairs in the country would be higher than this, and a total figure of 90,000–100,000, while being a very rough estimate, is not impossible.

The main method that we used to understand the lived effects of the deregulation of au pairing was interviews with those directly involved in the sector. We carried out in-depth semi-structured interviews with 40 au pairs and 15 people who host au pairs (none of the au pairs interviewed were hosted by the hosts interviewed). Our original intention had been to interview 40 hosts, and to talk to more hosts based outside London, but this proved impossible. Hosts were either too busy or reluctant to talk about the subject. For some who we approached the topic clearly touched a nerve and polite enquires were met with rude or even abusive responses. While this strength of feeling was revealing in some ways, it was also problematic as it has limited the range of host opinions and experiences we were able to hear about. The hosts who did agree to be interviewed were, without exception, desirous of being 'good' hosts. They were thoughtful, caring and engaged in the lives of the au pairs living with them. They were also recruited to the study through personal networks and snowballing and are likely to be a more homogenous group than au pair hosts as a whole.

The au pairs interviewed came from 15 different countries, all in Europe. The most important countries numerically were the Czech Republic (six interviewees), Germany (six interviewees), Romania (six interviewees) and Spain (five interviewees). The au pairs ranged in age from 18 to 29 and had been au pairs for between two weeks and five years. While most of the interviewees had been au pairing for six to nine months, three had been an au pair for five years and about half had worked for more than one family, with three having also been an au pair in a country other than the UK. Nineteen had high school as their highest level of education, eleven had university qualifications including six with professional qualifications or postgraduate degrees. Only nine of the forty were based outside London and its environs, and a further four had moved from a first au pair role outside London into London itself. We asked au pairs about their reasons for au pairing, and for coming to the UK, their work and remuneration as au pairs, their relationship with their host family and their future plans.

The host families we met were quite varied in composition but had similarities in terms of location and employment patterns. They were all based in London and the Southeast, except one, which was in Cambridgeshire. There were eleven households with two parents present and four with a lone parent. All the lone parents worked full time but in only three of the two-parent families did both parents work full time; five families followed a traditional 'one and a half worker' model, with the father working full time and the mother part time; in two further households, it was the mother who worked full time and the father part time; and in two households the father worked full time and the mother did no paid work (one of these was a student). We spoke to whoever in the household identified as hosting the au pair; for the most part this was women (12 of the 15 hosts) but there were also three men amongst our host interviewees, one of whom was a lone parent. The make up the families varied from one child and one parent to two parents and four children and the children varied in age from new born to 18; however, most of the children were of primary school age. We asked hosts about their daily routines, why they had chosen to host an au pair, any other childcare arrangements they had tried and the sort of relationship they cultivated. For those who had hosted a number of au pairs we asked them to tell us about their previous au pair arrangements too.

Interviews with au pairs and hosts were transcribed verbatim and coded both 'top down' for themes which we had identified in advance and 'bottom up' for themes which we had not anticipated but which emerged during the interviews. For example, the issue of negotiating childcare and relationships with children, which we explore in Chapter 6, was something which we had identified as important before interviews began, whereas the question of how much time au pairs spent cleaning and how they felt about this, was something which emerged very powerfully in interviews, we discuss its importance in Chapters 2 and 6. We have allocated pseudonyms to our au pair and host interviewees, which we use throughout this book. The names were allocated alphabetically in order of date of interview (those interviewed first have a pseudonym closer to the beginning of the alphabet), thus no attempt has been made to convey nationality, ethnicity, age or class status through the choice of names. The only characteristic we have kept constant is gender, with male and female interviewees being given pseudonyms that are, respectively, commonly male or female in British English.

The third method that we used to learn about au pairing in twenty-first-century Britain was to talk to key informants with knowledge about the sector or a related sector. We talked to representatives from BAPAA, the Low Pay Commission, the TUC, the Home Office, Migrant Rights Network, Kalayaan (a charity that works with migrant domestic workers) and Migrant Rights Centre, Ireland, who were carrying out a campaign around au pairs' rights in Ireland at the time. Talking to these experts allowed us to build our knowledge base about the broader context of au pairing from those involved in the sector and working on related issues. We also fed our research back to this group after we had finished so that they could benefit from our findings.

All research has its limitations, and a project such as this one, which is the first large-scale investigation into a largely hidden and unregulated arena, is no exception. As well as being unable to talk to less scrupulous hosts, we were also unable to reach the most isolated au pairs, such as those who were not participating in language classes or online discussion groups. We also found it difficult to involve au pairs and hosts outside London and the Southeast and did not speak to anyone based in Wales, Scotland or Northern Ireland. Therefore, while we discuss au pairing in the 'UK', because this is the unit for which policy is relevant, in terms of our in-depth findings, we actually know nothing about the experiences of hosts and au pairs outside England. However, despite these limitations, we thought the methods were extremely successful. We gathered a large amount of new and fascinating data. Using this variety of methods enabled us to view au pairing in twenty-first-century Britain from a variety of perspectives, and it allowed us to gain both an overview of the sector and detailed knowledge about what it feels like to be involved in au pairing.

Throughout the book more stories of the problems with au pairing surface than 'happy stories'. This is for three reasons; first, it reflects what we found when we talked to au pairs and hosts; second, there is a reasonably large, global industry dedicated to convincing both potential hosts and au pairs of the benefits of the sector. An online search for 'au pair' will generate thousands of pages of pictures of happy young women, caring for equally happy young children, accompanied by text that sells the arrangement; happy stories are readily available to those who want them. Third, the purpose of this book is to examine the effects of the deregulation of au pairing in Britain. That means it is necessary to reveal the problems and potential for problems in the sector, even if these do not affect all participants all of the time. In most areas of life, we don't wait until something fails 100 per cent of the time before declaring it in need of repair. The fact that au pair arrangements sometimes, even often, do work, that au pairs and hosts are happy with the deal that they strike and the relationship they have, is great, but it is not evidence that these arrangements will always work or that the system could not be improved. Rather, we argue the sector is urgently in need of regulatory attention and reform.

Our book begins with three chapters that set out the historical and social context within which au pairing is negotiated and experienced today. This context is important because, we argue, the problematic nature of au pairing and the elusiveness of equality within the au pair–host relationship are results of structural issues, which have their roots in the very foundations of the housework/work divide and in the global-scale inequalities which underpin the international division of domestic labour (Parreñas 2000). Chapter 1 sets out a short history of au pairing, locating this form of domestic labour in two important historical traditions of service: the idea of 'family membership' for domestic workers and the preference for white 'others' to become servants in British homes. Chapter 2 explores the theoretical context of why au pairing is not considered to be work and the relationship between social inequalities and paid domestic employment. It shows how the denial of domestic labour as a form of 'real' work is linked to the gendering of domestic labour. When domestic work is done for pay, class and racial stereotypes which portray working-class and migrant women as 'naturally' suited to these tasks can make the 'work' involved in domestic labour more, rather than less, apparent. In Chapter 3 we then set out the social context for the contemporary growth of au pairing in the UK: the growth in paid domestic work worldwide, the influence of government migration and care policies, the organisation of paid work, gendered inequalities at home and the importance of childcare cultures in shaping demand for particular forms of childcare worker.

We then present findings from our empirical research. Chapter 4 asks the question 'What is an au pair?' It explores in detail what au pairs do, what their hosts think they ought to do and whether au pairing resembles a relationship of an equal 'host' and 'guest' rather than an employer and employee. This chapter also examines 'cultural exchange' – this is what is meant to define au pairing and separate it from 'real' work. We argue that where it is present it is an important benefit and can be valued by both au pairs and hosts, but it by no means characterises the majority of au pair–host relations. Chapter 5 develops the analysis of the importance of online spaces for shaping the au pair sector at a time of deregulation. It draws on interviews with au pairs, with hosts, with representatives from au pair agencies as well as time spent 'hanging out' in virtual au pair chat rooms, both eavesdropping on and contributing to conversations between au pairs about their understanding of what being an au pair should or does involve and about experiences in the UK. It looks at the changing role of au pair agencies and explains why the rise of online agencies has been particularly detrimental in the context of deregulation. Chapter 6 explores how au pairs in Britain experience equality and inequality in their day to day lives. It shows how relatively mundane aspects of au pairing, such as how much cleaning is done and to what standard, become significant in conveying a sense of belonging (or not) and how powerfully interactions between hosts and au pairs can convey a sense of inequality. In Chapter 7 we examine host families' motivations for hosting an au pair – what is the problem they are trying to solve? And why is an au pair the best solution? In response to these questions we heard about the demands of highly flexible employment and the impossibilities of collective childcare arrangements, gender inequalities in the distribution of domestic work and financial imperatives. We also examine how hosts negotiate hierarchies within their homes, how they try to be 'good' hosts, how they avoid being parents to au pairs and how they use national stereotypes when hiring au pairs in order to produce particular types of relationship. In the conclusion we highlight four themes which animate our discussions: the importance of history, the importance of housework, the importance of government policy and the importance of paid work. We also examine the implications of our findings for au pairs and hosts and for policy makers, returning to the question of the effects of deregulation. Bringing the findings of our study together with research on au pairs in a number of other countries allows us to highlight the protections which are needed in the UK.

1 | A SHORT HISTORY OF AU PAIRING

Au pairs have long been an important part of the British solution to a perceived 'servant problem'. A problem which is as much about the tensions arising from having 'other' people within the private home as it is about finding a supply of suitable and supplicant labour. This chapter explores the context for the development of au pairing in twentieth-century Europe and in post-war relations between Northern European countries. The history of au pairing is a little-researched area despite a recent burgeoning in both popular and academic interest in lives 'below stairs'. Yet the research that has been done shows that au pairs were important figures both in British middle-class family life and the popular imagination in the post-war years.

In its formal incarnation au pairing has only a short history. The Oxford English Dictionary records the first usage of the word to date from 1897, when the *Girls Own Paper* (16 October) described 'an arrangement ... frequently is made for an English girl to enter a French, German or Swiss School and teach her own language in return for joining the usual classes. This is called being *au pair*'. The first record of its use as a verb 'to au pair' dates only to 1963, but the word, like the practice has longer roots. The history of the word is as an adjective describing an arrangement between parties paid for by the exchange of mutual services. In the early twentieth century, the term 'au pair' was often used in advertisements for mothers' helps or 'lady helps' to indicate that the successful applicant would be treated as an equal within the family. It also indicated that no substantial wage would be paid and where the post was for a companion to a lady with limited means it meant that expenses would be shared (Holden 2013). Au pairing as we see it today, therefore, has its immediate antecedents in these types of mutually beneficial domestic relationships but it also has a more complex history relating to practices of lifecycle service, informal exchanges between families and more formal types of domestic service such as the 'maid of all work', who also undertook childcare, the governess and, most obviously, the nanny.

Au pairs as a group of *migrant* domestic workers also have ante-cedents amongst earlier groups of domestic workers and the chapter traces past trends for British households employing domestic servants from other European countries. In the nineteenth and early twentieth centuries Irish women were the most numerous non-British domestic workers. Later, special schemes were designed by the British govern-ment to ensure a supply of 'acceptable' domestic workers to British homes. The post-war 'Baltic Cygnet' scheme, which placed Latvian refugee 'volunteer workers' as domestic workers in Britain, was one such. Latvian women, like Irish women before them, were seen as appropriate domestic workers because they were white but not British. They had just the right degree of similarity and difference to be accept-able within the families they would serve, a theme which is echoed in the au pair scheme.

Au pairing became prominent, or visible, with the decline of residential service in the post-war years but no simple history of subservient British servants being replaced by middle-class au pairs from neighbouring countries exists. There are continuities between au pairs experiences and those of earlier servants and between au pairs and other domestic workers working at the same time. The rise of the au pair did not represent a clean break with a hierarchical and formal servant-employing past but rather a slow evolution of existing practices of lifecycle service and foreign exchange. Au pairing builds on traditions of swapping daughters between households as a form of education and of domestic servants being considered as family members. When seen in the *longue durée* of domestic service the history of the au pair provides a crucial link between earlier histories of recruitment of European servants and the acceptance of domestic work as a migrant labour niche today (Liarou 2015).

This chapter traces the development of au pairing from these earlier forms of childcare and cultural exchange and also examines the importance of au pairs' status as 'equals' to the families for which they work. It begins by examining the antecedents of the au pair by looking at the history of who provided childcare in private homes, focusing on the figures of the 'maid of all work', the governess and the nanny. It then looks at the precursors of the unpaid/cultural exchange aspects of au pairing by examining the history of lifecycle service and exchange, and then moves to look at the history of white migrants being favoured for domestic work in Britain. We then detail the early development of the au pair scheme and changes to the formal au pair scheme from the 1970s to early 2000s.

Domestic work, childcare and being part of the family

Au pairs are a distinct group but also part of a historical continuity of domestic workers involved in providing childcare and living as 'part of the family'. In more elite houses the governess and the nanny might have figured, and these have clear affinities with au pairs today. In less wealthy households the most common form of domestic worker was the 'maid of all work' who undertook cooking, cleaning and laundering as well as childcare if there were children present. For all these domestic workers there could be some ambiguity in their position within the family. Governesses in particular, but nannies also, were meant to be 'ladies' or gentlewomen who would be able to instil the correct manners and attitudes in the children they cared for. Their treatment by employers distinguished them from 'servants' but they were still enmeshed in household hierarchies which located them as inferior to 'the family'. Maids of all work could also be included as 'part of the family', sometimes because the households they worked in were too small to allow the physical separation and distinctions on which stricter hierarchies relied.

Like au pairs today, foreign governesses were sometimes chosen by Victorian families because their foreignness could help to by-pass the problem of social difference (or sameness) that arose from having a 'lady' as an employee in the house. A French or German governess's references to her family, her clothes and accent could not place her socially with the preciseness that those of an English governess did and so could not be as easily used as evidence of her gentility. Her paid employment was less of an embarrassment (Hughes 1993).

Political unrest in France, Germany and Italy at the end of the 1840s brought a stream of middle-class refugees to Britain, some of whom ended up as governesses. According to the 1861 census there were 1,408 foreign governesses in Britain, the majority from Prussia, France and Switzerland (Hughes 1993). Prestige was also attached to French governesses in the Victorian era, and Kathryn Hughes (1993 p49) comments that Frenchwomen were an exception to the rule that Catholics would not be accepted as governesses in Protestant British homes: 'the moral threat of their presence was offset by the prestige that came with having one's daughters taught a modern language by a native speaker'.

There was also discrimination against foreign governesses, particularly Catholic ones, with one advice writer claiming that to allow a French governess into the house was to open 'a wide flood-gate to frivolity, vanity, and sin' (Mary Maurice 1847, quoted in Hughes 1993 p106). Foreign governesses could be taunted or blanked by other domestic staff and by the children they were in charge of.

In the pre-war era there is a continuum between informal forms of childcare performed by domestic servants, more specialist nursery maids and children's nurses, nannies and then later mothers' helps and au pairs. Nannies quite often occupied a liminal position within the families they worked for: not exactly servants, but not exactly not. Katherine Holden (2013) records the very complicated place nannies had – often adored by their charges and depended upon by their employers, they were still marginalised. Like governesses in an earlier period, nannies were traditionally middle-class women, or 'ladies', who were thought to be an appropriate influence on the children they cared for.

In the eighteenth and nineteenth centuries in Britain, the majority of servant-employing households had just one maid who carried out all work including childcare (Delap 2011). While looking after children may have provided some compensation to servants in more elite households that had multiple staff, Carolyn Steedman comments that for most servants, in more modest households 'a good place was a place without children' (2009 p228). Children created work, such as the very considerable work of laundering nappies, and they also created friction and disturbed domestic hierarchies. Servants complained at being ordered around by young children and mistresses worried about who should order and who obey – the servant or the child? In the eighteenth century, as in the twentieth and twenty-first, parents used advice manuals to help them in raising children and these often represented servants as people with little judgement from whose bad influences children needed to be protected if they were to be raised correctly (Steedman 2009).

As well as being related to the roles of governess, nanny and maid of all work, au pairing has roots in a long history of lifecycle service and the swapping of daughters, and sons, between families as part of their preparation for adult life. From medieval times, domestic service in a household other than the servant's natal one was common (Steedman 2009). Young men and women lived as members of the families they worked for and provided both farm and domestic labour. As Charmian Mansell (2018) notes, during the period 1550–1650, the workloads of most English women in service were not made up of chores that we would currently consider domestic, but instead also included brewing beer, picking apples and fetching wood as well as indoor tasks. In the late nineteenth and early twentieth centuries there was a practice of sending daughters of middle-class families to the homes of friends, or friends of friends, in other European countries to learn language skills and the housekeeping skills it was imagined they would need after marriage.

In addition, as Caroline Steedman comments (2009 p18), 'In the English eighteenth century, there were powerful Christian narratives to promote the thesis that master and servant were really relations'. Biblical texts promoted the idea that a master was some kind of a father into the nineteenth century. In fact, 1785 legal guidance 'Laws Concerning Masters and Servants' declared that 'Master and Servants are Relatives'. There is, therefore, a long tradition of including domestic workers as quasi family members and of treating them differently to other employees. Their location within the private sphere of the home adds to this, and this equivocal position is carried forward to the au pair schemes of today.

Au pairing and the British history of employing white 'others'

In order for the fiction of family membership to work in servant-employing households, it is necessary that domestic workers are both similar to, and also different from, their employers. One way in which this negotiation of similarity and difference has happened within Britain is through the favouring of white domestic workers, including white migrants. Even when there has been an influx of black people into the British labour market, such as slaves and former slaves in the eighteenth century, or Caribbean migrants in the 1960s, they have not been numerous as domestic workers and white migrants have been favoured for this work instead. As McDowell (2009) has commented there are hierarchies of whiteness in the British labour market, and these hierarchies become evident when trends in domestic employment are examined. Like Irish domestic workers and Latvian 'Volunteer Workers' before them, au pairs are part of an established history of employing white 'others' to carry out domestic work in Britain. Bronwyn Walter argues that

In order that the 'English' home could be clean, and the mother freed to devote her energies to her children's upbringing, working-class, including migrant, women provided invisible services. Their 'whiteness' helped to produce this invisibility and obscure the dependence of constructions of Englishness on the labour of Irish women. (Walter 2004 p484)

Before the twentieth century the numbers of international migrants in domestic work were relatively low, but there were still significant international flows of domestic servants to Britain. Jean Hecht (1954) reports that in the eighteenth century, there were large numbers of servants from France, and smaller groups from Switzerland, Italy and Germany. They were employed both because they could help their employers to adopt the latest, French fashions and because they were seen to be more servile than their British counterparts. Furthermore, many thousands of black servants were brought to Britain from the Caribbean and India by returning colonial families. Until 1772, there was also a trade in slaves directly from Africa to England, for use as domestic servants. Given the availability of slave labour for domestic work, what is striking is how few, rather than how many, black servants there were in Britain in the eighteenth century. Rather than being used as cheap labour for the most labour-intensive or dirty tasks, or by the poorest employers, black servants, who were overwhelmingly male, were employed as footmen and in other public-facing, liveried roles in the most aristocratic homes. They were seen as representing the luxury of the exotic and demonstrated their employers' fashionable taste through their presence alone. In contrast, European servants, particularly from France, were much more often female, and they were employed largely as 'body servants', that is ladies' maids who were able to dress hair and make clothes after the latest fashions. There were also French men employed as chefs and as valets (Hecht 1954). These servants were, therefore, involved in the most intimate care of their employers in ways which black servants were not.

During the nineteenth century, it was Irish women who were seen as naturally fitted to domestic work. Domestic service was the most important occupation for Irish women in Britain and Irish women were the largest group of migrants recruited to this work (Walter 2004). In the second half of the nineteenth century, as opportunities for English women improved and demand for servants increased, Irish women were increasingly in demand. There was also a rise in the status of Irish migrants who were increasingly well-educated. Young, single, educated, rural women were attractive servants in a way that married women from urban areas who had tended to migrate earlier had not been and English families turned to them in large numbers (Walter 2001).

Over the course of the nineteenth century Irish women became a much more important and sought-after source of domestic labour in Britain and there is some evidence that the desirability of Irish servants was related to their position as both acceptably different from and similar to the white, middle-class British families they served. Bronwen Walter (2001) has argued that Irish people in Britain were 'othered' through discourses of both class and race – discourses which drew upon each other with the expansion of colonialism. The Irish were portrayed as a 'race apart' through their place in both British slums and the colonised island of Ireland – both spaces seen as occupied by degenerate races in need of civilisation (see also Ignatiev 1995 on portrayals of the Irish in the USA). At the same time, Irish women were imagined as the same as white British employers because of their whiteness and through myths of the homogeneity of the British population in pre-war years. These myths were supported by British foreign and immigration policies which often denied the border with Ireland despite the tortured history of its existence. For example, Irish people were allowed to travel freely to Britain and to enter the workforce immediately on their arrival. Migrants from the Caribbean, members of the Commonwealth with ostensibly stronger ties to Britain, were treated much less favourably. There has been a discursive interchangeability between 'immigration' and 'race' which has hidden the lives of white migrants in Britain (Webster 1998). However, as Walter (2001 p107) argues 'the failure to acknowledge difference does not mean that "othering" has disappeared. Indeed, there are strong continuities in representations of Irish people in Britain which coexist in reworked forms with denial of difference'.

During the 1950s fierce debates took place about whether to include the Irish in immigration controls or not. '[The Irish] were finally given the status of freedom of movement on the grounds of expediency, because of the difficulties in controlling the border in Northern Ireland and because of the value of a flexible labour force' (Walter 2004 p482).

By the mid-twentieth century Irish women had become recognised as archetypal servants and were therefore allowed inside a boundary that was being drawn between those belonging inside and outside the home/homeland. But this was a measure of expediency at the domestic level just as it was at the national scale. The Irish were in the process of being defined as 'white' through the hardening of the official black/white binary in the 1960s but despite apparent homogeneity, the category contained a diverse range of identities who were not necessarily protected from ongoing racialisation. (Walter 2004 p288)

Analysis of 1881 census suggests that Irish women made up 3.4 per cent of the servant workforce in London (more than numbers of Scottish and Welsh combined) and that numbers had grown since 1851 (Walter 2004 p478). 'By the 1930s Irish servants were viewed as indispensable to the English economy' (Walter 2004 p479). A memo from the British Minister of Labour in 1932, which shows that the British government was considering the repatriation of Irish workers due to the depression, states, 'there is no doubt that under present conditions the total number of workers born in the Irish Free State with the possible exception of those engaged in domestic service could be replaced rapidly and without much difficulty by workers born in Britain' (quoted in Walter 2004 p479). There were other reasons why Irish women became concentrated in domestic service. First the Catholic Church encouraged them to enter service as it saw this as teaching them skills of home-making and child-rearing fitted to women. Second, Irish women were widely discriminated against in factory work. As a result, domestic service remained the major area of Irish female employment in the first half of the twentieth century, contrary to the general trend among the peer group of British women, whose employment in personal service in England and Wales fell from 42 per cent to 23 per cent between 1901 and 1951 (Walter 2004 p480).

The second half of the twentieth century saw large labour flows to the UK – including flows of relatively poorly paid and unskilled labour, female labour, people directly recruited to do domestic and care work in institutional settings – but these flows were of black people from the Caribbean and they were not seen as an appropriate solution to the 'servant crisis'. For labour in middle-class homes, another source of workers was needed. As Bronwyn Walter comments (2001 pp108–109):

Migrant women filled the full-time jobs for which female labour was required, particularly in textile mills, domestic service and various branches of the expanding welfare state. White migrant women were permitted to work inside the homes of indigenous English women as nannies and cleaners, but black women were not seen as suitable for this work. Instead they were distanced from the personal lives of white English people and given public domestic work such as hospital cleaning.

As shortages of servants became more acute the government more deliberately developed schemes to increase their supply. While no doubt there would still have been substantial demand for 'traditional' servants if they had been available, the post-war era also brought a new context for domestic work. There was an impetus towards equality and the questioning of hierarchies that servant employment had relied on which made live-in service in particular distasteful to both workers and employers. Additionally, the figure of 'the housewife' replaced 'the mistress' as the desirable role for middle-class women (Delap 2011). Class standing and feminine accomplishments were to be displayed through the running of the home and raising of children, rather than just the conspicuous consumption of leisure. These changes meant that new forms of domestic employment became popular as fitting both practically and ideologically with middle-class life. The part-time 'daily' or 'char' is one form that domestic work increasingly took, but another was service as a form of cultural exchange. This is largely the origin of the au pair scheme but this was not the only scheme importing domestic workers from Europe.

Linda McDowell (2005) has produced a detailed and sensitive account of the lives of Latvian 'European Volunteer Workers' (EVWs) who came to Britain at the end of the Second World War. They were recruited directly from labour camps, where they had been taken by the Germans and were seen by the British government as a solution to labour shortages in 'female' jobs in hospitals, sanatoriums and private households.[1] During the 1930s permits had been given for domestic workers from Austria and Hungary, particularly to young Jewish women, who were essentially refugees but were given leave to enter Britain as labour migrants. After the war the transformation of displaced persons and refugees into much-needed labour happened on a larger scale, between 1946 and 1949 83,000 migrants from Central and Eastern Europe were permitted to enter the UK, doubling the foreign-born population of the UK during those years (McDowell 2009).

The UK developed the 'Baltic Cygnet' scheme, originally to recruit women from the displaced persons camps to work in hospitals, but later extended it to other forms of domestic work, including in private homes. British discourse around the development of this scheme focused on the attributes of women from various different countries and how appropriate their bodies would be as workers and citizens of the UK. Ministry of Labour officials travelled to the camps in 1946 to assess the suitability of women from Latvia, Lithuania and Estonia to be domestic workers in institutions and homes in the UK. It might seem surprising that supplying domestic workers could be such a priority at a time of increasing social equality and severe labour shortage but demand was still high and it was thought that as domestic workers would live in they would not compete for housing and they would therefore be neither visible within the community nor place further demands on housing stock (McDowell 2005). Women workers were also imagined to be more acceptable to the trade unions as they would not be in competition for 'men's' jobs.

The name 'Baltic Cygnet' conveys much about how the UK government hoped the EVWs would be seen. As McDowell (2005 p98) puts it, the name presents

> a vision of vulnerable yet attractive young swans, redolent of purity, sailing across the water to the UK and emerging from their drab protective colouring as cygnets into the full beauty of an adult swan under the guidance of the British state or public.

The whiteness and youth of the cygnet, both suggesting purity and vulnerability, cannot be overlooked. In its naming of the scheme the British state is clearly signalling the benign and acceptable whiteness of these workers' bodies. As 'cygnets' EVWs were also presented as innocent and virginal and, therefore, as suitable wives for white, British men and as potential mothers of future Britons.

As white protestants and often of middle-class origin, Latvian EVWs were favoured over other migrant groups, including white Irish women. EVWs were represented by the UK government as strong, young workers with a common European heritage, and this was in contrast to both Irish women (whose Catholicism and long history as degraded 'others' disadvantaged them) and to black women from the Caribbean.

A memorandum from the Foreign Labour Committee after a visit to the camps in Germany recorded the advantages of Baltic women:

> The women are of good appearance, are scrupulously clean in their persons and habits ... There is little doubt that the specially selected who come to this country will be an exceptionally healthy and fit body ... and would constitute a good and desirable element in our population. (quoted in McDowell 2005 p99)

It was whiteness which fitted Latvian women both to the work they were steered into and to the role as possible wives of British men and mothers of the next generation. The entry of European migrant workers and Irish migrants 'was regarded as less contentious than that of Caribbean migrants by both government officials responsible for immigration policy and by the UK public at large because "they passed an unwritten test of racial acceptability"' (Paul 1997 pxiii quoted in McDowell 2005 p93; see also Webster 1998).

The emergence and development of au pairing

Au pairing emerged in the post-war days of 'the middle-class sense of entitlement and loss associated with being servantless' (Delap 2011 p132). 'Foreign girls' were seen as a solution to the shortage of British servants and they came to Britain under various schemes and migration regimes such as part time au pairs and full time 'domestics' and 'mothers helps'. The differences between these roles was not always clear in practice but during the twentieth century the au pair emerged as a particular type of domestic 'help', whose status as quasi family member rather than servant was particularly in keeping with post-war democratic ideals (Liarou 2015). As Lucy Delap says (2011 p133),

> The idea of light household tasks undertaken by a young 'visitor' in exchange for language learning, plus room and board had been available in Europe since the 1890s, but it was not portrayed as a solution to the class tensions of the servant problem until considerably later.

Au pairing thus developed as a solution to both a practical and ideological problem.

The au pair scheme developed from the post-war movement of Swiss, German, Austrian and Danish women who travelled to the United Kingdom to take up domestic posts that British women would no longer fill (Liarou 2008). Initially it was imagined that daughters would swap homes, each going to live for a period with the other's family, but this aspect of the scheme never caught on and the UK – or perhaps more precisely England – tended to host more au pairs than it sent abroad. The au pair would be an 'extra pair of hands', an equal to her host family and not a servant, and she was imagined to come from a 'good' family and might employ domestic help herself in the future.

From the outset au pairs occupied a contradictory position, expected to do denigrated work that had previously been done by servants in the households they went to, but also imagined as relatively privileged and flighty (Liarou 2008). Au pairing was specifically portrayed as a solution to the class tensions of the servant problem. Lucy Delap (2011 p133) quotes the *Manchester Guardian* of 1958, which stated that it hoped the au pairs would solve

> a delicate social problem for the professional and middle classes who cannot quite afford a full time domestic and whose accommodation is limited so that it is easier for the housewife to have someone around her of her own standing. One does not apologise to social equals.

But au pairs did not necessarily solve the awkwardness of servant employment and rules about how to behave were few.

The status of the au pair, 'not quite a guest and not quite a servant' (Delap 2011 p133) was always rather unclear. *The Spectator* commented in 1950 that the new 'home help from abroad' created even more difficulties than the maid. There were ambiguities between the role of au pairs and that of other domestic workers from overseas. A survey undertaken in the London suburb of Hendon in 1957 found large numbers of 'foreign girls' employed as au pairs, domestics and mothers' helps. The authors found little difference between the au pairs and the full-time domestic workers; they classified 80 per cent of them as middle class and a large majority came from Germany. The survey authors commented:

> Most girls are aware that they are taking the place of the pre-war 'servant' and they often resent it. There is little difference in attitude between au pair girls and full-time girls. They think of themselves as students, as typists, as glamour girls, but not as domestic workers … [Yet] if their employers wish to regard them as servants they have no protection. They are legally and actually, in the same position as old-fashioned 'servants' were. (Williams and Flower 1957, quoted in Delap 2011 p134)

Lucy Delap (2011) highlights that post-war claims of a servantless middle-class life were perhaps overstated. A 1964 study of university-educated women found that over 90 per cent of them employed domestic help of some kind, including residential servants, mothers' helps and au pairs.

Even in these early days au pairing was not clearly distinct from other forms of domestic 'help' and there was evidence of au pairs being exploited and abused. Liarou (2008 p221, quoting a report from the British Vigilance Association) comments:

> [By 1958] the 'Au Pair' system 'has become a means whereby girls under the age of 18 are employed to do almost exactly the same duties as regular domestic servants, with no insurance benefits or legal protection'. By the early 1970s this criticism amounted to what was called the 'Pink Slave Trade' as cases of economic and sexual exploitation of au pair girls were coming to light, and the government undertook to look at the arrangements for admitting them to Britain. On the other hand, au pair girls were accused of 'free-loading, laziness, arriving pregnant or ill to take advantage of free treatment on the National Health Service'.

The Times estimated that around 17,000 such workers were coming to Britain each year in the 1950s, and numbers grew in the 1960s and 1970s (Delap 2011).

The au pair scheme was formalised at a European scale in 1969 when member states of the Council of Europe signed the 'European Agreement on "Au Pair" Placement', otherwise known as the Strasbourg Agreement. The agreement was a response to the already existing practice of au pairing rather than an instigation of it. The scheme aimed to address what had already been identified as the problem of au pairs lacking social protections (Liarou 2015). Britain was never a signatory to the agreement but its tenets did shape the British au pair visa

The scheme then allowed young women, and it was specifically restricted to women at the start, to travel to another European country for a maximum of two years to provide 'help' to a family in return for room and board and a small amount of pocket money. On one hand, au pairing was seen as a way to travel and meet interesting people, but simultaneously it was a source of concern about abuse and overwork. In 1971 Joan Vickers, Member of Parliament for Plymouth, noted that '[au pair] girls are semi-servants for people who cannot afford servants, who do not like doing the work themselves, and who in most cases do not pay National Insurance or selective employment tax' (Delap 2011 p134).

The complaints raised by au pairs and their hosts in the 1950s, '60s and '70s foreshadow issues raised in our research in 2012–2014. The 1957 Hendon survey recorded complaints from au pairs about the food they were given and eating arrangements, nomenclature and lack of opportunities to practise their English. Hosts at the time complained about the lack of privacy arising from the au pair arrangement as well as the delicate negotiation of status differences. In 1961 *The Observer* addressed the 'au pair problem' concluding that 'one may prefer to see one's friends without an extra presence, and to be able to be alone with oneself or one's marriage partner is the essence of home' (*Observer* 30 April 1961, quoted in Delap 2011 p135).

Changes to au pairing since the 1970s

From 1969 to 2008 the UK au pair scheme reflected the European Agreement on 'Au Pair' Placement, which was part of the Strasbourg Treaty (see http://conventions.coe.int/Treaty/en/Treaties/Html/068. htm) and was formalised through the 'au pair visa'. Details of the scheme were set out by the Home Office as the authority that issued visas. Au pair visas were available only to people from Europe and, originally only Western and Central Europe (see Cox 2006). The au pair visa specified that au pairs must be unmarried and without dependent children; aged 17–27 years and could stay in the United Kingdom for up to two years but must leave the country within a week if they are not living with a 'host family'. In addition, the Home Office stipulated that au pairs had to be engaged in cultural exchange and improving their English. They could do 25 hours of 'light housework' or childcare per week plus an additional two evenings of babysitting but should not be in sole charge of very young children. In exchange for this the au pair would receive 'pocket money' (the Home Office advised £65 per week in 2008. It cautioned that if an au pair was given much above this amount this would suggest that the person was 'filling the position of domestic servant or similar, which would require a work permit' (Home Office website, quoted in Newcombe 2004 p16)), have their own bedroom and be provided with meals. The visa was not a work permit and the official construction of the au pair avoided other tropes associated with employment – the au pair receives pocket money not pay, and lives with a host family rather than an employer. While it was never a requirement in the UK that au pairs were placed via agencies, in the early years of the formal scheme au pair agencies were regulated and expected to help enforce the Home Office rules.

As the EU expanded and treaties allowed EU and European Economic Area (EEA) nationals access to the UK labour market, the number of au pairs needing a visa declined. In November 2008 the au pair visa scheme was closed as part of the United Kingdom's move to the Points Based System that encompasses all visa and work permit categories. Despite the fact that a relatively small percentage of au pairs needed visas by 2008, the existence of the visa, and its subsequent abolition, have been important in delineating the au pair role and the rights of au pairs. The existence of the visa required the Home Office to define au pairing, for example to set expectations on host families and au pairs, to suggest pocket money rates and to delimit the hours an au pair should work and these guidelines applied to all au pairs, not just those with visas. Official advice to au pairs and host families was provided by the Home Office through their website and in leaflets and it was a requirement that all au pairs entering the United Kingdom should be given a Home Office leaflet. The advice provided by the Home Office was re-circulated by agencies and language schools as well as between au pairs and host families. Whilst there were still many abuses of the scheme, and it is estimated that a minority of au pairs worked within the boundaries set out by the Home Office (Búriková and Miller 2010; Búriková 2015; 2016; Cox 2006; Cox and Narula 2003), their guidelines did provide an official basis for delimiting the au pair role, which, theoretically at least, provided some legal protection.

Since November 2008 au pairs in the United Kingdom have officially been integrated into Tier 5 of the Points Based Immigration System. This is the tier that covers youth mobility and temporary workers. While au pairs are now mentioned in those roles covered by the Tier 5 Youth Mobility Scheme (YMS) (a category open only to nationals from a very small number of countries, most of them English-speaking), there is no longer any detail given by the Home Office on what 'au pairing' does or does not involve; no suggestion of pocket money, appropriate tasks or living conditions.

The increased supply of low-waged labour from the A8 countries[2] combined with the deregulation of au pairing has created markets for au pairs and other domestic workers that did not previously exist. Families with much lower incomes are now taking on au pairs to perform a very wide range of tasks (see Busch 2011; 2012). The landscape of au pairing has changed considerably in recent years with au pairs becoming much less distinct from domestic workers and less likely to be involved in any form of cultural exchange or language learning. UK migration policy has facilitated the employment of domestic workers and has constructed certain people as appropriate to provide cheap labour in denigrated work in private homes.

Conclusion

This chapter has outlined the historical context of au pairing, showing its antecedents in international exchange schemes for young women, forms of domestic employment, such as the nanny, governess and maid of all work, that complicated the relationship between employee and family member, and a preference within the UK for white domestic workers, such as Irish servants and the Latvian 'Volunteer Workers'. This multi-faceted heritage hints at some of the confusions and contradictions that characterise contemporary au pairing. Are they primarily domestic workers or exchange students? Are they employees or members of the family? Are they 'different' outsiders or 'similar' and unthreatening white women who can belong in British homes?

As this chapter has shown, even in its early incarnations au pairing was problematic, and these contradictions shaped experiences of both hosts and au pairs. News reports reveal that worries about whether au pairs were 'pink slaves' or 'glamour girls' go back over 50 years. Policy and practice from the UK government did little to deal with these problems. Even though there was a visa, and with it a definition of an au pair, introduced in response to the 1969 Strasbourg Agreement, the UK was never a signatory to this agreement and had a rather 'light touch' approach to regulating the scheme, leaving the protection of au pairs to voluntary organisations.

The next chapter begins to put UK au pairing into its contemporary context. It examines the global growth in paid domestic employment in recent decades, and the particular ways in which the organisation of home and work in Britain has created demand for this form of domestic labour.

Notes

1 It is interesting to note that Helma Lutz (2011 p13) describes how German women were recruited as servants to other countries in large numbers in the early twentieth century. In part these women were recruited because as white women they were seen as appropriate wives for settlers. However, under fascism, the exaltation of the German woman as mistress of her own home opposed the imagining of women as servants in other people's homes. A programme of 'Maidservant Repatriation' from the Netherlands was instigated in 1938 and special trains brought German maids home. In the Second World War women from occupied eastern territories (Russia, Poland, Ukraine, Czechoslovakia etc.) were conscripted and an estimated 100,000 of these women were assigned to German private households to perform 'forced labour in the nursery' (Lutz 2011 p14).

2 Czech Republic, Estonia, Hungary, Latvia, Lithuania, Poland, Slovakia and Slovenia.

2 | INVISIBLE WORK AND HIDDEN INEQUALITIES: GENDER, CLASS AND NATIONALITY IN AU PAIRING

This chapter provides the theoretical context for the following chapters and is organised around two interlocking themes: the question of why au pairing is not considered to be work and the relationship between inequalities and paid domestic employment. These themes are interlocking because the denial of domestic labour as a form of 'real' work is inextricably linked to the gendering of domestic tasks and women's traditional responsibility for unpaid domestic labour in the home. When these tasks are done for pay, the fact that this is 'work' does not necessarily become clearer but can be further obscured by class and racial stereotypes which imagine working-class and migrant women as appropriate domestic workers, 'naturally' suited to that work, and therefore, not doing 'real' work or using real skills when they do those jobs. The specific construction of au pairing complicates this picture yet again. As outlined in the previous chapter, rhetorics of equality and belonging in the family define the au pair role and have deep historical roots and, while au pairs are almost always migrants, they may not be from countries or families poorer than their hosts; in the UK they are almost always white and imaginings of sameness amongst white, European populations can disguise difference and discrimination.

To tease out these inter-weaving themes and layers of complication we look at au pairing in the context of unpaid and paid domestic work. The chapter is divided into two main sections 'Invisible Work' and 'Inequalities'. In the first of these we explore how the gendering of domestic labour and the creation of the housewife role have made reproductive work invisible and undervalued. The 'non-work' status of au pairing has deep historical roots which are interlocked with women's oppression at work and home. In the second section we look at the inequalities which shape the paid form of domestic work – particularly class and race/ethnic hierarchies. Within this context of multiple, deep-rooted inequalities, the prospect of au pairs living 'as an equal' with their hosts seems distant indeed.

Invisible work

Au pairing is, at the most basic level, a form of labour migration within which the labour to be performed by the migrant is denied. This is, on the face of it, rather odd; even schemes like the 'Working Holiday Maker Visa' admit to the possible combination of 'work' with travel for other reasons. What is perhaps most odd is the persistence of the 'not work but cultural exchange' framing of au pairing over many decades and throughout almost all territories which have any definition of the role (see Cox 2015c for a comparison of au pair schemes. The notable exception to this trend is the USA where au pairs are defined by tax regulations as working but have an immigration status as students).

The denial of the work au pairs do is much less odd when it is put in the context of broader social constructions of housework and childcare as activities which exist outside the world of 'work'; tasks which are done for love rather than money and which belong in the private sphere of home and family not the public sphere of employment. In Chapter 3 we outline our argument that gender inequalities within homes create demand for au pairs not because women work outside the home in larger numbers than previously, but because men and women do not share housework and childcare equally and responsibilities for caring labour have been left with the private family rather than met socially through welfare systems. In this section, we foreground this argument by looking at the historical roots and wider implications of the gendering of responsibility for reproductive labour. Women's assumed responsibility for housework and childcare is both a practical problem and a symbolic one, an issue of status. While this work remains the individual responsibility of private families and while men are not seen as responsible for these tasks, this work remains low status and doing it is part of women's subordination. Many women, who can afford to, seek to escape this work by paying other people, almost exclusively other women, to do it. The effect of employing domestic workers is that domestic labour becomes distributed by class and ethnicity as well as gender (Uhde 2016), and the inherent problem of its devaluation is further than ever from being addressed. As Zuzana Uhde argues, the jobs which are created through the marketisation of care work are poorly paid and low status, they do not allow workers to achieve status through financial success nor do they give social recognition as valuable; 'In this context the commodification of care thus contains a paradox: by opening certain possibilities of financial reward, it institutionalised

[a] double misrecognition of care as both non-productive work and paid work that cannot be a source of social recognition' (Uhde 2016 p687).

In order to understand why domestic work is not considered to be work, and the profound implications of its gendering, we need to go on what might seem to be a detour away from looking at the organisation of paid domestic work in the twenty-first century to look at how 'housework' as a distinct set of tasks came into being and how their separation from 'work' has underpinned women's position in society. This section begins by examining how the industrial revolution and subsequent urbanisation separated 'work' and 'home' and created housework as a specific set of activities and the housewife as a distinct role. It then looks at first wave and second wave feminist responses to this gendering of domestic labour and feminist arguments about women's responsibility for domestic work to show how the invisibility of au pairs' labour is part of much broader processes of denying the value of reproductive work. It finishes by looking at the effects of the gendering of domestic responsibilities on women's experiences of work outside the home, to show how assumptions about women's 'natural' place and talents still saturate the world of work.

The contemporary relationship between home and work is historically specific rather than natural or inevitable. The transition from feudalism to capitalism and associated process of industrialisation profoundly affected the organisation of work and home, by separating out paid, 'productive' labour from unpaid work in the home (Barbagallo 2016). This, in turn, produced the modern understanding of home and housework and the housewife as the person who should do this work. Before industrialisation 'home' and 'work' were not physically separate spaces for most families and reproductive labour was not easily distinguishable from what are now seen as 'productive' tasks (Hall 1995 [1973]). The majority of men and women worked, with their children, on subsistence farms doing the work necessary to maintain themselves (Hayden 1981). In urban areas families also worked as units, in households which contained apprentices or others who worked alongside them. John Tosh (2007 [1999] p18) gives the example of David Macmillan who as late as 1833 took a post as a salaried shopman with a Cambridge bookseller. Macmillan lived in the home of his employer, ate all his meals with him and went to the family chapel on Sundays. This integration of an employee into the home and family of employer was quite normal. In these circumstances, there was a gendered division of labour within households but no great physical separation between work and home. Nor were tasks clearly divided between those which were for subsistence production, reproduction and production for sale. A woman might spin wool while watching her children, and that wool might be used in domestic production of cloth or sold to be woven elsewhere. She might prepare meals for apprentices or labourers who were part of her household alongside providing food for 'family' members. Both men and women could be involved in producing food and other items that would be sold as well as those for home use.

The process of industrialisation, and with it urbanisation, separated home from 'work' for men and in popular imaginings of what 'work' meant. It is not the case that women were not engaged in paid, 'productive' work, but that the work of home fell to them whatever their other responsibilities were and that the separation of 'work' and 'home' defined women's participation in life outside home. As Ann Oakley (1976 p32) succinctly puts it:

> The most important and enduring consequence of industrialization
> for women has been the emergence of the modern role of housewife
> as 'the dominant mature feminine role'. Industrialization affected
> the roles of men as well as the roles of women. But while for men
> it enlarged the world outside the home, chiefly by expanding the
> range of occupations available to them, for women it has meant an
> involution of the world into the space of the home.

In this new urban, industrial order, 'work' was separate from family life. Work became something that happened outside the family home that was done for monetary reward and for itself. The family ceased to be a productive unit and instead an ideal arose, first among middle-class households, and then later amongst working-class families too, that the man would be a sole wage earner and his wife and children would be dependent upon him (Oakley 1976; see also Johnson and Lloyd 2004). For this ideal to be realised the 'work' of housework had to be understood as something unproductive, and quite different from *real* work. The middle-class ideal also included domestic servants who would ensure the idleness of wives, an idleness which was an important statement about the status of husbands (Tosh 2007 [1999]). As Anne McClintock comments (1995 p94) 'In short, gender is not a separate dimension of identity to which one adds, accumulatively, the dimension of class. Rather, gender is an articulated category, constructed *through and by class*' (emphasis in the original). This association between class status and the not-doing of housework also meant that household tasks became increasingly hidden from public view; their importance and extent were denied at the same time as the results of that work became more socially important and fastidiously managed (Sambrook 2002).

The practical reorganisation of home and work was exacerbated by new ideologies about women's 'natural' place, which reinforced the idea that the home was where women belonged. During the Victorian period, as the disruptive effects of industrialisation became clear and old notions of hierarchy were undermined by the ideology of the free market and individualism, middle-class women were given the role of moral protectors of society. Women were increasingly portrayed as more moral, more pure and more clean than men and they had to be kept so by being segregated in the private home. The only work for women was that which protected the purity of others – particularly domestic work (Davidoff 1995).

Ann Oakley (1976 p43) writes of England:

> Until the early 1840s, the ideology of married women's economic dependence on men and their restriction to household work and childcare, existed only in embryonic form. The daughters and wives of upper- and middle-class men had not been expected to work for some time. Productive work was denied them, as were the duties of household work and childcare. 'The practice of female idleness spread through the middle class until work for women became a misfortune and a disgrace'. Working-class women were not restricted in this way. Although opportunities for women's productive work had diminished, there was as yet no generally accepted ideology of women's situation to justify the contraction of their roles as productive works on moral, social, economic or political grounds.

From the 1840s this situation changed and the new ideology which emerged was one that emphasised the housewife role as the only 'natural' and moral role for women. It is from this point in time that legislation starts to be introduced banning women from certain forms of paid employment, particularly factory work and mining (earlier legislation had restricted children's work which had had a practical effect on many women's ability to work outside the home, but it had not itself restricted adult women working). Debates at the time stressed the moral and physical peril to women of working outside the home, the threat to their children and to the 'proper' division of labour between men and women (Oakley 1976). By the early years of the twentieth century the housewife role had become the expectation and the norm for working class married women, even when employment would have improved the family's standard of living. 'From the perspective of women's situation, this change to housewifery among working-class women is the most dramatic result of the industrial revolution' (Oakley 1976 p50).

While women's paid work outside the home was increasingly presented as a moral peril, the number of women in paid domestic service grew as did the amount of work involved in keeping a respectable home for middle-class women. From about 1850 to 1950 domestic service was the single most important occupation for women and girls in Britain, employing over a million women until the mid-1930s (Davidoff 1995). These labours – paid service for the working class and household management for the middle class – were seen as highly desirable and morally appropriate occupations for the two groups of women, but they were also only equivocally considered as work. Leonore Davidoff (1995 p89) comments 'because it can never be really accepted that women's efforts in housework and houscshold management should be measured in monetary terms, the worth of all women's work is affected'. She goes on to quote the Registrar General discussing changes in the way that women's work had been classified in recent censuses:

> In 1881 and earlier, daughters and other female relatives of the Head of a Family, who were described as assisting in household duties, were classified as unoccupied. In 1891, however, it was considered that the nature of daily occupations of such persons being thus evident, they would be properly reckoned in Domestic Service … In deciding on the rules of guidance of the clerks at the recent census (1901) however, we came to the conclusion that, on the whole, it would be better to revert to the method of 1881. (Census of Population General Report 1904, quoted in Davidoff 1995 p89)

The British authorities were, it seems, unable to imagine housework as work, even when the 'daily occupations of such persons was evident'. This quote also reveals the possible slippage between *female* family members and domestic servants, a slippage which echoes in the construction of au pairing as family membership.

This confusion on the part of the British authorities encapsulates nineteenth- and twentieth-century views of housework. It was impossible to understand housework as work, and impossible to understand middle-class women as involved in domestic service. By 1901 the separation of home and 'work' had been accomplished as had the coding of housework as unproductive and low status. The figure of the housewife had been successfully created, and this figure would shape the lives of women, and men, at home, in work and in public life.

In contemporary Britain, as in many other countries, women's responsibility for reproductive work still has far-reaching consequences, even though women are increasingly part of the formal paid workforce too. The assumption that women ought to carry out housework and provide care for children and the elderly is still very much alive: for example, in 2012, 33 per cent of those surveyed for the British Social Attitudes Survey thought that women should stay at home to provide care for pre-school children (Scott and Clery n.d.). This assumption has profound effects on women's lack of equality in paid work and the public sphere and it underpins the organisation of paid domestic employment.

The assumption that reproductive labour is 'naturally', rather than socially, women's responsibility feeds the notion that reproductive work should take place within the family. Raising children, caring for adults and generally keeping life and limb together is imagined to be the private business and private benefit of each individual family rather than society as a whole. The result is that vast amounts of socially useful work are done for free by families (see the 'unpaid work calculator' provided by ONS Digital (ONS 2016). ONS estimate that in 2014 £1.01 trillion of unpaid work was carried out in the UK, equivalent to 56 per cent of GDP. Women did 60 per cent more unpaid work than men, 26 hours per week compared to men's 16 hours).

The ideological assumption that women are naturally suited to housework and childcare has far-reaching consequences within the arena of paid work and public life (Hochschild 1989). Women's responsibility for work inside the home has never meant that they are not also involved in paid work outside the home, or in other people's houses. However, this responsibility for reproductive work, and particularly the social construction of women as the appropriate people to do cleaning and caring labour has had an overwhelming effect on the types of paid work that women tend to do. This is most obvious in the large proportion of women employed as paid domestic workers, and it is also true of the tasks that women do in non-domestic settings. Women are much more likely than men to be involved in paid work which involves tasks similar to housework; cleaning, caring and cooking. Jarman, Blackburn and Racko (2012) carried out research in 30 countries and found that in all of them women were concentrated in traditional 'female' roles. For example, in the USA in 2009 97.8 per cent of all pre-kindergarten and kindergarten teachers and 92 per cent of all registered nurses were female, whereas only 1.6 per cent of all carpenters and 2.2 per cent of all electricians were female (Hegewisch et al. 2010 p2). Hegewisch et al. (2010) also found that occupational segregation between the genders fell between 1972 and 1996 in the USA but has hardly changed since then. Women with the lowest levels of education are most likely to be in gender-segregated jobs.

Occupational segregation matters not only because it means that women and men may be funnelled into work which is less than ideal for them as individuals but also because a significant share of the gender wage gap is accounted for by the differences in men's and women's occupations. There is a negative relationship between the proportion of women in an occupation and the average earnings of the occupation – that is, the more women there are in a job the more likely it is that the job will be poorly paid. There are many reasons for this but it has been argued that when women do cleaning and caring tasks the skill or difficulty of those tasks is overlooked (Cox 2010). Women's traditional responsibility for reproductive roles in the home means that the ability to carry out care work and similar jobs is seen as a 'natural' aptitude rather than an acquired skill, and is therefore not deemed to be worthy of reward.

The outcome of this deep entanglement between women's presumed responsibility for domestic work, its invisibility and the widespread discrimination against women in the world of paid work is important in a range of ways. First, understanding the history and social context of the current organisation of domestic roles sheds light on why the gendered division of labour in the home has been so slow to shift despite widespread changes in women's expectations of work outside the home. Second, this practical and ideological frame shapes the conditions of domestic workers and au pairs, including the legal construction of their work and migration statuses. The ideology which presents women as naturally belonging in the home, also presents domestic tasks as something distinctly different from work. This ideology allows for au pairing to be defined as a form of cultural exchange, not work; it also allows for other domestic workers to be subject to highly restrictive visa regulations and for all au pairs and almost all domestic workers to be denied basic labour rights, including minimum pay, restrictions on working hours and protection by health and safety regulations (see Cox 2012; ILO 2011). Last, revealing the current organisation of domestic work as historically specific rather than natural or enduring shows that it can change in the future and greater equality in this arena is possible. Reproductive work does not have to be the private concern of private families, it does not have to be undervalued, poorly rewarded or denied as a real and important form of work.

The employment of paid domestic workers in the private sphere cements the notion that individual families and households are responsible for reproductive labour and this further hides the social value of reproductive work. As Silvia Federici (2012 p71) puts it:

> The employment of a domestic worker, moreover, makes women (rather than the state) responsible for the work of reproduction and weakens the struggle against the division of labor in the family, sparing women the task of forcing their male partners to do this work. (See also Romero 1992)

All of this means that hosting an au pair can be simultaneously imagined as the perfect solution to families' needs for someone to do substantial amounts of housework and childcare and as 'not work'.

Inequality

Gender inequalities are linked to the organisation and performance of domestic labour in its paid and unpaid forms, but when domestic work is paid for, other forms of inequality also become important in its organisation: the forms that it takes, how it is valued and, crucially, who does the work. In this section we trace how income, class and status inequalities have shaped demand for paid domestic workers. While income inequalities appear to have a relatively clear correlation with increasing demand for domestic labour, status differences play out in more subtle ways in the organisation of au pairing. Equality in social status (if not much else) was, historically, at the heart of the au pair concept, and it is still something which is negotiated by host families and au pairs today. One of the ways in which hosts and au pairs make sense of why someone of 'equal status' is carrying out poorly paid and poorly regarded work is through focusing on differences in race/ethnicity or nationality. After outlining briefly the history of how racial/ethnic differences have shaped paid domestic labour markets, we look in detail at the 'invisible' ethnic hierarchies which shape au pairing in the UK. We label these hierarchies 'invisible' both because they are subtle and because they are largely between different white groups.

Whilst au pairing is not technically classified as domestic 'work' – because au pairs are not classified as 'workers' – it is worthwhile considering the burgeoning of this role in the light of the recent, that is since c.1990 (see Higman 2002, Figure 2, p25), growth of paid domestic work worldwide (see Chapter 3 for more detail on this growth). The historian Barry Higman has carried out extensive analysis of trends in the employment of domestic workers in contemporary times and earlier periods (Higman 2002; 2015) and located these trends within economic and political context. Drawing on the work of other historians and of economists, and using the example of Australia, Higman (2002) has traced how periods of growth and contraction in the numbers of domestic workers relate to economic trends. He shows that when unemployment is high and the wages of the low paid fall, the number of domestic workers grows as their labour becomes affordable to those who do have (better paid) work. This is, he suggests, because demand for domestic workers is a constant: 'Latent demand becomes effective demand when domestic assistance is easily affordable' (Milkman, Reese and Roth 1998, quoted in Higman 2002 p20). Like the period of the 1930s' Great Depression, when numbers of domestic workers reached a peak, the recent period has been one of very high levels of income inequalities both within nations and internationally; turning latent demand for domestic workers into effective demand at a global scale.

Higman (2015) also shows that the effects of patterns of income inequalities on the numbers of domestic workers are not entirely simple. Countries with extremely polarised incomes – that is where income is distributed unequally among the top 1 per cent – have lower rates of domestic employment than those where the 1 per cent share wealth more equally. He comments, 'Domestic service grows best in societies where a substantial middle class coexists with significant inequality, rather than where the concentration of wealth is extreme, or where true egalitarianism exists' (Higman 2015 pp33–34).

In his 2015 analysis of domestic service in relation to patterns of colonisation he identifies a number of possible influences on the number of domestic workers employed in a country today. Chief amongst these he argues is a history of slavery: those countries which had long histories as slave-based plantation economies (particularly Latin America and the Caribbean) have the highest numbers of domestic workers today. He also highlights that amongst the 116 countries for which data is available, those nations which have a history of involvement in colonisation – as either colonised or colonisers – have higher rates of domestic employment today than those which have no such history.

The UK in the second decade of the 2000s does have extremely polarised incomes (Dorling 2015), with an income distribution more like that of the USA than of other European countries. However, it also has a substantial middle class, who have seen their incomes grow faster than those in lower deciles. Steve McIntosh (2013 p4) comments that while there has been polarisation in jobs, with those at the bottom and top of the distribution growing and those in the middle shrinking (with the greatest growth numerically being in caring and personal service jobs), 'There is little evidence for wage polarisation – the growth in wages has been highest for high-ranking jobs, followed by middle-ranked jobs, and lowest for low-ranked jobs'. So, while the UK has not seen the growth in numbers of paid domestic workers that have been seen in the USA or southern European countries in recent years, the economic and social conditions for such a growth are there. Since 2008, this broad climate of inequality has been shaped by the imposition of 'austerity' policies in the UK and other European countries, which have also shaped the conditions of au pairing.

Class is an important dimension of the organisation and experience of paid domestic work and au pairing, but class relations within au pairing are not straightforward, as in some ways this is a form of domestic work which is constructed to hide class differences between employer and employee rather than to highlight them. As outlined in Chapter 1, the relatively high status of au pairs was originally seen as part of their attraction, something that would make sharing intimate spaces easier to negotiate (Delap 2011) and the negotiation of class sameness and difference still shapes au pair–host relations today.

The employment of domestic workers has long been implicated in class relations and the maintenance of status differences (Anderson 2000; Cox 2006). Within paid domestic work, class is both about the ability to pay someone and about the maintenance and enhancement of status; employing a domestic worker is not only a simple practical solution to a practical problem, but also an act which creates and maintains class positions (Ray and Qayum 2009). As Ray and Qayum (2009 p10) put it with reference to contemporary India, 'Domestic servitude, then, must be seen as an institution that produces cleanliness, meals and child care, as well as class'.

Social status can also be achieved and communicated through the physical work of au pairs and domestic workers, as they produce the appearance of the house and the competitive advantage of adults and children. Historically the work which servants did to create clean, ordered homes was a very important element of the way in which they ensured the status of their employers. Before electrical appliances and running water were widely available, cleanliness could only be achieved through the use of large amounts of physical labour; a well-kept home, therefore, bespoke the ability of the owner to command that labour. In contemporary times, status is more likely to be communicated through conspicuous consumption and the ownership of houses, furniture, furnishings and clothing that are time-consuming to maintain. Research shows that people who employ domestic workers are less likely to take into account how time-consuming or difficult it is to maintain their clothes or furnishings, than those who do domestic work themselves (Cox 2006). Additionally, employing domestic labour can increase status by freeing up time for employing families to do things other than housework. Adults are able to work long or flexible hours to shore up their position in paid employment, and perhaps more importantly, they are able to work without being distracted by home, particularly the needs of children. This is an approach to work which the housewife traditionally made possible for men, but which few women with children have been able to adopt. Middle-class children are raised to be 'successful' and au pairs (and other domestic workers) are a key element of this, facilitating unending rounds of enriching activities, helping with homework, musical instrument practice and additional languages (Cox 2011). This investment when children are young is designed to ensure their competitive advantage in education and then, later, employment so that they will be able to maintain their class status (Macdonald 2010).

However, the relatively low cost of hosting an au pair, compared to paying for a live-in nanny or housekeeper, combined with the lack of alternative workable forms of childcare, means that hosts are not always wealthy nor unequivocally and confidently middle class. The au pair scheme was originally meant to ensure that middle-class families could continue to access help in the home despite a shrinking domestic labour force, and while this was seen as a democratisation of relations between 'servants' and their employers, the scheme did not originally imagine any democratisation of access to help in the home. However, it seems that hosting an au pair might in some circumstances have become something that families who are not well off may be doing.

At the same time, the status of au pairs as 'not quite' workers has been noted as part of their attraction in some contexts. The veneer of equality which is inherent in the concept of au pairing makes au pairs acceptable to some host families who would be less comfortable employing a nanny or housekeeper. This is perhaps best illustrated in the Nordic countries where au pairs, although small in total numbers, are an increasingly important element of middle-class domestic life. In these countries, where class and gender equality are socially celebrated aspirations, the employment of 'servants' would be unpalatable for the majority of households (see for example Bikova 2010; Gullikstad and Annfelt 2016 on Norway; and also Berg 2015 on Australia).

The international scale at which au pairing, and other forms of paid domestic work, are organised further complicates the question of class. Once arrived to live with their host families, au pairs will often find that they are distinctly not equal to their hosts, but many au pairs, like many other migrant domestic workers, are highly educated and from middle-class backgrounds (see interesting studies by Bikova 2015 and Aguilar Pérez 2015 on experiences of middle-class au pairs). Downward class mobility in migration has been commented on in the literature on migrant domestic workers (Cuban 2013; Parreñas 2000; Pratt 1999b; Salami and Nelson 2014). It is not uncommon for migrant domestic workers to be from middle-class families and to have good levels of education, even to have employed domestic workers themselves. Through the process of migrating and becoming domestic workers they find themselves to have decreasing social status even if their income increases. This is particularly pronounced for migrant domestic workers from low- or middle-income countries as the differences in pay between their home country and destination make this occupational 'down-grading' worthwhile in simple economic terms, if not psychologically.

For au pairs, this process of contradictory class mobility is common because of the way that various au pair schemes are delimited and imagined. Au pairing is used by middle-class young women as a way to travel, see the world and improve language skills or cultural accomplishments (see Bikova 2015 on Filipina au pairs in Norway; Aguilar Pérez 2015 on middle-class Mexican au pairs in the USA; Cox and Busch 2016a; Cuban 2017a). The ideological and practical construction of au pairing means that this form of travel/work/living is not only aimed at a particular group of young, mobile and highly educated people, but also it is unattractive or inaccessible to others. Where formal au pair schemes exist, these tend to have age restrictions and rules about whether au pairs can be married or have children, which makes this form of domestic work less accessible to women who are looking to migrate in order to provide for their families (Cox 2015a; 2015c).

This slippery class context for au pairing at the individual level is important for the lived experience of au pairs and hosts. There is a rhetoric of equality, operating within a distinct power relationship that might be framed by confusion over status for all, as we explore in Chapters 6 and 7. Within this context of confusion and discomfort about class differences and similarities, racial or ethnic differences between domestic workers and employers can further obscure the class inequalities which structure domestic employment and can seem to naturalise the roles of employer and employee. It is to these differences that we now turn.

Invisible ethnic hierarchies

Migration for domestic work is an inevitable consequence of the interplay between global capitalism and structures of gender inequality (Uhde 2016). It is a process which results from and is shaped by inequalities at the global, national and household scales. There is now a large and excellent literature about the many ways in which racial and ethnic inequalities affect paid domestic employment in various different settings (see, amongst many others, edited collections by Haskins and Lowrie 2015; Lutz 2008; Romero, Preston and Giles 2014). This literature shows that histories of slavery and colonisation still shape the organisation of domestic employment in many parts of the world. Ethnic and national differences permeate relations between domestic workers and employers in almost all circumstances and have profound effects on who does which sorts of domestic labour and how they are regarded when they do that work. As paid domestic work is an occupation which is dominated by international migrants in most high-income nations, questions of racial/ethnic or national difference are also bound up with questions of citizenship and migration status for many domestic workers.

In order to understand the organisation of au pairing and experiences of au pairs and hosts in contemporary Britain, we need to add an exploration of how white identities become differentiated and how ethnic hierarchies are manifest within a relationship that is meant to be characterised by equality. This section starts by outlining two key ways in which existing literature has discussed race and ethnicity within paid domestic labour; the legacy of colonialism and the association of whiteness with cleanliness and blackness with dirt. It then goes on to look at literatures on white identities and the way that some white groups are not as equal as others. We argue that, as with Latvian Volunteer Workers, or Irish domestic servants before them (see Chapter 1), whiteness hides the inequalities of au pair–host relationships. There are hierarchies of whiteness in the British labour market (McDowell 2009) and they are evident in the experiences of au pairs. An examination of au pairing can also help us to understand the complexities of whiteness better, particularly at a time when many EU citizens are having to find new ways to belong in the UK.

Racial/ethnic hierarchies in labour markets are in no way unique to paid domestic work. However, in this sector they play out in particular ways because of the intimacy of the work involved, its closeness to dirt and, in many contexts, histories of slavery and colonisation which have shaped flows of domestic workers and expectations of who should do this work (Anderson 2000). White colonisers in the nineteenth century identified local people in colonised areas and former slave populations in the Americas as appropriate to do the hard work of domestic labour and to be close to dirt. In Europe, (former) colonial relations have shaped migration flows in the twentieth and twenty-first centuries, meaning that in many European countries (although not the UK) women from former colonies are numerous in domestic labour markets and seen as suitable domestic workers (Marchetti 2014).

Throughout the colonies, people of colour were portrayed as dirty but also tasked with keeping white settlers clean. Concepts of personal and domestic cleanliness were also part of the 'civilising' mission of Empire and used to structure unequal relations between countries. Anne McClintock (1995) has argued that through instilling routines of personal hygiene, and the marketing of British-manufactured soap, the management of cleanliness in newly colonised areas was a means of imposing social order and control. In colonial Africa advertising campaigns associated cleanliness with whiteness and 'civilisation' and darker skins with dirt and 'backwardness' (Burke 1996). For example, an advertisement for Pears' Soap from the 1890s has the text:

> The first step towards lightening The White Man's Burden is through teaching the virtues of cleanliness. Pears' Soap is a potent factor in brightening the dark corners of the earth as civilisation advances while amongst the cultured of all nations it holds the highest place – it is the ideal toilet soap.

In the centre of the picture is a naval officer washing his hands in a spotless bathroom while in the background there are images of steam ships carrying Pears' Soap to the colonies and of a clerically dressed white man handing soap to a grateful black man in a loin cloth who is seated at his feet.[1] The message of such advertisements is clear and it resonated with customers because of wider discourses that reinforced the idea that white Europeans were cleaner, better and more advanced than the peoples they were colonising. Unilever used the phrase 'soap is civilisation' in their advertising, despite the fact that the system of forced labour that they invented and used in Belgian Congo to produce the oils needed for soap manufacture is estimated to have halved the Congolese population through its brutality (Ally 2013).

This broader context shaped domestic service. Writing on one of the starkest examples of this, colonial South Africa, Shireen Ally (2013 p324) sums up this paradoxical relationship between domestic servants, dirt and colonisation:

> Domestic servants are at the centre of the most distinctive paradox of colonial cleanliness. Settler colonialism discursively premised itself on Africans as filthy savages, while white colonists depended on those same 'dirty' heathen blacks to keep them Christianly clean. Black servants were forced to use separate utensils so they would not pollute their white masters' things with their embodied dirtiness, yet incongruously, black hands spent all day in contact with – polishing, scrubbing, and dusting – the things that made white colonists white:

the shining furniture and splendid homes that bestowed Victorian virtue on settlers. Perhaps more significantly, the 'dirty' labouring hands of black servants spent their days keeping white bodies, literally, clean. Black servants bathed white settlers' babies, laundered colonials' clothes, hauled and emptied their chamber pots. Whites were made clean through this tactile intimacy with 'dirty' black hands. In sum, white cleanliness was intimately dependent on unclean black labour. Nowhere was the racialised moral scaffold of colonisation and cleanliness seemingly more incongruous.

Whilst South Africa is a particularly clear example of blackness being explicitly and repeatedly associated with dirt and whiteness with cleanliness and civilisation, a similar pattern appears in many other countries. It is not only in the recesses of history that this happens. We find the same pattern of domestic workers being cast as dirty and polluting due to their ethnicity but still responsible for producing the cleanliness which signals the superiority of their employers today. Sabrina Marchetti (2014 p110) quotes an Afro-Surinamese domestic worker, who, explaining how she got her job in the Netherlands, said simply, 'Because they couldn't find any white person to clean shit'. Similarly, a detailed study of imaginings of pollution amongst employers of domestic workers in Brazil (Barbosa 2007) found that notions of cleanliness, dirt and pollution were used to restrict the behaviour of domestic workers and to establish physical separation between the domestic worker and the rest of the house. Domestic workers are given bedrooms which are behind the kitchen area and out of sight of visitors. The room is generally constructed from materials which emphasise hygiene and are easy to clean, for example by having tiles on the floor rather than wood parquet. The domestic worker's bedroom is also often used as the storage space for cleaning equipment such as vacuum cleaners and the domestic worker may be expected to wash in the sink in the utility room which is also used to clean the dirtiest things in the house. There seems to be a confusion between the domestic worker as a person and the tools that are needed to do domestic work and with other objects that are considered dirty. Domestic workers in the study were not allowed to wash their clothes in the same washing machine as their employers or to eat from the same crockery or cutlery. As Livia Barbosa (2007 p30) comments, high standards of hygiene are expected of domestic workers at all times and to be dirty at work is a criterion for firing a maid, therefore the separation of domestic workers from employers 'does not have to do with the presence or absence of dirt itself, but with the idea of pollution'.

The stigma of working with dirt means that domestic workers find themselves trapped within a vicious circle, which defines domestic cleaning as low status because it is done by women, and women as low status because they deal with dirt. Migrant women and women of colour are additionally caught in a cycle that characterises them as appropriate people to do dirty work, and thereafter stigmatises them because of their contact with other people's dirt.

Sabrina Marchetti (2014) has used the concept of 'coloniality of power' (from Quijano 2000) to understand the concentration of black women in paid domestic work in contemporary Europe. She argues that in order to understand the concentration of migrant women in paid domestic work, we need to go beyond theories which describe the labour market and to look at the way that colonial legacies shape contemporary labour hierarchies. Using this lens, Marchetti argues, we can see how the cultural assumptions of colonialism did not vanish with the end of formal political control, but rather 'coloniality' shapes relationships between people today, and shapes the ideas, values, images, attitudes and social practices which circulate. For migrant domestic workers, this legacy is manifest in the segregation of labour markets and the concentration of migrant women in dirty, low-status work. Past relationships between former colonisers and colonised echo in contemporary representations and imaginings of who is available to do which sorts of work for whom.

The precise ways in which migrant workers are imagined and labour markets stratified varies over time and space, producing unique, geographically and historically specific hierarchies of domestic workers. In addition to the association between racialised groups and dirt, which tends to mean that people who are most discriminated against are allocated the dirtiest work, people of certain nationalities or ethnicities are also portrayed as being 'naturally' good domestic workers. They may be considered as particularly caring towards children or elderly people or particularly fastidious housekeepers. Filipino domestic workers, for example, have been marketed by their national government as 'supermaids', 'compassionate, loving super-workers' (Guevarra 2014 p131). This positions them in particular ways in labour markets, making domestic work more easily available to some nationalities and creating ethnic niches within domestic labour markets (Marchetti 2014). The resulting domestic labour markets vary from country to country (see for example Cox 1999 on the UK; Stiell and England 1999 on Canada; Marchetti 2014 on Italy; and the Netherlands and Nesbitt-Ahmed 2016 on Nigeria), but the result is that people, particularly women, who are from a national group which is concentrated in domestic work can find it difficult to enter other forms of employment (Pratt 1999b). Additionally, it must be remembered that the majority of domestic workers globally are not international migrants (Ray and Qayum 2009). Domestic workers can also be internal migrants moving from rural to urban areas and are often members of ethnic groups which are discriminated against.

Ethnic stereotypes combine with migration rules and policies (see Chapter 3) that restrict workers' access to labour markets and steer them into domestic work under conditions which limit their agency (Anderson 2009; 2010; 2014). In different countries and at different points in time, therefore, we see policy, cultural expectations and social norms combining in different ways to create domestic labour markets that are stratified on the basis of nationality, race/ethnicity, religion or caste. At the time of our study, au pairs in the UK were, for the most part, people who had free access to the UK labour market, were not from visible ethnic minorities, nor from countries that were former British colonies. In order to understand their experiences of au pairing and their location within hierarchies of domestic workers, we need to look in more detail at the construction and differentiation of whiteness in Britain in the twenty-first century.

In contrast to the countries where colonial histories have produced strongly racialised domestic labour markets, Britain has favoured white migrants as domestic workers (as outlined in Chapter 1). During our study the au pairs we met were not differentiated from hosts by visible racial differences; almost all au pairs were white and from European countries as were most of their host families and the hosts we interviewed. Instead, what comes to the fore in our study is the importance of national stereotypes, inequalities in citizenship status and the small rumblings of anti-European xenophobia which have since exploded around the EU referendum of June 2016 (see for example Weaver (2016) on the murder of a Polish man in Essex and the rise of hate crime against Eastern Europeans since the 'Brexit' vote). In this section we explore the on-going construction of whiteness in the contemporary UK, its relationship to UK migration policies and European 'belonging'.

Whiteness is not an absolute, undifferentiated or unchanging category, it is, as Noel Ignatiev (1995) says, something you 'do'. It can be claimed, denied, negotiated and bestowed on and by different groups through political and cultural practices, government policies and representations (Fox, Moroşanu and Szilassy 2012). As Alastair Bonnett comments (2008 p17) 'the history of whiteness is one of transitions and changes. This history is also a geography. It concerns the way the world has been imaginatively seized, its parts compared and its centre and periphery established'. Across time and space various national, religious and cultural groups have been considered, and considered themselves to be 'white'.

Within the category 'white', there are degrees of whiteness that position different white groups within a hierarchy of acceptability; whiteness is not just about skin colour but also about class, religion, status and language (Bonnett 2008; McDowell 2009). Historically, this can be seen in the treatment of the Irish in Britain. The Irish have been represented as racially inferior in England since at least the twelfth century. In the nineteenth century 'scientific' studies of different 'races' were made to establish equivalences between African and Irish characteristics and the 'facial angle index' was used to 'prove' the 'white negro' status of the Irish. Religious difference was used to politically exclude Irish people from belonging in the British nation, and their Catholic religion was seen to represent both a political threat and an inherent difference in character from a rational, individualist Protestant majority (Walter 2001). 'Racial oppression does not depend on a difference in phenotype' as Ignatiev (1995 p216) so succinctly puts it.

In the twentieth century whiteness became almost exclusively associated with European origins (Bonnett 2000), leading to a reciprocal association between whiteness and Europeanness (Fox et al. 2012) and also differentiation amongst white Europeans on the basis of nationality (McDowell 2008). In the context of twenty-first-century EU enlargement and relatively free movement of labour amongst EU member states, 'degrees of whiteness' (Fox et al. 2012 p680) exist amongst EU workers in Britain. Fox et al. (2012) have analysed British immigration policy and tabloid media articles to show how (white) European migrants have both been welcomed into the British nation in preference to other (non-white) migrants, and differentiated on the basis of nationality and degree of 'Europeanness', and therefore whiteness. Romanian migrants in particular have been represented in highly racialised ways in the press after having been 'symbolically denuded of their whiteness by an immigration policy that refused to recognise them as full Europeans with the associated rights (and colour) such a status would have otherwise availed them' (Fox et al. 2012 p685). While EU migrants have an advantage over non-white migrants, a 'new hierarchy of desirability' (McDowell 2008 p62) has been constructed in the UK labour market.

It is within this new, shifting hierarchy that the au pairs and hosts in our study found themselves. Putatively similar on the basis of shared European belonging and legal right to work in the UK, au pairs were practically differentiated by nationality. Romanian and Bulgarian au pairs were affected by the immigration rules that treated them differently to nationals of other EU member states at the time we were doing our research and Romanian au pairs were particularly affected by the negative stereotyping noted by Fox et al. (2012). However, stereotyping was not restricted to any national group, but pervaded the au pair sector, affecting access to (good) posts, rates of pay, work done and more. Europeanness, and associated whiteness, gave young European women (and a few men) access to au pair roles in Britain, but minute differentiations and assumptions on the basis of nationality sorted them into different experiences of au pairing (Cox and Busch 2016b).

Conclusion

In seeking to provide a theoretical context to understand the organisation of au pairing in the contemporary UK, this chapter has ranged widely, from the origins of 'housework' as a specific form of unpaid labour, to recent discrimination against some groups of EU migrants in the UK labour market. This wide lens has been necessary because au pairing is shaped by multiple forms of inequality that work together to shape who hosts an au pair, who becomes an au pair, the work that they do and the conditions in which they work.

We have argued that au pairing involves invisible work and hidden inequalities and it is necessary to illuminate these concealed aspects of its conceptualisation and organisation in order to understand the experiences of au pairs and hosts. The work done by au pairs is denied because of the type of tasks that they do. To understand this denial, we need to understand the relationship between housework, the gendering of responsibility for this work and how 'work' has been understood since the industrial revolution and the concomitant physical and financial separation of home and work became common for men. The deep roots of the misrecognition of reproductive labour – deep not only in historical terms but also in their significance in the reordering of daily life – mean that assumptions about the nature, value and 'right' organisation of domestic labour are also deeply held. They underpin government policy in diverse areas including immigration, child and elder care, planning and housing provision and affect social and cultural expectations. Overcoming these assumptions, therefore, is hardly easy. So, even when housework is done for pay, it is not clearly visible as work and it is relatively easy for anyone who does this work to slip from the category 'worker'. Au pairing is, therefore, not an odd relic of an earlier practice of exchange between families, but is a distillation of the contradictions inherent in the contemporary organisation of reproductive labour.

The premise of equality between au pair and host can hide the various forms of inequality that are so important to the operation of the sector. Income inequality fuels the growth of all forms of paid domestic employment, creating both a demand for services and a supply of labour. Within this context of putative equality, confusions and contradictions around status are important in shaping the labour market, drawing relatively highly educated women into au pairing. This, in turn, shapes the experiences of hosts and au pairs, and the ambiguous class status of au pairs further hides the real work that they do.

In many forms of paid domestic labour, inequalities between employers and employees are also manifest in terms of race/ethnicity. Racial/ethnic differences can obscure class differences (and similarities) and can be used as a way to rationalise and naturalise the roles of employer and employee. The association of dark skins with dirt and white skins with purity is one way in which this rationalisation and naturalisation happens. Understanding the relationship between status, dirt, gender and ethnicity is important to understand the experiences of au pairs as they negotiate different aspects of their role and their relationships with hosts. We have also drawn on literature which analyses hierarchies amongst white migrants in the UK workforce and which highlights differentiation on grounds of nationality. The on-going, shifting and often subtle racialisation of European workers in the UK is the context within which au pairs in Britain live.

Note

1 http://wwnorton.com/college/
history/give-me-liberty4/img/ch/17/
CH17_05.jpg.

3 | THE TWENTY-FIRST-CENTURY GROWTH IN DEMAND FOR DOMESTIC LABOUR

Having located au pairing in historical context we now look at the contemporary circumstances of au pairing in the UK including the more general expansion of paid domestic work worldwide. This chapter explores these global trends in the growth of privatised forms of child (and elder) care to locate contemporary au pairing in the UK in a broader geographical and social context. We do this to emphasise that au pairing is a form of paid domestic labour, even if it is constructed by policy makers and actors in the industry as something other than work. The chapter begins by outlining the resurgence in the numbers of paid domestic workers at the end of the twentieth century, a resurgence which took academic observers by surprise and which is commonly explained as a response to increasing numbers of women, particularly middle-class women, engaging in paid work outside the home. We then complicate this explanation by looking at the broader context of childcare in the UK, showing how government policies have supported the growth of a privatised domestic labour force, through a lack of investment in the collective provision of care, the promotion of ideologies which locate responsibility for care with families, particularly with mothers, and the use of migration schemes – such as au pairing – to mould workers to fit the domestic labour force. One outcome of the growth in migration to undertake domestic work is the creation of 'Global Care Chains' which link families across the globe. In the second part of the chapter we look in more detail at the complexities of family life and how changes in women's working patterns, a lack of change in men's attitudes to housework, a lack of flexible public childcare combined with parenting philosophies such as 'intensive parenting' which increase the work of childcare have all fed into demand for paid domestic and care workers.

The global growth in paid domestic labour

The period since the 1990s has been a time of growth in the numbers of domestic workers employed around the world and the increase in the number of au pairs and au pair schemes can be seen as part of this growth. The burgeoning numbers of domestic workers took observers by surprise at the end of the twentieth century as for two decades scholars had assumed that domestic service, particularly in its live-in form, would disappear altogether because of 'social progress', household technologies and the development of welfare states (Sarti 2014). 'World War I was assumed by many scholars to have been the point at which the history of domestic service in "developed countries" came to an end' (Sarti 2014 p292). The sociologist Lewis Coser had proclaimed that the role was 'dying' in a 1973 article somewhat unfortunately titled 'Servants: The Obsolescence of an Occupational Role'. Many scholars studying domestic service had subscribed to a theory put forward by the economist Ester Boserup (1970) that employment in domestic work and other personal services grew during the 'intermediate' stages of economic development, with the expectation that as economies develop the sector will decline. However, in the 1980s and early 1990s the trend in the numbers of domestic workers, which for the countries of the Global North, had been declining since the 1930s, started to change.

The International Labour Organization (ILO) estimates that there are at least 53 million domestic workers worldwide and the number could be as high as 100 million, 83 per cent of whom are women. As the ILO explains, even at its lowest estimate 'if all domestic workers worked in one country, this country would be the tenth largest employer worldwide' (ILO 2011). Whilst numbers of au pairs are tiny compared with these global totals, their numbers are growing in tandem with other forms of paid domestic work.

Growth in the numbers of domestic workers, and particularly the very large numbers of *migrant* domestic workers, has been part of a much broader globalisation of manufacturing and services which has seen increased flows in goods and people around the world. Rather than the numbers of domestic workers being described as part of national level economic development, they are now understood to be located within global-scale trends, where inequality between and within nations is crucial to understanding the numbers of people entering domestic work, where they come from and where they go to (Sarti 2014). The large numbers of women migrating to take on paid domestic work have made domestic workers the iconic female migrants (Uhde 2016). 'The growth of "new" domestic work has involved the expansion of arrangements that were long considered "old", "traditional", and not appropriate in "modern" societies, such as, in particular, the co-residence of employers and employees under the same roof' (Sarti 2014 p307).

The tasks which domestic workers and au pairs undertake are labour intensive and neither well respected nor well rewarded. They consume many hours of people's time but are also considered to be unskilled; something that anyone, or at least any woman, can do. Domestic work is, therefore, exactly the sort of work which has been globalised, that is moved to low-wage economies in order to take advantage of cheap and plentiful available labour, but rather than children and houses being neatly packed up in container ships or the holds of airfreight planes and sent, like the components of a car or a mobile phone, to be worked on in a low-wage location, domestic labour is globalised by moving low-paid workers around the world. The growth of au pairing, in the UK and elsewhere, can be understood within this broader context of a resurgence in paid domestic employment worldwide.

Globalisation has affected the movement of domestic workers into childcare not only by facilitating the movement of people around the world but also through the spread of neoliberal ideologies which have underpinned the withdrawal of the state from care provision and broader processes of urbanisation and class restructuring. We see an increasingly similar pattern of privatised childcare across the globe as even nations which have traditionally shunned private solutions and invested in state support for childcare, such as the Nordic countries (Isaksen 2010), are moving towards increased use of private childcare. We now see flows of migrant domestic workers and au pairs to these countries which, until the late 1990s, could be characterised by both plentiful publicly provided childcare and social attitudes that rejected the employment of privatised forms of domestic work. As Lutz and Palenga-Möllenbeck (2012 p19) put it

> at the end of the twentieth century Eastern Europe and Western and Southern Europe – despite their very different histories – arrived at a nexus in which labor market participation was seen as an adult citizen's duty, while states were not or no longer prepared to deliver the necessary support for the balance of waged and care work.

To this constellation of European states we could add that North America and many parts of the rapidly developing economies of the

Global South were moving in a very similar direction (see for example, Glenn 2010 on the USA; Nesbitt-Ahmed 2016 on Nigeria; Ray and Qayum 2009 on India).

Mirroring policies which encourage universal workforce participation and private solutions to the needs for child and elder care, are migration policies which produce a supply of care workers. UK employment and immigration policy have worked together to produce a new 'servant class' unable to access even minimum wages. Williams and Gavanas (2008 p15) have shown how the phenomenon of female migration into domestic and childcare work 'can be understood as part of the dovetailing of childcare regimes (state policy responses to changes in family and work) with migration regimes (state policy responses to changes in work, population movement and change)'. Opportunities (or not) for migration to carry out domestic work are, therefore, directly related both to state policies on childcare, family leave etc. and to cultural expectations about how domestic and care work should be done and who should do it. The resulting migration policies seek to produce particular types of labour (low waged, 'unskilled', insecure) performed by particular migrants (women, often from specific countries) that are seen as appropriate to the type of work and undemanding to the state (Walia 2010).

Au pair schemes, including the UK's lack of regulation since 2008, are examples of migration policies which produce appropriate workers. Domestic workers and au pairs are 'moulded' by specific and highly restrictive migration rules (Anderson 2010) which reflect national care and migration regimes. Looking at migration schemes around the world, we find that for the most part such rules give domestic workers fewer rights, for example to permanent settlement or family reunification, than other migrants and impose stricter controls on their behaviour (Ozyegin and Hondagneu-Sotelo 2008). Most commonly this includes stipulations that domestic workers live in their employers' homes but there may also be regulations that govern aspects of a domestic worker's private life, such as restrictions on personal relationships. Migration regulations can also act to empower employers to impose additional, even stricter, conditions on domestic workers which can cover aspects of dress, hairstyles and most other areas of life (see Cox 2012 for an overview). Requirements that workers live in and those that tie a worker to a particular employer – as is the case with au pair schemes in Norway, the USA and elsewhere, increase employers' or hosts' power over domestic workers and au pairs to enforce such rules. Migration schemes developed expressly to allow the import of domestic labour rarely give domestic workers protection against low pay and long hours of work. For au pairs this most clearly happens through their positioning as 'not workers', a status which specifically excludes au pairs in many countries from protections under labour laws.

These examples demonstrate that the UK au pair scheme is not unique in constructing precarity for domestic workers. Through their specific restrictions, or by turning a blind eye, migration regimes create workers with particular characteristics, able to command particular pay and conditions (Anderson 2010). In the case of domestic workers and au pairs the characteristics demanded are generally low cost to employers and insecurity. Migration regimes achieve this in a range of ways – from tightly regulating the migration of workers and giving them only limited rights to creating conditions which encourage the supply of undocumented workers who are inherently insecure, or as in the case of UK au pairs, by creating a non-worker category that only migrants can fill.

The internationalisation of the care workforce, and the trend towards migrant domestic workers providing care for children within private homes has led to the development of what are termed 'Global Care Chains' (GCCs) a concept which lays bare the differential impacts of migrant care work on the children of the migrant worker and the children of her employer and around which public concern for migrant care workers has been catalysed. A 'care chain' is created if a migrating care worker recruits someone, usually a woman, from a still poorer household to look after her own children. That woman may be a paid worker or an unpaid family member and she may then need to pass care for her own children to someone else. As we go 'down' the chain the monetary value of the care labour decreases until it is unpaid and at the end of the chain an older daughter may substitute for her mother and care for her younger siblings (Yeates 2012). Au pairs are imagined to be outside GCCs, because they are not thought to have any caring responsibilities in their home countries. The focus that GCCs give to migrant domestic workers as mothers has had the effect of overlooking the experiences of migrant domestic workers who do not leave children behind and has been used by policy makers to justify support for au pair schemes.

Global Care Chains (GCCs) reveal not only the process of the globalising of care, but also the lived experiences of this globalisation for care workers and their families and the stark inequalities between women. Global Care Chains leapt to prominence following Arlie Hochschild's (2000; 2003) writing on the transfer of care from poor families in the Philippines to wealthy families in the USA, when Filipina nannies leave their own children behind in order to take up jobs as domestic workers abroad. She likened the care chain to a commodity chain, whereby care was extracted from poor countries and consumed in rich ones. Thus, it is poor women and their children who bear the costs of a global shortage of care, through the loss and pain they suffer due to separation. Parents and children in the rich world benefit from the easing of work-family balance conflicts and the flow of 'surplus love' from poorer countries.

Hochschild's account of the 'importation of care and love from poor countries to rich ones' (2003 p17) highlighted the emotional pain felt by migrant workers who care for other people's children yet are separated from their own children for many years at a time; 'a choice freighted, for many, with a terrible sadness' (2003 p22) as she describes it. Hochschild calls the love which such women give to the children that they care for and are unable to give to their own children 'a global heart transplant' (2003 p22). She argues that children left behind suffer both physically and psychologically, they are ill more often than their classmates, express anger, confusion and apathy and do less well at school. Rather than love being something that does not run out, a renewable resource, Hochschild argues that these findings show that love is in fact a scare resource which is extracted from the South and consumed in the North.

The idea of a care chain or care drain is linked to gendered norms for caring responsibilities. It would be easy to conclude that the migration of mothers to carry out care for other children, many hundreds or thousands of miles away, could only lead to trauma and negative consequences for their own families. However, this assumption naturalises women's role as carers and also naturalises one particular, Western, version of mothering. Mothering can take many forms and there are many possible care arrangements for children. There have been studies which have focused on the relation between financial support for children left behind and their educational performance and shown this to be positive; others that have looked at the negative effects of the absence of mothers and those which argue the outcome of the care chain is neither simply positive nor negative (Lutz and Palenga-

Möllenbeck 2012). Studies have also highlighted the possibilities of mothering from a distance. This includes many forms of contact such as Skype calls, which, as they are often free, can be both frequent and long. Some migrant domestic workers will stay online to family all day on their day off and cook and eat meals 'with' them (Madianou and Miller 2011). Parents can supervise homework by Skype and send text messages to remind children to pack the right things for school or eat a healthy lunch. However, there are limits to such contact for many families and distant contact is not the same as presence and not all employers allow workers to call frequently or to use computers. Time differences may make contact awkward and very young children are least able to communicate with their parents this way.

The GCC concept brings to light the very different things that childcare can and does involve. For middle-class parents in the Global North who employ migrant carers, the priority can be to reproduce a form of care based on an ideal of intensive mothering which accords large amounts of time to children and involves them in 'enriching activities' in order to ensure that they will achieve in measurable terms and be given the foundation which will enable them to be financially successful in later life (Macdonald 2010). For migrant workers, the priority might be providing materially for their children through their remittances and expressing their emotions in that way (Mckay 2007) while they stay in contact and care for their children using information and communication technologies. Yeates (2009) argues that the GCC approach could be strengthened by including a broader conception of care – one that attends to nursing care and care for elderly people, as well as childcare in collective settings. This conceptualisation would expose the important role that governments and institutions play in triggering care chains and shaping the globalisation of care, recognise the diversity of migrants' familial circumstances and counter the heterosexism evident in the original approach (see also Manalansan 2006).

Au pairs are always imagined to be outside these sorts of chains; they are thought to be more like gap-year students than mothers and they are not thought to be motivated by the desire to earn money to send as remittances. While for very many au pairs (and other domestic workers too) this is the case, it is also a situation which has been legislated into existence rather than arising because of the nature of au pairing. An examination of the attempts to exclude mothers, and other people with dependents, from au pairing, reveals the closeness between au pairs and other migrant domestic workers. In most formal au pair schemes internationally – that is schemes which have rules that set out who can and who cannot be an au pair and under what conditions – people who are married or who have dependent children are specifically excluded from being able to apply for au pair posts or visas. The best studied example of this is Norway, where concerns over 'mommy robbery', as the importation of migrant domestic workers was termed, have been expressed in the press (Stubberud 2015a). One result of press outrage at the experiences of au pairs who had left their children in the Philippines was that in 2012, Norway closed its au pair scheme to parents (something which Denmark had already done), this means that some au pairs now lie about having children and risk having their visas revoked if they are discovered to be mothers (Stubberud 2015a). In the absence of other, legal, routes for labour migration from au pair-sending countries, the result is not that au pairs are outside GCCs or that Norway and Denmark are not implicated in draining care from poor families, rather au pairs are more likely to work in situations which make regular contact with their children difficult and hazardous.

Hochschild's (2003) account of the pain that migrant workers feel caring for other people's children appears to distinguish migrant women involved in privatised childcare from those involved in other forms of care work and overlooks the myriad dependencies and responsibilities that people have. Mariya Bikova (2010; 2015) has written about the care relationships that Norwegian au pairs from the Philippines are involved in and she argues that these are better thought of as 'care circulation' (after Baldassar and Merla 2014) than more simple chains. As she demonstrates, it is not only mothers who are involved in providing care for friends and relatives, and it is not only mothers who are a loss to their communities if they migrate. Au pairs can be part of a 'socio-emotional commons' (Bikova 2015 p90) that is depleted if they leave their homes.

The large and growing numbers of migrant domestic workers worldwide have led to a burgeoning of scholarship on the causes of this growth and the experiences of migrant domestic workers. Au pairs need to be considered as part of this broader group of migrant paid domestic workers and au pair schemes need to be understood as part of broader trends in government policies to produce a supply of low-waged domestic labour with limited rights. Like other live-in domestic workers their experiences are shaped by a broader policy context, international inequalities and the specific circumstances of the host family they live with.

The mysterious absence of work–life balance

The growth in the numbers of paid domestic workers worldwide is generally explained as being due to changes in women's work outside the home, particularly the increasing numbers of women with young children who are now in paid work and the numbers of middle-class women who work in career structured jobs which demand long hours and commitment (see for example Ehrenreich and Hochschild 2003; Gregson and Lowe 1994; Macdonald 2010). Policy makers in some countries have justified the importance of the au pair schemes on this basis, even in countries which are otherwise antithetical to low-waged labour migration. For example, the Social Democratic mayor of Copenhagen (Denmark) wrote in a leading magazine about the city's policies to support female executives:

> But it is not even necessary for modern women to be faced by the dilemma of family and career … In special cases, the local council can even offer a subsidy for au pair and cleaning services as part of the salary package. We will create good possibilities for more female executives. We simple have to make it possible for women to make it to the top. (Quoted in Stenum 2010 p40)

Even in the 'woman friendly' (Bikova 2010) Nordic countries the assumption is that women are responsible for reproductive labour and that au pairs and other domestic workers are taken on in order to make working outside the home possible, or palatable for women.

While it is undoubtable that a great many families who host au pairs will reason similarly to the Mayor of Copenhagen and that individual women will experience an au pair or domestic worker as relieving them rather than anyone else of a domestic burden, it is also worthwhile to be sceptical of explanations which appear to assume that childcare would or should always 'normally' be carried out by mothers. An explanation of the growth in the employment of au pairs and domestic workers which highlights increasing rates of women's paid workforce participation works only if we note that while this change in women's lives has happened in many countries, it has not been met by a concomitant change in imaginings of men's responsibilities, or by a great increase in state provision of care. In other words, it is not that the increase in numbers of women working outside the home causes a childcare crisis and with it a demand for au pairs and other domestic workers, but the enduring assumption that women are still responsible for child-care despite the fact that they are now more likely to work outside the home.

Citing the growth in women's paid employment as a reason why more au pairs, nannies, babysitters or cleaners are employed overlooks all the other possible arrangements for childcare and housework that could be made. It silences questions about why men do not do more in the home, why working patterns are so family unfriendly and who cares for the children of families who cannot pay others. In order to fully understand the increase in numbers of paid domestic workers and au pairs it is necessary to also consider the broad context within which families try to negotiate the demands of home and paid work, including working patterns, state withdrawal from social welfare provision, attitudes towards childcare, ideologies around mothering and the rise of labour-intensive competitive caring.

The majority of au pairs in the UK are involved in providing childcare as well as doing housework. Parents' working hours – including things like shift patterns, the need to work extra hours at short notice or just long hours of work – have an effect on the demand for au pairs, the relationship between hosts and au pairs and on au pairs' wider experiences of life in the UK. The long and flexible hours that British parents work are an important element of the context of au pairing in this country and something which was evident in the advertisements for au pairs which we analysed (see Chapter 4) and which permeated interviews with host families (see Chapter 7).

Parents in the UK work long hours compared to many of our European neighbours but the pattern of this work is highly gendered with men's workforce participation increasing when they become parents while the likelihood of women being in paid work, particularly full-time work, falls. In 2011 average working hours for full-time workers in the UK were 42.7 per week, the highest of the large economies in Europe (Greece and Austria had longer hours). At the same time the average of all hours worked – that is by both full-time and part-time workers was in the middle of the range for European countries, reflecting the large number of part-time workers in the UK (Stewart 2011). The pattern of part-time and full-time work is gendered; in

2013 men in the UK worked an average of 44 hours per week and only 12 per cent were in part-time work, while 42 per cent of women were in part-time work (ONS 2013). Parenthood also affects men's and women's working patterns differently. Fathers are more likely to be in work than men of working age without children (91 per cent compared to 74 per cent, with fathers also less likely to be working part time than men without dependent children). The trend for women, however, is the opposite: mothers are less likely to be in paid work than women without dependent children (ONS 2013). In 2004 73 per cent of women without dependent children were in work, 23 per cent part time, compared to 71 per cent of married or cohabiting mothers who were in work, 42 per cent working part time (Walling 2005).

This pattern of a 'one and a half' worker model, where one parent works full time, often long hours, and one parent works part time, has increasingly come to characterise British families, particularly middle-class ones (Holloway and Pimlott-Wilson 2016). Comparative figures for the 27 EU member states in 2010 showed that only the Netherlands, Denmark and Austria had a higher percentage of mothers aged 20–49 in part-time work than the UK. In the Netherlands almost all mothers work part time and part-time jobs are widely available with employers being legally required to provide part-time contracts at the employee's request. In Denmark there is a similar long tradition of facilitating participation in both paid work and family life. However, in the UK part-time work is more likely to be taken on in response to economic pressures combined with a lack of affordable childcare and the work available is likely to be lower skilled and worse paid than full-time work (Miani and Hoorens 2014).

The 'one and a half' worker model can make hosting an au pair a particularly attractive way of providing childcare for those who can afford it. While there are no longer any fixed limits on the number of hours that an au pair can work (see Introduction), for many au pairs and host families there is still an expectation that au pairs should provide a limited number of hours of childcare each week, and are not appropriate for providing full-time care for pre-school children. The relatively low cost of hosting an au pair can also mean that this form of care is affordable even when one parent does not work full time.

In order to be useful, as well as being affordable, childcare has to cover the hours that parents need. In the UK increasingly long working hours, growing numbers of parents working outside 'normal' hours and an expectation of 'flexibility' in terms of hours worked, all make childcare hard to organise. Added to the demands of working hours can be complications of moving between work and home, particularly in large cities, like London, where commute times are long and in areas where high property prices make living near work impossible.

As one report found, 'At least one partner in 75 per cent of families on low-to-middle incomes and in 91 per cent of families on higher incomes works outside the hours 8am–6pm, once thought of as the normal working day' (Alakeson 2011 p3). These trends affect childcare arrangements and feed demand for the most flexible forms of childcare (Hill 2015). The situation in London is particularly pronounced because of higher than average rates of flexible working and a shortage of flexible forms of childcare. The Family and Childcare Trust (2015) found that there has been a growth in the number of Londoners who work outside standard nine-to-five hours, but childminder numbers are in decline and fewer parents in London are able to rely on grandparents to provide informal childcare than families in other areas.

An additional complication for Londoners trying to fit work around formal childcare is the long travel times many face to get to work. A TUC study in 2012 found that the average Londoner spent 75 minutes a day commuting, compared to 52.8 minutes for the country as a whole. Notably the time that women in London spend travelling to work has increased in recent years; men in the capital spend on average 77.2 minutes and women 72.8 minutes. Nowhere else in the UK do women spend more than 48 minutes per day on average on their commute to work (O'Doherty 2012). When added to long and flexible hours such journeys can make the use of group childcare with set hours impossible.

Men's involvement in and attitudes towards housework and childcare have changed over the last 50 years, even while gender inequalities persist. One of the most noticeable changes is in the time that fathers spend with their children (Kilkey, Perrons and Plomien 2013; Aitken 2016). Between 1975 and 1997 British fathers' time spent caring for their children rose 800 per cent; from 15 minutes to two hours on average per working day. By 2005 31 per cent of fathers were working flexitime to spend more time with their children and the number of 'home dads' doubled between 1993 and 2011. These figures do need to be understood in the context of wider parenting culture, which has seen both mothers and fathers spend more time with their children

– a move which has been cemented by policies which favour such an approach (Faircloth 2014b).

However, the UK still lags behind many Northern European countries in terms of men's involvement in childcare and housework, and state policies to support gender equality in the workplace and at home. Women do on average 60 per cent more unpaid work than men; they spend nearly twice as much time as men doing cooking and housework and more than twice as much time doing childcare (ONS 2016). Long, non-standard working hours, a lack of access to high quality part-time work and long commute times all conspire to make combining childcare and professional life difficult in the UK. This can have the dual effect of leading women to withdraw from their careers after they have children, and/or paying for flexible, privatised childcare and other domestic services. In a comparative study of middle-class parents in Amsterdam and London, William Boterman and Gary Bridge (2015) found that compared to their peers in London, gentrifying middle-class parents in Amsterdam had better access to subsidised childcare, the right to work part time and typically had only a 20-minute commute to work by bike. They conclude:

> Where there was evidence of more equitable childcare sharing in the Amsterdam case (with lower childcare costs and more family friendly employment practices) in London the childcare regime was consistently strongly divided along gender lines – regardless of whether it was in urban, suburban or semi-rural neighbourhoods. In the London case inflexible work regimes and high childcare costs mean that a traditional gender norm around full-time male employment is reinforced. (Boterman and Bridge 2015 p258)

As the figures for women's workforce participation and the prevalence of part-time work amongst mothers suggest, women are still expected to take a larger role in childcare and housework than men in Britain. This unequal division of labour is another factor that encourages the employment of paid domestic workers and au pairs, as women feel unable to cope with the demands on their time (see Chapter 7). Additionally, as Kilkey et al. (2013) have found, new, parenting cultures can actually create demand for paid services in the home, rather than otherwise. As fathers prioritise spending time with their children they may choose to outsource tasks that they would previously have done themselves, such as DIY. The result is that while there has been some equalling out of domestic tasks between male and female partners in heterosexual households, this has been partial and there has also been a trend towards outsourcing amongst households who can afford to pay others, which is fed both by an unequal gendered division of labour and the ways that some fathers have adopted new approaches to parenting which emphasise spending 'quality' time in child-centred activities. An au pair can solve the problems families face of co-ordinating multiple forms of care, fitting housework around paid work and children and negotiating an unequal division of domestic labour.

Childcare in the UK is expensive, patchy and too often inflexible. According to an OECD report childcare costs in the UK account for just over a quarter of parents' take home pay, the second highest figure for the OECD and well above the average of 11.8 per cent (Jowitt 2014). The UK government provides limited childcare for three and four-year-olds and some subsidies for childcare for children under two years old or of school age. While the number of hours covered by free care have increased in recent years, publicly funded provision falls a very long way short of providing the hours or flexibility of care that is needed by parents who work full time. Families who need full-time care are expected to piece together a patchwork of state and privately provided care paid for through a mix of subsidies, tax-efficient vouchers and hard-earned cash. This pattern of poor provision, inflexibility and complexity means that for many families formal or group childcare outside the home is not suitable and/or is more expensive that hosting an au pair.

During the period of this study all three to four-year-olds in England were entitled to 570 hours of free early education or childcare per year. This is usually taken as 15 hours each week for 38 weeks of the year. Two-year-olds whose parents are claiming certain benefits or who have particular needs, for example due to disability, are also eligible for free early education childcare (gov.uk 2015). In Scotland provision was slightly more generous at 600 hours of free early education for all three and four-year-olds but in Wales children were entitled to only 10 hours per week and in Northern Ireland to only 12.5 hours per week for one year. Parents working over 16 hours per week but on low pay were also entitled to 'Childcare tax credits' to help pay for childcare provided in 'approved' settings – that is by a registered childminder or in a nursery, after school club or playscheme. Some parents could also get childcare vouchers. This is a way of paying for childcare from pre-tax income and relies on employers being involved in a scheme and the childcare being provided by an 'approved provider'. In 2015 each parent could take up to £55 per week of their pre-tax salary in childcare vouchers, giving a maximum annual saving of £930 (MSE 2015). Vouchers can be used to make up some of the cost of the extra hours three and four-year-olds might spend in nursery over and above the free hours provided by government, to pay for an after-school club for older children or to pay for nursery, a registered childminder or OFSTED (the Office for Standards in Education) registered nanny for a younger child.

Parents who need long or flexible hours of care are, therefore, expected to use a complex mix of free, subsidised and market-cost provision depending on the age of their child and the costs and availability of different types of care in their local area. Each year the Family and Childcare Trust carry out a survey of childcare costs in the UK. In 2015 they found that only 43 per cent of local councils in England reported that they had sufficient childcare available to meet demand from working parents and that childcare costs had consistently risen above the rate of inflation, with the cost of a part-time nursery place for a child under two rising 32.8 per cent over the last parliament (Rutter 2015 p3). In 2018, despite an increase in the number of hours of free childcare that three and four-year-olds were entitled to, they found that the cost of childcare had increased by 7 per cent since 2017. Only half of all local authorities in England and Wales had enough childcare for parents working full time and only 14 per cent of local authorities in England had sufficient provision for parents working atypical hours; no local authorities in Scotland or Wales reported that they had sufficient provision for this group (Harding and Cottell 2018).

The costs of childcare vary between types of care and between regions. As Table 3.1 shows, costs in London are substantially higher than they are in other regions. There are also very large variations within regions, between local authorities, and even between providers in the same local area. Reports suggest that a full-time nursery place in London costs somewhere between £14,000 and £22,000 per year (Hill 2015) a cost that meant nearly a quarter of parents in the capital were thinking of giving up work or reducing their hours (4Children 2015).

TABLE 3.1 Price of childcare for children under three by region

| | 25 hours per week of care | | | | 50 hours per week of care | | | |
| | Nursery | | Childminder | | Nursery | | Childminder | |
	Under two	Two	Under two	Two and over	Under two	Two	Under two	Two and over
Great Britain	£122.46	£119.47	£107.41	£109.44	£232.84	£229.33	£217.30	£216.10
England	£124.73	£120.66	£110.61	£109.95	£236.19	£231.75	£218.22	£217.06
Wales	£116.18	£116.02	£100.22	£100.38	£218.73	£220.77	£202.61	£203.10
Scotland	£109.68	£108.60	£114.33	£112.75	£205.18	£200.66	£228.00	£224.85
English regions								
East Midlands	£109.61	£109.53	£94.36	£94.35	£202.05	£201.86	£188.52	£188.49
East of England	£122.20	£122.13	£106.41	£104.28	£226.35	£229.84	£209.96	£206.05
London: Inner	£183.56	£174.47	£155.14	£154.11	£342.78	£323.40	£307.77	£305.58
London: Outer	£145.44	£134.03	£135.71	£135.36	£269.06	£258.96	£260.65	£261.36
Northeast	£122.30	£118.11	£106.20	£106.02	£215.77	£208.17	£204.30	£203.92
Northwest	£101.83	£101.19	£88.98	£90.89	£194.67	£193.66	£175.92	£178.88
Southeast	£141.70	£131.16	£121.82	£120.12	£267.36	£260.86	£243.64	£240.24
Southwest	£116.36	£119.22	£108.18	£107.35	£233.77	£232.64	£213.49	£211.92
West Midlands	£108.52	£106.41	£98.72	£97.09	£213.03	£208.53	£196.29	£193.72
Yorkshire and Humberside	£105.30	£103.37	£96.16	£95.78	£206.40	£203.51	£190.29	£198.39

Source: Harding and Cottell (2018 p6 and p8).

In the UK children typically start compulsory schooling at the age of four, and the school day will last from around 9am to 3.30pm. This pattern of schooling means that for children of school age the problem of childcare does not disappear and finding 'wrap around' care – that is before and after the school day – can be difficult and expensive as can finding childcare during school holidays. As Table 3.2 shows, the average cost of after school care (until 6pm) for one child in Great Britain was £56.38 at an after-school club or £62.25 with a childminder; in Inner London this rose to £71.75 and £88.04 respectively. These costs multiply when more than one child is involved and do not include the cost of before school 'breakfast clubs' or other activities such as sports clubs or music lessons which are also used as forms of childcare (Harding and Cottell 2018).

Care for school-age children can also be a particular problem during school holidays. The Family and Childcare Trust found that in 2017 the average weekly price of holiday childcare in Britain was £124.23 per child (Cameron and Kiss 2017). They also found that the majority

TABLE 3.2 Weekly price of an after-school club or childminder for children age 5–11

	After-school club	Childminder (to 6pm)
Great Britain	£56.38	£62.25
England	£56.82	£62.95
Wales	£50.64	£54.47
Scotland	£56.74	£61.92
English regions		
East Midlands	£50.90	£60.48
East of England	£65.76	£43.60
London: Inner	£71.75	£88.04
London: Outer	£53.16	£88.32
Northeast	£56.34	£51.25
Northwest	£48.84	£50.78
Southeast	£58.55	£67.13
Southwest	£55.28	£61.17
West Midlands	£57.93	£59.71
Yorkshire and Humberside	£54.78	£58.62

Source: Harding and Cottell (2018 p13).

of local authorities in England do not have enough holiday childcare places available, and shortages have increased. Holiday clubs provided by the private, voluntary and independent sector make up the majority of provision but these are significantly more expensive than local authority provision. As a result, parents rely on practices such as 'shift parenting', where each parent uses their annual leave in turn to cover holidays, meaning that families do not have time off together, informal care from relatives such as grandparents, or reducing working hours so that one parent works term time only (Cameron and Kiss 2017).

As a response to the increasing demand for flexible, extended or non-standard hours of care, there have been a small number of initiatives that aim to provide collective 24-hour care for the children of working parents. For example, a small number of private nurseries now offer 7pm–7am sleep over service that parents can use on a flexible basis. This is aimed at professionals who may work non-standard, or simply very long hours and who need childcare beyond the 'standard' 7am–7pm day (Barbagallo 2016). For older children of well-off families there is also the very traditional option of boarding schools and 'flexible boarding' has been a growing offer in the twenty-first century. Flexible boarding is seen in part as a response to parents' working patterns as children can board for part of a week or different days on different weeks in the term. The Good Schools Guide reports that 'Thursdays and Fridays [are] the most popular. This is not surprising as it means parents can enjoy a night out without having to find a babysitter (and not have to get up on Saturday morning for the school run)' (Good Schools Guide 2018).

Barbagallo (2016) also details a scheme aimed at a different group of parents – an extended-hours childminding service introduced by the London Borough of Brent in 2014 (see www.brent.gov.uk/services-for-residents/children-and-family-support/childcare/flexible-child-care/ for details). The Brent scheme is unusual in that it was established to support low-income parents who are on zero-hours contracts, work irregular hours or night shifts, or who need childcare at short notice. While organising paid work and childcare is difficult for most families, and there has been increased attention in recent years paid to the increasing flexibility demanded of people working in professional and creative occupations, it is important not to overlook the fact that flexible work, shift work and night work have long characterised low-paid jobs, including jobs in the care sector, traditionally done by working-class women and often by migrant women of colour. For these workers shift work or night work might be a solution to childcare problems and Barbagallo (2016 p192) comments that in their experience of combining precarious work with childcare, Black women's experiences can be read as pre-figurative:

> There is something to be recovered in Black women's experiences of work in the post-war period and their struggles against its precarious, low-paid, devalued status; when we consider the current conditions of many working parents, particularly working mothers who face the difficulties of combining work and care and are trapped in low- paid and often low-status work, we find the contemporary conditions of many working mothers in the past experiences of Black women workers.

Social research, which takes a 'whole economy' perspective – that is, it considers reproductive activities as well as 'productive' work and sustainability, has shown that organising childcare is a key issue for middle-class families in British cities (McDowell et al. 2006). Helen Jarvis' work on 'successful cities' (Jarvis 1999; 2005; Jarvis and Pratt 2006) shows the difficulties of negotiating work and reproductive labour in places where the demands of work are for 'flexible' and 'competitive' workers in cities which are large and growing. The practical problems of moving (multiple) children from home to school to after-school activities to home again all make organising work difficult (particularly for women who this problem normally falls to) and they can make the use of collective childcare untenable. Hosting an au pair can be a solution to an otherwise unsolvable problem for parents of small children

Childcare cultures and the rise of competitive mothering

Au pairing takes place within a cultural as well as a practical context. Alongside the concrete issues of working hours and childcare provision, demand for au pairs is affected by attitudes and cultural assumptions about what constitutes 'good' childcare for middle-class children. Interest in the practice of 'parenting' – a word which is itself relatively new – has escalated in recent decades and parents find themselves monitored, advised and admonished about every aspect of their engagement with their children. As Lee et al. (2014 p2) summarise the current state of affairs:

the message to mothers (and also fathers) is that the health, welfare and success (or lack of it) of their children can be directly attributed to the decisions they make …, 'parenting' parents are told, is both the hardest and most important job in the world. Tomorrow depends upon it.

One outcome of this focus on the importance of parenting practices has been a move towards 'intensive parenting', particularly amongst middle-class families in UK and US settings. Sharon Hays (1996) coined the term 'intensive motherhood' to describe an ideology which encourages mothers to spend huge amounts of time, energy and money in raising their children. One particularly contradictory aspect of this new culture of childcare is that it has arisen at the same time as women have been increasingly engaged in paid work outside the home. Rather than women's move into the workplace going hand in hand with them spending fewer hours caring for their children, mothers actually spend more time with their children today than they did in 1981. Research has found that practices which were considered perfectly normal in 1960s Britain – leaving children unsupervised to play, letting them go out alone or letting older children supervise younger ones – would be considered neglectful today (Edwards and Gillies 2013, cited in Faircloth 2014a). The expectation is that parents should constantly be with their children and engage them in structured activities which will aid their 'development'. While the practices of intensive mothering are not followed by all mothers, they become a normative standard against which mothering practices are evaluated. A result of this and the time-pressed context within which this culture has emerged is that mothers are tired, overstretched and torn between home and work. Not only are parents expected to spend more time with their children but also the quality of that time has become more intense (Faircloth 2014a), filled with activities that parents hope will ensure the successful development of their children against standards which are, of course, unreachable. Barbagollo (2016 p8) has commented that every mode of production produces particular modes of motherhood and subjectivities of motherhood, with these 'particular families are created, particular childhoods are experienced, particular types of consumption occur, particular wage structures are dominant and particular political subjects are produced'. However, the apparatus of motherhood is not stable, it is often in crisis and contested in various ways. There is not necessarily any congruity between the political, practical and cultural expectations of motherhood.

Intensive parenting has become the cultural context within which most families in the UK are now expected to raise their children; however, it is not experienced or implemented by all families in the same way and there are distinct class differences to parenting practices. The logic of intensive parenting derives from the developmental paradigm, an approach to child development which posits that experiences in early infancy have lifelong implications in terms of health, intellectual development, happiness and wellbeing and which leads to a form of 'parental determinism' in that the actions of parents in relation to their children are constructed as having 'profound significance for the future of individual children and also society as a whole' (Lee 2014 p71). One aspect of this is a belief that childcare in infancy will affect later educational success, and therefore, the ability of offspring to access well-paid work in the future. This characteristic of intensive parenting seems to particularly affect middle-class parents who want to ensure their children have the very best chance of financial security in the future but do not have the wealth to guarantee this themselves (Macdonald 2010). Middle-class parents are also better able to devote resources to the sorts of activities which exemplify intensive parenting, such as cultural activities, sports clubs and extra tutors.

In the UK, as in the USA, the chauffeuring of children to endless rounds of enrichment activities has increased the work of mothers:

> Katz (2008 pp10–11) argued that anxiety over political economic futures in the Global North has led to an intensification of parenting and a 'supersaturation of resources in particular children', resulting in the phenomena [sic] of the 'overscheduled child' whose every minute is filled with productive activities designed to ensure their success in a changing world. (Holloway and Pimlott-Wilson 2014 p614; see also Macdonald 2010)

In their study of parenting in the English Midlands, Holloway and Pimlott-Wilson (2014) found that 94.9 per cent of middle-class families took their children to enrichment activities off school premises compared to just 52 per cent of working-class families. The parents described these activities as being a way to build their children's confidence, expand social networks and build social capital, and the time involved in chauffeuring children between activities, staying to watch and cheer on, or even becoming involved in leading activities such as cubs and scouts, meant that family life became more child-centred. Faircloth (2014b p191) comments:

> Current [UK] policy measures around work–life balance … could be said to be less about trying to effect gender equality than about a self-conscious policy goal to encourage both parents to spend more time with their children. One paradoxical outcome of this is that, rather than women being enabled to do more work outside the home because their partners are on hand to look after the children, such policies could simply extend the logic of 'intensive parenting' to men, thereby doubling the labour for both parents.

There are also local 'childcare cultures' (Vincent, Ball and Kemp 2004; McDowell et al. 2006), local moral geographies of mothering and 'gendered moral rationalities' which shape British cities. For many of the people taking part in our study an au pair providing childcare was not only convenient but also chimed with childcare philosophies that saw home-based care as preferable to collective settings, particularly for very small children. As Kate Boyer, Suzy Reimer and Lauren Irvine (2013) have shown, attitudes towards nurseries are not always good and nursery workers are imagined to be uncaring, ill-educated and purveyors of working-class culture and associated bad habits, such as regional speech patterns, which middle-class parents don't want their children to pick up.

In a study of migrant domestic workers providing childcare in the USA, Cameron Lynne Macdonald (2010) describes what she calls 'competitive mothering', a form of intensive parenting which supports the idea that each family, or more specifically each mother, is expected to transmit the economic, social and cultural resources needed to reproduce or enhance a child's class status. Competitive mothering can underpin the demand for paid, privatised childcare in the home because parents want to ensure that their children are given every opportunity to benefit from individual adult attention and are exposed to a wide range of stimuli and learning opportunities. Hiring a domestic worker or au pair to do childcare rather than putting a young child into collective day care can mean that parents are able to provide a form of childcare which most closely resembles what they think they would provide if they were doing all their childcare themselves. This includes taking children to various educational activities appropriate to their age, familiarising them with museums, galleries and other 'high culture' activities. Childcarers may also be expected to teach children a foreign language or a musical instrument. Older children can be ferried by a domestic worker or au pair to after-school enrichment activities such as music and dance classes and domestic workers are often required to supervise and help with homework.

The quest for a 'mother substitute' who will further a competitive mothering agenda, tends to favour a particular type of worker who will pass on, or instil, class advantages. Macdonald (2010) found that employers wanted childcare workers who would help their children to develop cultural capital so that they could succeed in the future. Parents did not want their children to pick up 'accents' from childcare workers who sound working class or who spoke the 'wrong' sort of Spanish. They wanted children to listen to classical music, to feel at home in museums and to mix with the 'right' kind of children, and they hired domestic workers who could make this happen.

Joan Tronto has written extensively on the ethics of care (1993) and the undervaluing of care work (see 2002 and 2011 for example). Her work is instructive in illuminating the way that 'doing the best' for one's children is necessarily caught up in broader processes of social inequality. She uses the concept of 'competitive caring' to explain that while care remains a subordinate value and activity within a competitive society caring well for your family necessarily 'will make one an enemy not a friend of equal opportunity' (Tronto 2006 p10).

> In a competitive society what it means to care well for one's own children is to make sure they have a competitive edge against other children. On the most concrete level, while parents may endorse a principle of equality of opportunity in the abstract, their daily activities are most visibly 'caring' when they gain special privileges and advantages for their children.

Far from being in some way separate from or outside the norms of capitalist, market relationships, care at home is shaped by them both directly and indirectly. This is not only in the most obvious ways, such as the pay and working conditions of childcare workers, but also in less obvious ways – such as what it means to provide care. The competitive mothering projects of middle-class childcare employers produce advantage for their own children (and themselves) at the cost of other children, including those of the workers they employ.

One factor which underlies the prevalence of competitive mothering within certain middle-class families is the conflict that working mothers feel about their roles and their strong desire to address these conflicts by showing that their children do not suffer because of their employment. Parents are all increasingly expected to be engaged in paid work, even when their children are very young, and women are both expected to aspire to having fulfilling careers and forced into work through punitive welfare measures (Glenn 2010). At the same time, families are seen as having full responsibility for their childcare needs. Strong discourses of families' – read mothers' – responsibility for childcare, translate into guilt and confusion for women who do not care for their children full time themselves. While equally strong discourses on the importance of paid work create similar conflicts for parents who do not engage in paid work. These powerful emotions, and conflicts then shape the terrain on which relations between employers and childcare workers are negotiated.

> [Mothers] are caught in an impossible dilemma that renders *all* of them inadequate, whether they engage in full-time paid employment, part-time work outside of the house, or opt to be stay-at-home mothers. As one mother in LA explained, 'Everything about being a mother is fraught with guilt. If I put my kid in daycare, I'm guilty, if I have a nanny, I'm guilty, if I stay at home – guilty, if I work – guilty'.
> (Rosenbaum 2014 p131)

We saw evidence of these conflicts, self-doubt and guilt in our discussions with host mothers and also in online discussions on fora such as Mumsnet (see Chapter 5) where 'mums' could seek support and forgiveness from others in similar situations.

Competitive mothering is closely related to ideas of the 'perfectible child' which are popular in child-rearing manuals consumed by North American middle-class mothers. These manuals put forward the idea that children benefit from 'intensive mothering' in the first three years of life, and that there is a unique and special bond with the mother. They argue that if enough attention and effort and correct mothering is invested children are 'perfectible'. Any shortfall in children's happiness or accomplishments (at any point in their future lives) is, therefore, evidence of a mother's failure (Macdonald 2010). One outcome is that mothers will focus on measureable outcomes and goals for their children, such as the age at which a child talks, walks or can read, in order to reassure themselves they are not bad mothers. This focus translates into prioritising their child's competitive advantages as a means by which to measure the success of their parenting strategies.

The supply of migrant domestic workers has been met by increased demand for privatised forms of childcare and other domestic work in many countries. This increased demand cannot simply be explained by women's increased participation in paid work outside the home, but is rather the result of changes in the workplace, in the provision of and attitudes towards group care and in childcare cultures. For middle-class families particularly, the combination of long and unpredictable working hours, unequal divisions of household labour and a commitment to intensive parenting have all fed demand for au pairs and other domestic workers.

Conclusion

This chapter has placed the UK au pair scheme in the broader context of the growth in paid domestic work which we have seen across the globe in the last three decades. Both the supply of migrant domestic workers and the demand for their labour have been affected by changes in women's expectations of paid work, and policy responses to this. The terms 'supply' and 'demand' suggest the operation of simple market mechanisms, but as this chapter has shown, the conditions which have encouraged the growth of au pairing in the UK, are as much about cultural preferences and public policy as they are about economics. While au pairs are a very particular group of domestic workers, it is important to put them in this context in order to understand the work that they do as real work, work which is important to their host families and the children they care for. In the next chapter we look at how these fierce forces shape the au pair role, particularly as it is described by host families advertising for an au pair on line. In the context of so many competing influences, what is an au pair?

4 | WHAT IS AN AU PAIR?

In the Introduction we set out the technical definition of what an au pair should be in twenty-first-century Britain. In this chapter, we explore in detail how government and agency guidance translates into the norms and expectations of au pairs and hosts. What do au pairs really do? What do their hosts think they should do? And to what extent is this really a relationship of 'guest' and 'host' rather than employer and employee? In examining these questions, the chapter develops the argument that au pairing, rather than being an unproblematic example of cultural exchange between equals, is better understood as a particular form of poorly paid childcare labour, which sometimes includes opportunities for au pairs to develop skills, networks and relationships which they value as important aspects of their experience.

The chapter describes a situation 'on the ground' that runs contrary to the official language that has surrounded au pairing from its inception and questions the idea that au pairs are distinctly different from other groups of childcare and domestic workers. To do this we first describe the general pattern of au pair conditions we found from analysing advertisements on Gumtree.com and look at how these compare to official guidance on au pairing and to what might have been thought of as nanny posts. We then look at the notion of 'cultural exchange' – the thing that is meant to define au pairing, remediate for poor pay and enable some kind of 'equal' social status between au pairs and hosts. We first explore the views of au pairs about cultural exchange. There are some good things about being an au pair, according to our participants, and these seemed to cluster around cultural exchange and language learning. Even some of the au pairs who felt that they were being exploited conceded that the benefits of being able to explore the UK and/or improve English-language skills or enrol in other further study courses were significant. Next we hear from hosts we interviewed, many of whom agreed that they had decided on an au pair because it was either the most satisfactory or the 'only' way in which they could reconcile the demands of their paid labour outside the home with the logistics of childcare and household maintenance responsibilities. In other words, they were not primarily motivated by the desire to engage in cultural exchange, but some found it a rewarding aspect of au pair hosting.

Advertised demands: shaping the au pair workforce

One of the first steps we took to try to understand what it means to be an au pair in contemporary Britain was to look at advertisements for au pairs on Gumtree.com. In the absence of any official data, this gave us an overview of the sorts of working hours, tasks and remuneration that hosts were prepared to offer. Our headline findings were that the average working week being advertised was 38.7 hours long (including babysitting) and that 31 per cent of advertisements were asking for an au pair to work more than 25 hours a week. While only about half of the advertisements which we looked at (507) stated the hours that were needed, of these nearly 100 (10 per cent of the total) wanted an au pair to work 50 hours a week or more, nine requested 70 hours or longer and the longest working week was 80 hours. About 80 per cent of the ads specified that they wanted an au pair to do cleaning, some offered extra pay for cleaning, most included it; about 65 per cent specified that duties would include cooking and about 15 per cent specifically mentioned that duties would include care of pets. However, the significant work that au pairs would be doing, both implied and detailed explicitly, was childcare. Some ads set out what this would consist of – 'sole charge week days, half day Saturdays and babysitting', or 'female wanted to look after our three gorgeous boys' – others just gave the ages of children or the number of children present, implying that this was relevant for the au pair's work.

In remuneration for this the average pocket money offered was £108 per week (although again only half of all the ads revealed the amount on offer). Fourteen per cent offered below the recommended £85 pounds per week, and it was striking that there was no correlation between the hours to be worked and the amount of pocket money offered in return. For example, three ads posted next to each other illustrated this very well: the first offered £100 per week plus own bedroom and bathroom for 45 hours work looking after four children, one of whom was under three and one of whom was under one; the next offered £100 per week plus own bedroom for 50 hours work looking after one child under three; and the third offered £110 per week (no information given about bedroom or bathroom) for 25 hours work looking after three children, none of whom was under three years old. The lowest pay offered was £0 – that is no pocket money, just room and board – for 30 hours work looking after a child under three years old and cooking and cleaning. The highest pay offered was c.£360 per week to care for two school-age children after school during term time and full time during the holidays, as well as cooking and cleaning. Both of these were described by the advertisers as au pair posts.

The average hours expected of au pairs, the duties outlined and pay offered in most of the ads gave the strong impression that in most situations, the au pair was the solution to making childcare and paid employment work. There were a small number (perhaps a handful) that mentioned 'mum at home' or that the au pair would be helping an existing nanny, and a small number which did not need childcare (two of these were asking for a carer for an older person, a few just wanted care for pets or just cleaning and help with another business, or it was not clear what was involved), but in phrases such as, 'help with our hectic lives', and 'basically we're looking for someone to make our lives a lot easier', as well as the constant mentions of 'busy' families the ads were like a window onto the stresses and strains of negotiating paid work and home. This is hardly surprising, given the context we set out in Chapter 2, of the prevalence parents working outside the home, the long and flexible working hours that British families face (Alakeson 2011) and the shortages of other forms of childcare (Family and Childcare Trust 2015).

The other thing which is not surprising about the ads is that they seemed like a window onto a female world. The ads were largely written by women and directed at women, where men made an appearance it was as sons, and one elderly man to be cared for. There was not a single ad that specified they were looking for a male au pair, and while there were a number looking for 'big sisters', no one seemed to want a 'big brother' for their children. This is not surprising because women are still responsible for the majority of domestic work and childcare in Britain (ONS 2016), whether they do that work themselves or organise someone else to do it. The increasing pervasiveness of the 'one and a half' worker model amongst middle-class families (Holloway and Pimlott-Wilson 2016), combined with the long, non-standard working hours and the lack of access to high-quality part-time work all conspire to make combining childcare and professional life difficult in the UK. As outlined in Chapter 2 this has the dual effect of leading women to withdraw from their careers after they have children, and/or paying for flexible, privatised childcare and other domestic services. As Boterman and Bridge (2015 p258) found, the childcare regime in Britain was consistently strongly divided along gender lines and 'inflexible work regimes and high childcare costs mean that a traditional gender norm around full-time male employment is reinforced'. The result is that hosting an au pair is particularly attractive, and that it is women who are responsible for organising that and making it work.

The ads were clearly targeted at a particular imagined audience – presumably made up of people who are suitable to be au pairs. This was evidenced in the specification of gender (about 15 per cent asked for women, none for men), age (some ads asked for 'over 21' or gave a range of ages, a very small number asked for 'older' or 'mature' applicants), nationality and language skills. A small number of ads asked for native English speakers, but a very large number asked for 'fluent' or 'good' English, suggesting that they understood their audience to be migrant workers. Others specified the nationality of the au pair they wanted and these varied, with no single nationality dominating. Two ads said they were African families looking for African au pairs and one said that African or Asian people were welcome to apply – something the advertiser clearly thought needed to be spelt out. The most common language asked for, in addition to English, was French, but Russian was also quite common. Mandarin, Arabic, Swedish, Finnish, German, Italian, Spanish, Romanian and Bulgarian were also asked for. The audience for the ads, therefore, appeared to be young, migrant women, mostly but not exclusively from Europe. The assumption that au pairs would be young, European women seemed to be unspoken, with hosts who wanted someone who did not conform to this assumption, articulating that preference overtly.

Examination of advertised demand revealed how far from the original Strasbourg Agreement rules some au pair posts had drifted. Thirty-three of the ads were for 'live-out' au pairs, one offered the au pair the sofa in the living room to sleep on, and another was to live with the host mother's parents. There were also a number of ads for 'au pair couple', which seemed to be wanting people to take over a traditional 'couple' role, where the woman is expected to cook and clean and the man do gardening, repairs and perhaps driving, this is a form of domestic employment which is most commonly found in quite wealthy country houses. For example, one ad stated:

[we are] looking for an au pair couple for the following: childcare, pet care, cleaning, laundry, babysitting, gardening, handyman work e.g. decorating, car care etc. ... we will also pay au pair salary each week.

A number of the ads wanted an au pair to provide care for pets as well as or instead of children. Mostly this was for dogs, but there were also a number who wanted someone to help with horses, including one from a family in Notting Hill, London which baldly stated 'must have horse experience'. Another, in Cornwall, offered 'Use of horse and kayak' as an additional perk.

It was also common for ads to specify that an au pair be responsible for duties that appeared to go beyond 'helping' with childcare and domestic duties, including shopping, cleaning windows and floors, washing and ironing, caring for relatives' children or care of stepchildren on weekends, waitressing for host's drinks/dinner parties, cooking for parties, gardening, teaching a child a language and more. One ad stated they wanted an au pair to help with the photo business run by the writer of the post as well as 'helping to run the home' – the au pair must 'have style,' take 'pride in their appearance' and the photos which applicants were asked to send were flagged as very important. The person writing the ad also specified that they wanted the au pair to like clothes and make-up and to enjoy 'going bargain hunting in charity shops'; there was no mention of children to be cared for. In keeping with the horse theme, one ad asked for:

solid horsemanship skills with proven record of safety with horses and children ... in order to exercise the horses you'll need to weigh no more than 11 stone ... You will need your own car. To apply please email [with] your pay expectations.

This 'host' also stated that they wanted English as first language and for the au pair to have a first aid qualification. The ad gave no indication of hours to be worked, but did state there were three children, one of whom is under three years old, in addition to the horses.

Examination of these ads also gave us a way to investigate whether there was a clear distinction between nanny (work) and au pair (not work) roles. In common with findings discussed by Anderson (2000; Anderson et al. 2006), Cox (2006) and Øien (2009), our analysis of the advertisements reflected a lack of clear boundaries separating au pair positions and employed childcare positions such as nannies. For example, whereas, under the terms of the au pair visa, an au pair was not expected to provide sole charge care for babies or infants, we found that 33 per cent of ads specified that they were looking for someone to care for a child under three years old, and 14 per cent for someone to care for a child under one year old. There were a small number of ads (12) that asked for au pairs to provide care for disabled children, including one wanting an au pair to care for two children with learning difficulties and one which asked for an au pair to help with the home schooling of an autistic son as well as providing other care for him; one used the job title 'special needs au pair' to describe the role. There is no reason why an au pair should not look after disabled children, and we met au pairs who had done this and particularly enjoyed the role; however, some of the ads suggested that quite high levels of skill and experience were needed (first aid training, experience with epilepsy, for example) and that families might be relying on au pairs rather than trained carers or specialist teachers. Similarly, 44 per cent of the ads asked for an au pair with prior experience and 26 per cent specified that they would only consider applicants who were already in the UK. Many ads described the 'salary' as negotiable or asked for applicants to state 'salary expectations' and used other language which framed the au pair role in the parlance of employment. This suggests, that rather than facilitating travel, cultural exchange and language learning, hosts were looking for competent, experienced childcare workers who were already familiar with the country and language.

These advertisements reveal how capacious the category 'au pair' has become; it is apparently used to cover any form of live-in work, or any form of domestic and childcare work whether it is live-in or out. One implication of this is the effect it has had on the work available to nannies. As we have explored in detail elsewhere (Busch 2012; 2015), the deregulation of au pairing appears to have created a situation where the category 'au pair' has absorbed the 'bottom end' of nanny work, leaving only the most highly skilled and paid nannies as distinguishable from au pairs.

The ads also gave some illustrations of the sorts of relationships those advertising wanted with their au pairs. Many of the people posting ads were clearly eager to give a good impression of welcoming, happy households and used phrases such as 'fun', 'friendly' and 'loving'. A number made reference to their good relationships with their previous au pairs and one ad was actually written by an au pair who was leaving, looking for her replacement and recommending the post. A small number specifically stated that the au pair would be treated as a member of the family, and some others described what they were looking for as a 'big sister' to the children to be cared for (see Hess and Puckhaber 2004).

However, some ads were very clear that they were not looking for a friendly or familial relationship, such as one which stated: 'Strictly no boy friend, girl friend business and clubbing and pubbing late nights … Strictly no TV watching' (although it was not clear if it was the au pair or the children being cared for who were not to watch TV). Another said, 'When you are not working you must be out or in your room so that the family can have some time together'. The au pair was clearly not imagined as a member of the family. Perhaps the most chilling was one which said: 'looking for a fun, honest and courageous au pair … Please don't contact us if you are not courageous'.

Some of the advertisements seemed to reveal 'au pair fatigue'; the weariness that comes over host families when they have to hire their fourth, fifth or even tenth or twelfth au pair (Búriková and Miller 2010). For example, one demanded (in capitals) 'Do not apply if you are LAZY'; another stated:

> We are looking for someone with experience and references, who is not a party animal (we made redundant our previous au-pair for that reason, for security reasons I can't have someone going out until 2am 4 times a week and being in the streets with my kids the next day). Canada, NZ, Australia, Ireland preferred for nationality.

And another, after giving a very detailed candidate checklist, stated 'Please read everything below VERY carefully', suggesting a jaded response to previous experiences of finding an au pair. Búriková and Miller (2010 p37) comment:

> One of the most important factors determining families' treatment of au pairs was simply how many au pairs they happened to have employed. Almost all families would admit to treating their first and second au pair very differently from the tenth or fifteenth … This is one of the reasons why au pairs return with such a diversity of experiences.

Families who are new to hosting an au pair are likely to be more attentive to and caring about an individual au pair's needs and experience, while those who have seen many au pairs come and go pay less attention. Similarly, more experienced au pairs are more likely to desire independence, while new arrivals may want support and to be absorbed into a new family. When the expectations of host and au pair meet the result can be a successful 'reciprocal exploitation of mutual interest that pays no regard to the idiom of the family' (Búriková and Miller 2010 p37) or a mutual desire to create a family-like relationship. However, as au pairs stay as au pairs for a shorter time than hosts are likely to be hosts, it is also quite likely that there are large numbers of jaded, weary, fatigued families hosting newly arrived and enthusiastic au pairs.

Analysis of advertisements for au pairs revealed that what an au pair 'is', is far from clear. Pay, conditions and types of work expected varied immensely between advertisers (except that there were no very high levels of pay offered). There is confusion and elision between nanny and au pair roles and there is variation in the type of relationship – family-like or otherwise – being offered by hosts. Given the relatively low levels of pocket money being offered for au pair roles, it appears that for households that were property rich, to the extent that they had a room (or a sofa) an au pair could inhabit, hiring an au pair could appear a relatively affordable childcare solution, especially when pocket money paid to an au pair was compared with average salaries earned by professional nannies (see Introduction). The language used by people advertising for an au pair was clearly indicative of the extent to which childcare in the UK was rhetorically valued, but the terms and conditions of employment reflected the low status and lack of economic value attached to this exchange (Anderson 2009 p411). The undervaluing of the labour of au pairs is a common 'double jeopardy' that migrant domestic workers face (Parmar 1982; Phizacklea 1983; Wills et al. 2009 p99) in that their work is devalued based on its coding as a low-paid migrant job, and then further undervalued because of its association with women and lower social class and lower-status people (Busch 2015; Tronto 2006).

Cultural exchange

The saving grace of au pair positions, the thing that both differentiates au pairing from 'work' and that compensates for low pay, is meant to be 'cultural exchange'. Therefore, in understanding what au pairing is, and whether it is, in fact, distinct from 'work', we need to look at what cultural exchange might be, and whether it is an important component of au pair–host relationships. For most of our au pair interviewees cultural exchange was almost entirely limited to improving their English, with very little inclusion in the life of their host family. However, where au pairs identified the elements that were good about au pairing, these were largely in the area of cultural exchange and learning English was a valued aspect of the experience. The hosts we interviewed had mixed attitudes towards 'cultural exchange': some understood it as a significant aspect of the au pair arrangement, but they were also clear that they hosted an au pair in order to meet their childcare and housework needs at a price they could afford, rather than because they wanted to engage in cultural exchange. Some hosts had enjoyed the cultural exchange aspects of having an au pair in their family while others also reflected that they did not think au pairs were seeking cultural exchange and they represented the exchange as being one of cheap childcare in exchange for board and lodging.

In all regulated au pair schemes around the world, au pairs are specifically described as being in some way involved in cultural exchange (see Cox 2015c for details). In some countries au pairs have to be involved in some formal study under the terms of their visa (e.g. USA, Norway) and in some situations it is also required that the host family must pay the cost of classes or contribute towards them. However, there is little detail as to what 'cultural exchange' might include and where any indications are given, they largely suggest that rather than an 'exchange', the au pair should learn about the hosts' culture, but not the other way around.

Yet the imagining of au pairing as a form of cultural exchange is enduring and it has effects. The representation of au pairing as cultural exchange means that different people, with different ambitions, can chose to be au pairs than those entering other forms of domestic work (see for example Bikova 2015 on middle-class Filipinas au pairing in Norway, and Aguilar Pérez 2015 and Geserick 2015 on middle-class au pairs in the USA). Across the world, au pairs do tend to be well-educated, from middle-class backgrounds, young and without dependent children of their own. They are rarely motivated simply by a desire to earn money but may well wish to achieve some form of personal development, such as improving their language skills or accomplishing personal growth through independent travel, at the same time as supporting themselves. Mirza Aguilar Pérez's (2015) discussion of the 'cosmopolitan dilemma' faced by Mexican women going as au pairs to the USA perhaps encapsulates the effects of the portrayal of au pairing as a form of cultural exchange most directly. She argues that Mexican young women are attracted to au pairing through the dream of seeing the world and living in an exciting cosmopolitan city. Their Facebook pages, which can be seen by friends and family at home, are full of pictures of themselves at iconic tourist sites in New York and other cities. However, many also have an alternative online persona with a pseudonym unknown to their families in Mexico but shared with other au pairs in the USA. Through this second profile they discuss the daily grind of au pairing, the disputes with hosts, the children's tantrums and the reality of life doing domestic chores.

Amongst the au pairs we interviewed there seemed to be strong desire for cultural exchange, in various different forms. This included learning/improving English, visiting cultural institutions and events, and just learning more about daily life in another country. Where these things were available they were highlighted as positives of the au pair experience, and something that made au pairs feel like 'part of the family'; when they were not, they very rapidly gave the au pair the impression that they were 'working' or a 'servant'.

Nicholas expressed his favourite parts of the au pair life in exactly the sort of terms the originators of the scheme might have recognised:

> One of the best ideas that I have free time and I am free to experience whatever I want. So the second one is being in a family. I think that's also a very gives you a good impression or appropriate impression about life here. You see how people live, how they spend their money, how they wake up in the morning, how they treat you when they are annoyed or unhappy.

When asked whether they had felt like a 'member of the family' and been engaged in cultural exchange, both Tina and Christina showed how important the relationship was between opportunities for cultural exchange and feeling valued and respected by the host family. Tina Said. 'They're always really nice … They have a little cottage in Wales and one weekend I could join them to go there and yeah, they're really nice'. Christina, from Latvia, reflecting on how happy she had been with a previous host family, said:

> They were such a traditional English family, I think you can see everything and learn a lot from this … They made me feel like really

special, like queen and I know sometimes maybe I wasn't superb but still there was superb respect which now I'm really grateful to them. I'm quite sometimes depressed when I think, so yeah for me it was amazing and I really appreciate what they did for me and always was very sensitive to what was happening with me and my family

Opportunities for cultural exchange, be that seeing how English people spend their money, or going to a cottage in the country, were very important in shaping the whole relationship between host an au pair. These quotes suggest that au pairs saw opportunities for cultural exchange as interesting and enjoyable and also as a sign of respect from hosts.

Au pairs were also often interested in taking advantage of wider cultural experiences, particularly those offered by living in a large city like London. When we asked au pairs what they liked best about au pairing 'London' came back as a frequent answer (along with liking the children they were looking after) (cf. Geserick 2016 on au pairs' dreams of seeing America). London is the destination of choice for au pairs moving to the UK, including those we interviewed. The bright lights of the big city and the dream of streets paved with gold have long attracted migrants. As London has been named 'the best city in the world to work in' (Dearden 2014 n.p.), the 'best for culture' (Hutchinson 2014) and the 'most stimulating' (Wygant 2013 n.p.), it is hardly surprising that it is a destination of choice for young people from Europe (Cox and Busch 2016a).

We found that many au pairs fixed on London as a destination in order to enjoy the shops, museums, clubs and general feeling of 'being there'. They perceived London to be exciting, tolerant and often very different from home. For example, when asked what was good about au pairing, Anna said, 'London is incredible and it's amazing' (cf. Conradson and Latham (2007 pp242–243), who argue young Australians and New Zealanders are also attracted by the buzz of London, the cultural amenities and the feeling of being at the centre of the world). The opportunity to mix with new people and try new things can be a great draw, as Búriková and Miller (2010) found in their work with Slovak au pairs in London. Their interviewees experienced a sense of freedom in the city and relished the opportunity to behave in ways which they would never behave at home, and so discover more about themselves. For hosts of course, being able to offer au pairs a base from which to experience so many things, is an added bonus.

Being able to study or practise a language is perhaps the most organised way in which au pairs are expected, or imagined, to take part in cultural exchange. In Britain, being enrolled in formal English classes was never a requirement of the au pair scheme, but the au pair visa did require au pairs to be either learning or improving their English, for example, through practising with their host family (this meant, for example, that native English speakers could not become au pairs while the au pair visa was in force, but this is no longer the case). Our research gave the impression that a minority of au pairs were attending English classes, but for many improving the standard of their English was still immensely important. We wished to discover whether au pairing was more likely to be seen as something other than an employment transaction by au pairs if there was a clear sense that there was something over and above a wage that was likely to come out of their experience. For example, the language acquisition aspect of being an au pair could provide an incentive for accepting pocket money and accommodation in exchange for providing childcare, housework and/or other services (Búriková and Miller 2010; Búriková 2006; Cox 2006; Hess and Puckhaber 2004). This exchange could be used to differentiate au pairing from other forms of paid employment.

> Well, I have – I don't pay rent and there's good opportunity for me to learn English, because I need this English. I don't want to be au pair all my life but that's a good start because you actually don't pay any bills and you – the money you have are only for you. So, the money I take, I invest them in courses, so, my qualifications getting better and I make new good contacts, which will help me to find a job. (Lisa)

As Lisa's comments suggest, being able to improve her English was compensation for low pay; the time she spends being an au pair is treated as an investment in her future. Similarly, Oskar, 26, from Romania explained that even though he felt being an au pair was 'exploitation', there were nonetheless advantages and these advantages were the reason he tolerated what he regarded as the exploitative conditions. He said:

> I've seen this as a first step, you know? Because if you don't have any relatives or you don't know anybody in the country it's like a first stop. Then you can go off and find something else. So it's a good way to get used to the way of the country you know to learn to improve your language.

For some of the au pairs we interviewed, their plan was not to stay permanently in the UK but to use their improved English, gained through au pairing, to allow a move to a third country – perhaps in a specialist job; air traffic controller, travel agent, shipping manager were all mentioned to us in this context. English skills were also part of at least one au pair's plans to move to the USA where the au pair scheme demands higher levels of English. Au pairing in the UK can offer the chance to do this and so is part of long-term, multi-cited migration plans (Cox and Busch 2016a).

Au pairs who could not access opportunities to improve their English, either because they could not go to formal classes or because the host family did not give them any opportunities to practise conversation (either because the family did not speak English at home, or because they simply did not speak to the au pair), could be highly frustrated by this. For example, Sasha commented:

> I wasn't allowed to do all the things which I wanted to do. For example, I wanted to go to college to learn English somewhere. I wanted to go on English courses and my first host family wasn't very happy about it because they said they can need me at any time so I have to be there for that, you know? I wasn't very happy with that.

Sasha left this host family and found another. Their demand that she needed to be available at any time in case they needed her was clearly limiting in practical terms as it stopped her learning English, but also very far from the 'spirit' of the ideal au pair arrangement.

At worst, rather than being an additional form of compensation which made up for low wages, the benefit of being able to gain a very valuable skill – such as improved English – could be a reason why au pairs would stick in positions where they were not happy. As Oskar commented, it helped him put up with exploitation; Paula, from Spain, focused on the projected material benefits that would result from her English skills. When discussing this aspect of her role, she pointedly explained that she dealt with the humiliation occasioned by the family's treatment of her by holding on to the sense that 'this is not all I am' (see Anderson 2009 p420). She said:

> For me the problem is not so much the money. I think that it is a transitory situation in my life. It is not really my life. And for me it is ok because I don't have to pay for my room or for food and I know

England is really, really expensive. And I will go back and I hope I will speak good English, so in my case it is different. It is different because I can choose.

The key point for Paula about being an au pair was that she expected to return to her 'real life' in Barcelona enriched, and this prospect allowed her to accept the injustice of providing care for what she saw as inadequate wages. Paula's recognition of the importance of temporality (Anderson 2009), and her emphasis on the importance to her of the collateral advantage of improved English and life experience were indicative of the more general point that the au pair role needs to deliver something in addition to pocket money and accommodation if it is to be something other than just a form of exploitative work. It is also worthwhile noting, with reference to the very varied pay rates for au pair posts noted in the discussion of advertisements above, an au pair arrangement might also have been entered into with reference to benefits such as the ability to attend English classes, so that the 'pocket money' received was not the only – or indeed the primary – reward attached to the role.

Hosts are not generally motivated to take on an au pair because they want to engage in cultural exchange. Almost without exception, host families need or want an au pair as a form of affordable and flexible domestic labour – normally to provide childcare (see Chapter 7). The cultural exchange part of the arrangement can be ignored by host families, entered into reluctantly, or it can be a pleasant surprise that becomes, as it is for au pairs, the most enjoyable part of the arrangement.

The hosts we interviewed understood that being able to offer an au pair post in London, particularly a central part of London or somewhere with good transport links, was an incredibly valuable resource. As one said 'Childcare is phenomenally expensive and then, so many people want to come to London that what you offer, your spare room, becomes a really valuable thing'.

Another host, Eleanor, said of her current au pair's motivations:

She wanted a new cultural experience. She wanted basically to meet London, go out. She comes from a small town. Just have fun really and she does. She really goes out. Friday night to Sunday, you don't see her and that was another thing. I said to her, 'you can go out, absolutely no problem. Go clubbing, I know you're after that' ... She just told us that she's going. She's got a job offer in New York ... She's actually going to spend another year au pairing but she comes from a small town in Germany so she's basically saying this is my opportunity now ... She's constantly – every weekend. She hasn't been one single weekend at home. It's constantly museums, galleries, whatever. She's always out with her friends. So, I think, you know, she's really used London a lot.

Reflecting the point made above, about au pairs valuing opportunities to engage in language learning and cultural exchange more than monetary rewards, host families also understood this and some knew that they could rely on the 'pull' of London as a highly regarded global city, to supply migrants willing to engage in low-paid jobs, such as childcare.

The literature on au pairing has highlighted the reluctance of hosts to participate in or facilitate cultural exchange. Cultural exchange can feel too much like hard work for hosts, particularly those suffering from 'au pair fatigue' after their first few au pairs (Búriková and Miller 2010). Hosts may then seek au pairs who are culturally similar, as Durin (2015) found in her research in Marseille. Au pairs wanting to share their culture can even be unwelcome to host families, as Elizabeth Stubberud (2015b) found: one of her au pair interviewee's attempts to introduce her culture to the children she cared for got her fired. Amongst our interviewees, hosts were generally well aware of the notion of cultural exchange within au pairing and made some efforts to facilitate it. Niamh explained her approach:

I'd support them for English classes, make sure that they are networked with other people. Make sure that they're seeing the sights of London or just experiencing things so sharing things that we're doing, that sort of thing and also just being there I suppose like a sort of counsellor or their point of contact so if ever they're worried about anything. So I know it's supposed to be a parental role but I think by the time they're here they're 18, 19 and it is about experiencing freedom but at the same time knowing that they've got a base and they know that if ever they need any help then I'd be able to find that for them.

She added, that she saw it as a particularly positive thing for her son:

It's a really positive thing I think to have a young person from a different country who teaches language or speaks different languages or exchange different things and explains them and to a certain extent [son] will correct them for words and teach them about things. So, I think that's probably actually quite a non-threatening way of learning a language because you're actually just exchanging it in that environment.

Another experienced host, Poppy, had a similar approach that directly linked making an effort to enable cultural exchange to the nature of the host–au pair transaction:

> But as I see it, if you're an au pair you're coming to improve your English. You need to have time to be able to study English and go to school and the family has to support you in that and the family, we're committed to spending time talking to our au pair, helping her with her English and helping her. When they start, I'll spend a day or two showing them the area, introducing them to other au pairs. I found out she liked football, I helped her find a woman's football club, all that kind of thing. A nanny I think is a straight financial transaction whereas with an au pair I think it's a very different experience. I'm committed to putting the time in to do that.

However, even amongst this self-selected group of 'good' hosts, there were signs of the effort that culture exchange could entail.

Arthur perhaps explained this best. His first statement when interviewed about hosting an au pair was 'I hate it'. He then went on to explain his belief that it was necessary to facilitate cultural exchange, but also, wearing:

> *Facilitator*: When you were thinking about a cultural exchange, did you think 'we need somebody in our house to look after the children and the help to make our household work, but we recognise that we can't afford a nanny or a paid child-minder, so we recognise that it's a cultural exchange kind of arrangement'?

> *Interviewee*: Yeah, and we've been very conscientious, even still even though I'm less conscientious than I was but making sure that the au pair was using her time well, making sure she was integrating, that she was making friends with people who were British so that she wasn't just hanging out with other Germans in her case. But I have to say I've become less conscientious.

> *Facilitator*: Have you become more disillusioned with the scheme?

> *Interviewee*: No, I think it worked. I think what it requires – I think it requires people to be really diligent and not abuse these young

women. We have heard horrific stories. As you know, we've heard horrific stories. I would hate to think that anyone who's been with us has gone off and told those stories of exploitation.

Facilitator: What do you think the au pairs are getting out of it? Do you think that it's a productive experience for them?

Interviewee: I think it's different. I mean, all of them, their language has improved which is what they've wanted. I think a couple of them have then wanted to work in my particular area, so a couple of them have then done acting courses or singing classes or something.

In a separate interview, Arthur's wife, Jo, explained that without cultural exchange the fact that they were paying pocket money for something which is work 'because they're looking after your child and that's childcare and that's work' would be exploitation. To further illustrate how confusing the construction of cultural exchange and family membership is within au pairing, another host, Lucy, after saying that she thought it was very important that au pairs were treated as part of the family, so that they were not exploited, and giving examples of how she always made it possible for the au pair to eat with the family as evidence of how she did this, then went on to tell a 'horror story' about an au pair she had fired. She gave as an example of the au pair's bad attitude the fact that the au pair had expected to join in a meal when Lucy had invited her friends over, and when she, Lucy, would be clearing the table and washing up. Lucy explained with shock that the au pair had expected 'literally to be treated as a guest', and clearly saw this as evidence of unreasonable behaviour.

As well as situations where hosts found cultural exchange hard work or an intrusion, we also spoke to hosts who had embraced the opportunities for themselves, their children and their au pairs, which this aspect of the arrangement encompassed. June explained that she had learned a huge amount from her au pairs, and that this aspect of the arrangement had been an 'unexpected bonus':

I think we felt it would be really positive for the children to be, to have somebody else living [with us] from a different country. I mean we live in London anyway so it's not like they're not exposed to multi-culturalism. Their school is about as multi-cultural as it gets, but I suppose to have someone live-in here and learning the language and everything has been, I think, been really interesting for them. Certainly, the first, one, two, three, four, five girls were all from

Eastern Europe or Northern Europe which were places that I didn't really know at all. I mean I didn't really even know about – that Estonia was a place. It's just that I mean a very, very [laughs] – huge geographical gaps. So for us it's filled in all of that and certainly a couple of the girls have been really interested in politics and things, the Ukrainian girls, so I know a lot more about the Ukrainian Government than I would ever thought I would know. So you do, you end up having those really interesting conversations but I don't think that was something that I was thinking of prior to having them. That's been a really nice bonus. So, oh I know about stuff now and if someone asks me about Ukrainian politics I can actually [make a comment] which is great. So that's been an unexpected bonus.

Jack, was a lone parent who spoke with great enthusiasm for his former au pair, showing how the two-way sharing of culture could work:

> But I think what – it was – there was some kind of – it wasn't cultural in the classic sense of being cultural but [au pair] was as interested in learning about London and learning English as she could be and every time they went out anywhere it was a whole adventure for the three of them to go and find out these things. Plus she would ask a lot of really interesting questions because she wasn't part of their culture. So she would ask but why are all the buses red, and they would have to have an answer for that, and there was all sorts of answers anyway. But I'd take them all off, we'd all go to the Tate or whatever it is at the weekends and have a look around. But she would explain to them continuously what my country's like, you know, we don't have this sort of thing in my country and we don't do this, that and the other. So what it did was it opened their eyes to other cultures being in London and London being a melting pot of different types of people. I remember particularly we had a – there was a world map on the wall. So whenever [au pair] went home, which was – she'd go home three or four times a year – the boys would put little stickers on the map as to where she was going to and draw lines and have little things. So they knew where Bulgaria was before anybody else in this country did actually, which was quite sweet.

June and Jack's comments show what a bonus cultural exchange can be for all involved when it works well. Not only did Jack's au pair learn about London and his children learn about Bulgaria but spending time with a Bulgarian au pair also helped the children to understand London, their home town, better.

The rhetoric of au pairing as a form of cultural exchange is reflected not only in official definitions of au pairing but also within the 'au pair business', the world of au pair placement agencies. The International Au Pair Association (IAPA) – 'the global trade association for the au pair community' (IAPA 2014a n.p.) – which co-ordinates au pair agencies worldwide and lobbies governments on au pair-related issues, is part of the World Student Youth and Educational (WYSE) Travel Confederation and it locates au pairing within student travel and volunteering schemes. It has as a stated objective 'to lobby governments to treat au pair programmes as cultural exchange and not as work programmes so that au pairs and their receiving host families are not subject to employment taxation' (IAPA 2014b). While the IAPA does not by any means oversee the majority of au pair placements, organisations like it and its members (individual agencies and national associations of au pair agencies) are extremely influential in shaping the information which is available to hosts and au pairs, and therefore in shaping the discursive environment within which au pairing takes place.

The fact that the IAPA is able to baldly state that the reason it lobbies for au pairing to be understood as cultural exchange is in order for au pairs and hosts to avoid taxes gives some indication of how instrumentally the concept of cultural exchange can be used within au pairing. In a report prepared for the Norwegian government, Cecile Øien (2009) found that if au pairing in Norway was to achieve its aims of cultural exchange, au pairs would only be able to work for eight hours per week. The fact that au pairs work for many more hours than this, even in the most generously regulated schemes, and could work for over 70 hours a week in countries without regulations, as shown by the advertisements discussed above, suggests that time for cultural exchange and the practices of cultural exchange are not prioritised within au pairing by regulatory bodies, hosts and often even au pairs themselves. However, as both our au pair and host interviewees explained to us, cultural exchange could work and could be both valuable and enjoyable.

Conclusion

In this chapter we have moved beyond official definitions of au pairing offered by government and the industry to establish what it means to be an au pair in contemporary Britain. The answer, based on the 1,000 advertisements we analysed is perhaps 'many different things, none of them very well paid'. The ads show that there is still some kind of central idea that an au pair is a young person (generally a woman), generally (but not necessarily) from overseas, who is involved in providing live-in childcare, cleaning and cooking, although she may be caring for horses or dogs instead of children and may be living out or at a relative's house rather than in her host's home. She is likely to be doing this for somewhere between 25 and 70 hours a week and is likely to be paid around £100 per week. She might be looking after children of any ages, and could be responsible for up to four children (and maybe also some dogs and horses). The 'soft' conditions that she is offered are also highly variable: her hosts might want someone who will be a 'big sister' or other, similar member of the family; they might be quite clear that this is absolutely *not* a quasi-familial, or even a very friendly relationship; or they may already be too fatigued to specify.

This analysis shows that a substantial proportion of au pair posts being offered in Britain are offering conditions a very long way from the original intentions of the scheme or the terms of the now defunct au pair visa. Government neglect of this area has allowed a 'race to the bottom', where a very wide range of roles, some of which would have been nanny jobs in the past, are now being presented as 'au pair' posts. The variety of positions being listed under this title, as well as the shockingly poor conditions being offered in some of them, demonstrates that the sector needs regulation.

Au pair positions are still very definitely shaped by the notion of 'cultural exchange' as an important element of the au pair experience and reward. From our interviewees we discovered that this aspect was incredibly important in shaping the relationship between host and au pair – is it one of respect or servitude? Au pairs also saw opportunities for cultural exchange, particularly language learning, as part of the reward for being an au pair, an aspect of their experiences which could ameliorate for low pay. Hosts were more likely to see engaging in cultural exchange as a chore, but even the most jaded of the hosts we met understood both the moral importance of this aspect of the relationship and its great value to au pairs. If cultural exchange is to remain part of au pair arrangements, it is extremely important that it is not just used in instrumental ways (as is implied by IAPA) but that it gives au pairs real opportunities.

'Wanted: one au pair. Result: 2,000 applications'. So ran the headline of an article in *The Telegraph* newspaper about a London-based mother who had advertised for an au pair on the website AuPairWorld (Murray-West 2012). The article drew attention not only to the volume of traffic flying around the cyber world of au pair–host matchmaking, but also to the extent to which prospective employers of au pairs in the UK were able to 'name their price' and pick and choose an au pair from a huge range of very able candidates (Murray-West 2012). Sites such as AuPairWorld and Au Pair.com, as well as Gumtree, host thousands of ads, with new listings added by the hour. People advertise for au pairs to live with them or work for them in the UK, au pairs advertise themselves to prospective UK families; au pairs and the families who host them covertly look for a 'better match' while they are already 'engaged', so to speak, and all these ads contain fascinating information about the terms and conditions common to au pair placements and about what families and au pairs are looking for.

In addition to the au pair–host 'matchmaking' service conducted online, au pairs also use Facebook, Instagram, Twitter, WhatsApp and other forms of social media to 'find their feet' in the UK, make new friends and arrange social outings (after we finished our research BAPAA launched a new app, 'AuPairs UK', to help au pairs link up). Au pairs we met also used forms of cyber communication to evaluate, compare and critique their own experiences and those of contemporaries by comparing 'good' and 'bad' families and swapping notes about what was 'reasonable' in terms of the pocket money on offer and the childcare and housekeeping duties expected of them (cf. Búriková 2015 on au pair gossip). Hosts of au pairs, meanwhile, used Facebook as well as websites such as Mumsnet and netmums, and more geographically specific sites such as the East Dulwich Forum, to discuss their experiences of hosting au pairs and to compare notes about subjects such as what kinds of household tasks au pairs could be asked to do, for how much pocket money, and how much and what quality of food hosts should be expected to provide for au pairs. In this way, the internet served as a kind of virtual 'back fence' that au pairs and hosts conversed over and which they used to assist them as they constructed the social and labour market fabric of au pairing, evaluated their own experiences and compared and contrasted these with those of others.

This chapter draws on interviews with au pairs, with hosts, with representatives from au pair agencies as well as time spent 'hanging out' in virtual au pair chat rooms, both eavesdropping on and contributing to conversations between au pairs about their understanding of what being an au pair should or does involve and about experiences in the UK. This material has been drawn upon to analyse the role internet communication has come to play in the experiences of au pairs and of hosts and to assess the extent to which the growth of internet communication in the placement of au pairs has altered the market place for this form of childcare and domestic work in terms of pay and conditions offered. In particular the chapter examines the role online communication has played in the construction of a virtual marketplace for au pair labour, and the implications for the regulation and oversight of the au pair sector in the UK if the internet continues to displace 'physical' agencies as a forum for negotiation and placement.

We argue in this chapter that the internet virtual marketplace has contributed to a buyers' market and a race to the bottom in wages and conditions for au pairs in the UK. The internet serving as a marketplace for au pair employment has also had the effect of shrinking the role of au pair agencies, which in the past had acted as unofficial regulators of the industry and provided one of the only 'safety nets' for au pairs. However, the negative effects of internet communication have been offset to some extent by the role online communication has played in allowing au pairs to gain agency by being able to virtually discuss wages and conditions. Also, the internet has in some instances served a valuable function in allowing au pairs who needed to make a quick escape or who had been thrown out by a host family to be rescued by compatriots or sympathetic online acquaintances. Finally, internet communication has provided a space where au pairs can socialise and build networks. This has been a valuable service as many au pairs have found it difficult to meet people without the assistance of virtual networks, as many have found themselves isolated inside domestic spaces with only young children for company.

Into the regulatory void: from au pair agencies to online matchmaking

We begin by taking a step back from the virtual, to look at the role that 'real world' agencies have played in regulating au pairing and why their replacement by unregulated, online sites matters. Previous studies have found that agencies specialising in the recruitment and placement of migrant domestic workers were key 'gatekeepers', setting conditions of entry for female migrant domestic workers (Bakan and Stasiulis 1995 p304; see also Cox 2007; Souralová 2012; Yodanis and Lauer 1997). Agencies have also been important sources of information about the rules of au pair employment and should, in principle, have helped to ensure that an au pair's working and living conditions did not violate the law. Until the rise of online matching services such as AuPairWorld, agencies were one of the main routes through which hosts and au pairs could meet each other and, in some countries such as the USA, agencies still play a key role in placing au pairs and facilitating visas. In this section we discuss the role that agencies have been able to play in protecting au pairs, what the limits to their remit and abilities are from this point of view, in the light of the rise of online matching for au pairs and hosts at the same time as deregulation of the sector. The result is a 'mess', as one industry representative told us.

Existing studies have found that in circumstances where agencies have a role, au pairs are not as likely to be at the mercy of the market and employers' whims in respect to their wages, conditions and experiences. Au pair agencies can provide a barrier between au pair and host and have previously been found to be effective in setting wages and conditions, even if these were not enforceable by law. In respect to the situation in the UK, this was the view put forward by BAPAA, a respected au pair agency trade association, which said of its mission:

> We are the only recognised Trade Association for the British Au Pair Industry … [We were] formed on a non-commercial basis with the sole purpose of setting standards for the Au Pair industry.

In an interview during our research a founder member of the organisation, said:

> We set up our NGO to be able to really set out the standards of what we think au pairing should be in this country because there wasn't … we're not regulated. So we set up to agree a code of conduct and a

standard for au pairing. [For example] [we] have taken on the mantle that we recommend that families give the 28 days holiday. Not all do. Because some of them pay for college, give them a car to use, give them mobiles, pay top ups, all sorts of things. Take them on their family holidays, treat them like an older daughter or son ... So these are the sort of issues that we deal with at the moment. We'd love for au pairing to be more regulated.

Since then, BAPAA has continued to respond to the lack of government regulation by refining their own guidance and trying to reduce ambiguity around the au pair role. As shown in the Introduction, the Association set out new guidelines on 'What is an au pair' in September 2017 (BAPAA 2017) and no longer supports the placement of people in 'au pair plus' roles (an 'au pair plus' is a highly ambiguous position in which someone is described as an au pair but works longer hours and may take on more responsibility, it is very difficult to distinguish from a nanny post except by the lower pay and lack of employment rights). BAPAA's position has been that given that au pairing in the UK has not been regulated by any government department, it has been up to au pair agencies – particularly those that are members of the association – to perform a public service by acting as the 'conscience' and, as far as possible, the non-official 'enforcers' of the industry.

However, not all au pair agencies in Britain are members of BAPAA, so even amongst 'real world' agencies the association's influence is somewhat limited. There are also structures in the industry that can encourage less scrupulous agencies to deprioritise the interests of au pairs. The most important of these is the fact that au pair agencies are businesses – they are not charitable organisations whose *raison d'être* is the wellbeing of au pairs. As such, the principal aim of agencies is to generate a profit (or at least break even) and the way that au pairing is organised means that au pair agencies earn income servicing the interests and requirements of hosts rather than au pairs. It is hosts who pay agency fees in the UK and who are more likely to be repeat customers over the years. Au pairs, on the other hand, are valuable only at the point when they are needed as placements, but the very large number of young people willing to be au pairs means they are a dispensable labour supply, as the newspaper quote at the opening of this chapter illustrates. Au pairs moving to the UK who use an agency will have paid an agency in another country who then passed their details to an agency in the UK. This means there is often no direct link between the au pair and the agency actually making the placement with a family.

The shortfall in agency assistance available to au pairs requiring protection from exploitative or troublesome hosts came up a number of times in interviews we conducted with au pairs. Louisa, for example, was placed by an agency with a host family in the USA. The child she was to care for appeared to Louisa to have developmental delays, which led to the child displaying emotional and behavioural immaturity. Louisa reported that the host mother, meanwhile, was drinking large amounts of alcohol throughout the day and night and gave Louisa the impression that she was suffering from mental health difficulties. The agency had not conveyed any of this context to Louisa when it assigned her to the family. After a number of weeks, Louisa contacted the agency, explained her situation and tried to get the agency to assist, or at least advise her. Louisa explained the lack of response from the agency in the following terms:

> I talked to the counsellor [at the agency] first and told her my problem, and the first things and sentences she said were, 'Are you really sure? Don't you think she's just doing …'. – And I said, 'No, really. She is doing that and that, and I explained to her the situation, like I explained to you, with the psychiatry, with the sleeping on the sofa, with how often she drinks, with how fast the gin bottle empties …'. She was, like, 'I don't know what you mean, what are you telling me? No, everything is okay'. I was, like, 'Okay … are you sure?' 'Yeah'. She was telling me no, everything is okay, because, obviously, my host mum, a drunk person, a drinker for seven years. I'm telling him, describing things like weaving, and she's telling me 'No'. So I was like really, oh gosh … The bad thing, though, is that the family, even though I told the agency – I mean I had forced them to not get them any other au pair, but my old host family got a new au pair without any problem, so you think the agency just wants to make money.

Louisa's story was far from unique in its account of agencies not intervening and failing to offer assistance to au pairs who reported difficulties in their placements. It is also telling that it took place in the USA where au pair agencies are perhaps the most strictly regulated and where the organisation of the au pair scheme requires them to have a role in all au pair placements, including quite substantial responsibilities for the au pairs they place, such as sponsoring visas and providing orientation courses.

In addition – and the primary focus of this chapter – there is a very large and apparently expanding online sector that exists outside any form of regulation. BAPAA acknowledges the significance of the market for non-agency placements, a founder member said:

> So there is a mess going on [in] that sector that we can't do anything about at the moment, because it is unregulated. A lot of the sites are run outside the UK, not based here. So you can't actually source where they've come from and what they're doing.

This 'non-agency' marketplace has taken the form of web-based direct contact between hosts and au pairs that avoid the higher charges and paper work – and the regulatory framework, such as it is – associated with traditional au pair agencies. The extent of this marketplace has been difficult to quantify as the number of websites displaying host and au pair profiles for mutual perusal is ever-changing. However, as mentioned in the Introduction, there are tens of thousands of people applying for au pair posts in the UK each year. The majority of hosts and au pairs we interviewed expressed a preference for using sites such as AuPairWorld or placing or responding to ads on sites such as Gumtree, rather than using a physical agency. In the case of employers, a common practice was that they had used an agency the first time they wanted to hire an au pair, when they were unfamiliar with norms and practices in the sector, but had then realised they could save money by looking through profiles online and contacting au pairs directly themselves. Au pairs felt that direct contact gave them more control over where they went and to whom. Below we look at 'the mess' that has resulted from lack of regulation and the evidence of this that could be found through analysis of internet traffic.

A buyers' market: matchmaking in the open market for au pairs

Families and au pairs who wished to bypass using an au pair agency had a number of options. They could sign up to websites such as AuPairWorld, where au pairs and hosts could look at each other's profiles. They could rely on word of mouth or ads posted in the window of local shops; or they could advertise their requirements or their services directly using listing sites such as Gumtree.com. In the course of our research we learned about how the market for au pairs in the UK – particularly the virtual internet-based market – functioned. Our data revealed a thriving internet-based buyers' market, particularly for hosts who lived in London. This move to internet-based placements matters because not only are online recruiters able to work outside national regulations (such as they might be), they are also powerful actors in representing migrant workers to their potential employers and thereby shaping who is and who is not recruited and by whom. As James Tyner (1999 p195) commented in relation to online sites placing Asian domestic workers, in this sector, the actor who controls lines of communication is able to construct the reality of migrants' experiences:

> Labour recruiters, therefore, through their marketing of female foreign domestic workers, retain a considerable amount of power in the representation of migrants. Consequently, developments in Internet technology portend significant implications for both the vulnerability and exploitation of migrant workers, as well as the provision of migrants' rights across the globe.

The expansion of online spaces for the recruitment of au pairs is therefore important both in terms of their existence outside regulation and the way in which they influence who might look like an appropriate or desirable au pair. Tyner (1999) argues that in the case of Asian domestic workers, this particularly reinforced the gendering of the sector and ethnic hierarchies within it, something we also found within the au pair sector.

That there is a buyers' market for the services of au pairs was made clear in the huge response hosts reported to their advertisements, compared with the very few responses au pairs reported receiving to their advertisements, as well as in the competition for placements that au pairs reported experiencing. So, for example, all hosts interviewed about how they went about hiring were clear that they received more applications than they had time to read. This was true of those who recruited an au pair using an agency, and even more the case for those who posted a 'family looking for au pair' profile on an au pair website or placed an ad on Gumtree.com. Au pairs who posted profiles on websites and/or paid for ads offering their services on Gumtree said they did not necessarily get any responses at all. One au pair, 25-year-old Beatrice, from the Czech Republic, described how she had become frustrated by the lack of uptake, so had engaged in a form of online marketing to increase her appeal. She said:

I searched for a very long time, I don't know, maybe four months, maybe more. I went to several pages, I created my profile and then I changed it several times because I was wondering why other girls with probably maybe nicer pictures has more views on the pages and mine wasn't. Even I had a degree, like working with children, I had working experience in after school centres, in summer camps. Then I went through these good profiles and I copied some ideas or some structures to make it more easy-going or maybe user friendly.

Beatrice's experience was indicative of something other au pairs also reported – that there was stiff competition for placements in the UK, particularly for placements in London and that her online appearance mattered. There are many thousands of young people from across the world who are keen to come to the UK and becoming an au pair has been an accepted way to achieve this aim. The UK has been a popular destination for the youth of the world because of the cultural pull of the UK, and particularly London; the economic, cultural and social value attached to high levels of English-language proficiency and the relative (with relative being the operative word) strength of the UK labour market, particularly for those who were thinking of using au pairing as a starting point to a more permanent migration to the UK, among other reasons (see Cox and Busch 2016a for more on the particular draw of London).

We found in the course of our interviews that people discussed different reasons for coming to the UK as au pairs and there was a degree of correlation between geographical region of origin and motivation. To summarise, the most common reason young people from newer EU countries in Eastern Europe gave for coming to the UK as au pairs was as a 'soft landing' point that marked the beginning of a more permanent migration into what was perceived to be a more dynamic jobs market, a more socially liberal society and a more culturally exciting place to be. Young (and not so young) people from Southern European countries such as Spain, Portugal and Italy were for the most part fleeing youth unemployment and stagnant economies. They aimed to improve their English while 'waiting out' the economic crisis back home or to establish themselves as professionals in the UK after a period acclimatising as an au pair. It was only those from Western European countries with wage structures and employment markets more comparable to the UK – such as France, Germany and Sweden – who were aiming to come to the UK to live and work as an au pair for a fixed period before returning home to continue work or study. The different motivations of the au pairs and the varying amounts of flexibility in what they were looking for in the au pair experience affected how they worded their profiles and ads, influenced the kinds of ads they would respond to and, in many cases, ultimately influenced how they were perceived and treated by host families (Cox and Busch 2016b). As we discussed in Chapter 2, ethnic/national hierarchies are common in paid domestic employment and one way in which they form is through subtle processes like the wording of 'position wanted' ads. Potential au pairs from different countries do not enter the labour market under the same conditions; this affects their individual treatment and feeds into imaginings of 'types' of au pairs based on nationality.

The hosts we interviewed also differed in why they were looking for an au pair, what they had to offer in terms of accommodation and cultural exchange opportunities, and what they thought they could get away with in terms of childcare and domestic work required versus pocket money offered. Some hosts hired an au pair because they genuinely felt that their childcare and domestic needs did not require the services of a nanny and/or a housekeeper and were keen to try to offer room and board and an element of cultural exchange in exchange for childcare and housework. Other hosts interviewed said they had sought to hire an au pair because they needed someone to do childcare and domestic work but they could not afford any other option but an au pair. What was clear from interviews conducted with au pairs and with employers was that there was no baseline level of what could and could not be asked and no bottom level of wage (or 'pocket money') that employers agreed upon. Instead it was very much up to the individual circumstances, requirements, values and beliefs of the employers what they asked au pairs to do and for how much money. It was also the case that there was no baseline in respect to acceptable conditions and wages for au pairs. What an au pair regarded as acceptable depended on the degree of desperation to find a post, the level of formal education reached and relative proficiency in English, and the general nous and streetwise demeanour, among other factors.

As outlined in Chapter 4, this free-for-all in how employers and au pairs understood what being an au pair amounted to was reflected in the varying hours and terms and conditions that people advertising on Gumtree mentioned and in the varying requirements laid out in the ads placed by prospective hosts on AuPairWorld and other such sites. Some advertisements for au pairs stuck quite closely to the way in which au pairing was described by BAPAA, and the regulations that used to be issued by the Home Office; other ads for au pairs did not.

In the Introduction we outlined the background to the au pair scheme as a way of allowing young European people to improve their linguistic skills and experience life in another country in exchange for 'day-to-day family duties' (Council of Europe 1969 p4). Au pairs that we interviewed were in many cases very clear about there being a mismatch between their perceptions of what the au pair role involved before they left home and the reality of the duties required. They nominated excessive cleaning, long hours of childcare (not only because they found it onerous but because the children being cared for were deemed to be unhappy to be left with an au pair as their primary carer and craved parental love and attention), inadequate pay and demands that they do everything and anything (e.g. work in the family business, serve food and drink at parties, visit aged relatives) as amounting to terms and conditions they found unappealing or unacceptable, and at odds with their perception of what being an au pair was supposed to entail. Whether au pairs were in a position to be able to sift through ads to find positions that most resembled au pairing as it was described in the Convention – and then to follow this up by talking at some length to the prospective host family – depended on a number of factors. Beatrice, who was 25 at the time of interview and had a university degree, said on this subject:

> It depends. There are many families and many expectations. Each family has something different on their mind what really au pair is. So you have to really discuss it clearly. If you are very young – I would say if I was at age 18 these things just wouldn't come across to my mind. Even I would read some scary events which happen to other au pairs or something it can really scare you on the internet. So you have to think about this carefully and you have to – but you never know.

The key point in the quote above is that Beatrice referred to each family having 'something different on their mind' about what being or having an au pair in the home entailed. The lack of regulatory environment around the employment of au pairs meant it was indeed a 'free for all'. And this 'free for all' gained added momentum with the space and potential for wide reach made possible by the internet.

Hosts were also aware of the scope for making up their own terms and conditions that online au pair recruitment forums allowed. At worst this could create conditions which were dangerous. Whereas licensed, legitimate agencies are inspected by the Department for Business, Energy and Industrial Strategy (BEIS) and need to be able to show that they have carried out basic background checks on au pairs and hosts, the same does not apply to online matching services based outside the UK or to private ads on platforms such as Gumtree. Margaret, an employer of au pairs in London, had had some experience of things going wrong, both in the case of au pairs she had employed and in the case of others she had met. Margaret described a situation where an au pair she had come into contact with through AuPairWorld had taken a position with a lone-parent family. When the au pair had arrived she discovered that the mother was suffering from cancer, that the boy she was to care for was disabled and required specialised care and that the previous au pair had been violently assaulted by the host's ex-husband. Margaret only knew of the au pair's plight because she had interviewed her after placing an ad on AuPairWorld, and then had stayed in touch via Facebook. Margaret said:

> Yeah, I think it's a huge problem because actually what happens in that situation? Does she contact AuPairWorld and blacklist the family? Are they really going to blacklist the family? Because AuPairWorld is quite difficult in terms of there is in this country no contract. Other countries on AuPairWorld have a contract to sign. I'm not sure actually what the legal standing of that contract is; I'm not actually sure that AuPairWorld has any – there's no real safety net. So I don't think there's a safety net for the families but I think the families, being adults and being in their own country, are in a stronger position than the young girls coming over.

The cyber marketplace for au pairs therefore contributed to the problems of an unregulated sector. Further, in the buyer's market, it allowed hosts to name their price and terms without reference to BAPAA or government standards and in this way contributed to a race to the bottom. Also, online ads allowed people to, for example, specify the nationality or gender they preferred for an au pair, reinforcing the stereotyping of domestic work, whereas this would be more covert if agencies were used or when print ads were more common, because of the regulation of printed media.

Strategic information gathering: au pairs gossiping in cyber space

- 48 Facebook groups helping au pairs to meet and make friends in London
- 11,500 YouTube videos made by au pairs for others
- 3,411 members signed up to LinkedIn
- 831 tags on Instagram

Zuzana Búriková (2015) has argued that 'gossip' is an important activity for au pairs, rather than being a social occupation, that it is actually strategic, and enables them to gather information about the sector from an otherwise isolated position. The lack of regulation and clarity about exactly what au pairing is means that au pairs have to work hard to gain information about standards and practices in the sector. The plethora of online fora used by au pairs shows that cyberspace is now the place where they go to compare notes, ask for advice and seek confirmation from other au pairs.

Many of the au pairs we spoke to said that the expectations of their employers and the reality of their daily lives left them unsure about whether what they were being asked to do was an acceptable part of being an au pair. For example, Edina, said:

> I just really didn't know about it. I think it is – I have a lot of friends who has a really good experience of that. I can't say that it's a bad experience but it's definitely not what I expected though. The children are – yes for example the youngest one calls me mummy because her mummy is never at home. So I'm the only parent for them and I am 20 years old and I have four children. Yes it's not what I expected really, it's too hard.

For many au pairs, those who were newly arrived in the UK in particular, the vagueness and loose guidelines around what they were meant to be doing meant that the role of the au pair was a work in progress – it was made up by au pairs and by families as they went along. This meant that au pairs had to formulate their responses – be that acquiescence, protest, non-cooperation or retreat – on their own and with very little reference to outside sources. In some cases, the flexibility around what role an au pair should perform in the home could work in the interests of the au pairs, but in many other cases it meant that the au pair became the family dogsbody who was expected to be on call day and night and to do all manner of household and non-household tasks.

Rather than discussing their placements in the language of legal employment – 'equality', 'exploitation' or 'fairness' – au pairs that we interviewed were anxious to gauge whether their placement was with a 'good' family or a 'bad' family and whether they were getting a good or a bad deal. Au pairs used conversations with each other to work out where their placement stood in a kind of au pair ranking scale of 'good' families and 'bad' families. Our findings in this respect chimed with Búriková's findings with respect to Slovak au pairs in the UK (Búriková 2015; Búriková and Miller 2010). Búriková argues that the conceptualisation of families as either 'good' or 'bad' points at a power imbalance inherent in the relationship and that it is up to the family to decide what the au pairs would do and 'whether the relationship would be exploitative or generous, friendly or cold'. However, the meaning of 'good family' went beyond the concept of exploitation. A 'good family' was not only a family that behaved ethically (i.e. that treated its au pair fairly), but also a family that was generally pleasant to stay with. Thus, when judging the 'goodness' of their hosts, au pairs were thinking simultaneously about the fairness of their working conditions, the social dimension of their relationship to their hosts, and about the more general context of their stay, including the number and age of the children, the locality, the proximity of a language school, and various other facilities available to the au pairs.

The information au pairs gathered from other au pairs allowed them to discover the real norms of au pair employment, how much these corresponded with the formal rules, and whether their particular experience was common or unique (Búriková 2015). This information was used to help au pairs decide whether what they were experiencing 'was usual (in terms of practice) and what was right (in terms of rules or ethics) with respect to the treatment of au pairs in general' (Búriková 2015 p44). This was very important for au pairs because they needed this information to decide whether the family they had been placed with were an aberration and as such if they sought another family in the UK they could expect markedly different treatment, wages, working hours or conditions (if these or other considerations were the key issues at stake). If they found that what they were experiencing was closer to the norm in terms of how au pairing was actually practised in the UK (and there are regional variations in wages, hours expected, space provided, extras such as a car, a mobile phone etc.), they could then decide whether to accept it, move into another employment field, return home or move on to another country.

So, for many au pairs the most effective and reassuring way in which they could gather the information they needed about the au pair institution and about the fairness of their working and living conditions was to make contact with other au pairs in the UK. Some of these meetings occurred in the course of their daily duties such as on the school run or at childminder groups they attended with younger children or at language classes if they were able to attend those. However, not all au pairs were living in neighbourhoods where they were able to meet fellow au pairs and many had substantial housework duties that confined them to the home. This meant the default means of communication with the world outside their host families became Instagram, Facebook, WhatsApp, Twitter and a range of other social networking sites:

> Facebook is very good to find other au pairs. There are lots of groups. Actually Facebook is the most helpful thing because many au pairs are on there. (Carla)

> I just read on the Internet, mainly on Facebook there are many groups of au pairs. So sometimes I read on there, yeah. (Edina)

> Oh, I don't know. It's a good experience. It's interesting, because every family's different. So meeting other au pairs we can talk about the families and how different they are. (Eva)

Aguilar Pérez (2015), in her study of Mexican au pairs in the USA, found that social media enabled au pairs to gather information, make friends and manage their communications with families at home. Their negotiation of social media was an important way in which they both improved their experience as au pairs and endured their disappointments. Social media allowed isolated au pairs to make virtual friends and to discuss the 'real norms' (Búriková 2015 p44) of au pair employment, how much these corresponded with the formal rules, and whether their particular experience was common or unique. One of the most important concerns of the au pairs was to determine the degree to which their relationship with their hosts was equal and non-exploitative. Even in advance of coming to the UK au pairs could monitor websites and learn about what to expect, as Serena told us:

> Before I become au pair I read a lot of comments on internet, on a website especially for au pairs and I read about their experience, what happened with them; good and bad stories. So, I was aware a little. I spent really a lot of time to get to know everything; advantages and disadvantages, what can happen and you know.

The ease of contact with other au pairs and the honest views about au pairing that au pairs share on line, which they may not always share with their families (Aguilar Pérez 2015), means that social media offered support and protection for au pairs, as well as facilitating the deregulation of their conditions.

Social media had another slightly contradictory role in au pairs' lives, in that it helped them to stay in touch with their families and friends at home and could be important in helping them stick out bad times, particularly when they first arrived and were most homesick. In this way, by easing links with home, it also eased the stay away from home. Studies of migrant domestic workers, particularly those who have left children behind, have shown how important online communications are for maintaining these transnational families and enabling domestic workers to continue 'mothering at distance' (Cuban 2017b; Madianou and Miller 2013). Our au pair interviewees were much less dependent on regular social media contact with their families than the domestic workers in these studies, and none of them had children of their own from whom they were separated. Rather than allowing them to continue to perform the role of a parent as many transnational domestic workers do, the au pairs in our study were more likely to use social media to continue to perform the role of child, turning to their own parents for support and affirmation when the demands of their new role were overwhelming.

Hosts online: Mumsnet and other stories

- 100 group discussions on Mumsnet about issues ranging from finding a good au pair, to basic costs and contracts and even how to fire someone

Au pairs were not the only ones using social media to figure out how to make sense of and get the most out of an au pair–host relationship. The 'real norms' of au pairing were also being worked through and established by online communication between hosts. Mumsnet and other online parenting communities have been shown to be important in supporting mothers by providing alternative sources of information while at the same time allowing them to have agency in the production of parenting-related knowledge. They have also been shown to allow mothers to 'try out' different versions of motherhood (Pederson and Smithson 2013). We found similar processes at work in discussion of au pair hosting, as hosts sourced practical advice, emotional support and compared themselves against others for reassurance.

Hosts that we interviewed and discussion threads on sites such as mumsnet.com revealed their concerns about what the 'market rate' was for au pairs in their city, town or neighbourhood and about getting good value for money in terms of childcare and housework duties specified and also less tangible issues such as how trust develops in this very intimate relationship. Eleanor, who lived in West London, explained that she had researched the 'real norms' of au pairing by going online. She said:

> Basically what I've done, I've gone on Mumsnet seeing what people do. Then I've gone on Gumtree and some other places to see what people are paying, what job – basically I've done all these couple of descriptions and thought, oh this is what that mum's paying and this is what does it involve. So I started creating a rough picture of what hours should I agree, what are the house rules and things like that.

Eleanor was aiming to be a good host in that she was also using her online research to reflect on what not to do. She explained:

> When I see an advert, you know, three toddlers for £100 a week. Well, I can't cope with one toddler sometimes and it's – driving the car, dropping them to the clubs, cooking a [good, organic] meal. I think a lot of them are under a lot of pressure, I would imagine. I think au pair experience can be very different for two different girls.

The discussion threads relating to hosting an au pair on Mumsnet made it clear that not all hosts were as concerned as Eleanor was with being a good host. Some hosts were seeking information on what was permissible in terms of ages of children and sole care. Other hosts were apparently preoccupied about au pairs who were exploiting their placement to their own advantage, with numerous online discussions about au pair strategies for taking employers for a ride. Other hosts were concerned about 'trust' issues. For example, one Mumsnet poster said:

But we are wondering if there is any tips/advice that we should consider from some seasoned pros that we may have missed. Has anyone ever asked their au pair to surrender their passport for safeguarding until trust has been built up?

Mumsnet discussions also revealed attempts by hosts to self-police the marketplace, confusion about what to do in cases of flagrant exploitation of au pairs and bewilderment that there wasn't a clear path to 'report' such cases. For example, the ad below was the subject of a great deal of discussion about the extent to which it amounted to exploitation and what could be done about it.

This is a great opportunity for the financially-savvy nanny. Although this role is unpaid, we estimate that the board & lodging package is worth at least £1000 net per month (given the cost of living in London). You will have no rent to pay, no bills and we provide all your basic food plus Wi-Fi & membership of Amazon Prime AND you will still have 4–5 free days in which to do another paid job!

The ad asked for more than 22 hours a week care for two children under 5 years old and offered no pay. Mumsnet posters were on the whole aghast, with a typical response being:

The idea of posting with the title, 'to keep an unpaid slave in my guest room to look after my children, as long as I give them yummy roast dinners' is very tempting though …!

And another posting:

Could someone direct me to government legislation which says why it's not legal? Maybe we can direct them to it.

These posts might serve to check, or at least give pause to, hosts who are attempting to impose the most exploitative conditions. They also allow other hosts, and 'mums' who do not host au pairs, to feel better about themselves because they are not behaving this badly. In the general atmosphere of guilt surrounding motherhood, which we set out in Chapter 3, this is not a small part of the function of these discussion lists (Pederson and Smithson 2013; Barbagallo 2016). Parents, and mothers in particular, are under extreme pressure to strive for completely unrealistic standards in their performance of their role as parents. Feeling that someone else might be doing it worse, or with less moral integrity, can be a comfort and can release some of the pressure that comes with contemporary motherhood, even for those who can afford an au pair.

Other concerns aired by hosts involved long posts about the extent to which 'their' au pair was lazy, greedy, stupid, immature, sexually rapacious or a combination of all of the above. For example:

> She came down with a cold, as did I, and she has barely left her bed since. I had to take the whole day off today to do the school runs, washing, cleaning, cooking etc. I am self employed, so it cost me hard cash.

And:

> Does Au Pair = Affair?

Hosts 'fished' for information on message boards such as those hosted on Mumsnet in order to justify behaviour towards au pairs, as well as to work out 'acceptable' standards of pay, hours worked etc. Often this information was required to prevent an au pair from immediately leaving to find a 'better' placement. However, it was also apparent that much of the au pair arrangement came down to the individual whims, prejudices, needs and feelings of the host, and these people required a forum to seek to justify their behaviour to themselves. So the internet acted as a sort of confession box in which questionable behaviour by hosts was validated or excused by a community of 'mums'.

> It's very early days with the au pair – she arrived on Tuesday. She's young and attractive and ds seems to really like her. I am 31 weeks pregnant, grumpy, sleeping badly and 40. My ankles disappeared weeks ago and I feel unattractive.
>
> Dh usually spends his evenings on the computer, leaving me to deal with ds, but he has become very interested in spending time playing with ds now that the au pair is here and spending time with ds. I'm feeling jealous and I hate it!

The question posed was should the mother sack the au pair and the answer from other 'mums' was a resounding 'yes'. The issue of whether au pairs would have affairs with host dads (or just be attractive to them) has had a great deal of currency (Cox 2007), but the ability to discuss this in a public but anonymous space is relatively new. It raised interesting questions about how the connectedness that the internet offered potentially alters the 'private' of the private sphere. Indeed, as Richenda Gambles (2010) has argued, online fora such as Mumsnet, which enable people to make the 'private' public, have the potential to blur the lines between public, private, personal and political spaces. Questions such as the one above, which in the past may not have been aired by a host mother, or may only have been shared with the most intimate friends, are now publicly (albeit anonymously) discussed. The outcome was that hosts could feel supported by a virtual community but may be being advised to do something that was morally questionable, such as sacking an au pair who had done nothing wrong merely because of a suspicion that 'dh' was attracted to the au pair.

The internet was also used by parents to talk about and compare and contrast attributes of au pairs from different countries. For example:

> u sound pretty reasonable but my worst times have been with
> Polish au pairs. I may be wrong about this but have had two and
> both were difficult and always talked about in my country. I also work
> with Polish people and whilst they are lovely they can be opinionated
> and do really believe Poland is the best. Criticism goes down
> very badly.

In this way, cyber communication between hosts, in common with the 'position wanted' ads place by au pairs, reinforced and reformed ethnic hierarchies of labour, in a sector where the imagined characteristics of different nationalities is extremely important. The combined context of ethnic stereotyping, which is common in paid domestic work (see Chapter 2), with online fora and lack of regulation, allows these sorts of rhetorics to flourish. The hierarchies of whiteness, which have characterised the organisation of paid domestic work in Britain for hundreds of years, continue to be remade in these most modern ways.

With au pairing, as with other topics, online discussion has the tendency to confirm people in their own beliefs. People seek out and join in conversations with others who they perceive to be like them. Au pair hosts feel isolated when dealing with the issues of managing their home and raising their children and what they want is often validation (although sometimes they really do want clear advice about legalities). The end result is that assumptions are unlikely to be challenged and there is no higher authority who can step in.

Conclusion

Au pairing in contemporary Britain is shaped by online interactions, between groups of hosts, between au pairs and hosts, and between groups of au pairs. These interactions are fed by the ambiguity and intimacy of au pairing. It is an environment where reliable information is hard to come by or to identify, but where the stakes for being poorly informed are high. Au pairs run the risk of being exploited, or even abused, and hosts similarly worry that the norms of au pair behaviour and expectations are obscure to them. Cyberspace provides a 'back fence' to gossip over where otherwise isolated people can share stories and compare notes. This sharing is powerful and can be important in undermining the worst behaviours in the sector, but it is also unregulated and not always well informed. As with all social media interactions, there is the danger of talking only into the 'echo chamber' of a community who share similar ideals. This means that there is no guarantee that outlandish expectations will be challenged, nor poor practice checked.

One of the most significant aspects of the organisation of au pairing today is the ease with which hosts and au pairs can find each other online. This has undermined the role of 'real' agencies, who now place only a small fraction of all au pairs. The corollary of this weakened role for agencies is that they are less able to act to regulate the sector or protect au pairs. Online agencies, websites such as Gumtree, and all the other ways in which au pairs and hosts can now connect, all make it extremely difficult for any non-government agency to ensure standards, or even communicate norms. The growth of online matchmaking has reinforced the problems that have come from deregulation and the 'mess' of the au pair sector.

6 | THE LIFE AND TIMES OF AU PAIRS

In chapter four we examined the multitudinous nature of what it means to be an au pair; the extensive and varied demands hosts make on au pairs and the wide variation in remuneration and conditions that au pairs receive. In this chapter, we look at what au pairs told us about their lived experience of au pairing and what happens within the host–au pair relationship to the notion of 'equality' that it is meant to define. The 40 au pairs we interviewed had, between them, worked for 66 host families in five countries. One of them had been au pairing for just two weeks at the time we met, but three of our au pair interviewees had been in the sector for more than five years. Not surprisingly, they had a wealth of diverse experience in terms of the households they had worked for, their locations and the tasks they had done.

The themes of equality, status and belonging within the family came out in various ways in our interviews, and in this chapter we examine the main activities which make up the au pair experience: cleaning, childcare and living in the host's house. In this discussion we contribute to the growing literature on 'intimate labour' (Boris and Parreñas 2010), a concept that has been used to understand many forms of paid and unpaid care work as well as sex work and other personal services and which, within discussions of paid domestic labour, highlights the interrelationships between affective, embodied work and inequalities of class, race/ethnicity and gender and the very particular ways these play out within the home. Working, as well as living, within someone else's home requires the negotiation of a very particular type of intimacy. As Anita Borner, a domestic worker quoted by Helma Lutz (2011 p54), puts it:

> Imagine you need a home help. You look for someone you can simply give your house keys to, and you can be sure she won't open your drawers or your letters and you'll come home and find everything tidy. It's very hard … She's supposed to fold your underwear, do your bedroom and make your bed – you can imagine what that's like? Really very specific. We go deep inside people's private and personal lives. Deep inside.

We start by looking at the importance of cleaning work to establishing the status of au pairs. Our interviewees were clear that they would prefer to do childcare and that being given responsibility for all the cleaning in the house communicated to them powerfully that they were not equal. We then look at the terrain of childcare within au pair–host relationships, what au pairs think of their hosts' child-rearing practices and how au pairs can be affected by parents' feelings of guilt. While not all au pairs live-in, the vast majority do, and sharing the intimate space of home with employers brings its own challenges. We examine the effects that living-in has on au pairs' feelings about their working hours, their control over food, physical intimacy and sexual harassment and how they judge the social standing of their hosts when they see them behind closed doors. What becomes clear, in exploring the experiences of au pairs, is that equality – and more often inequality – are not produced in simple ways through low pay or excessive working hours but are manifest and communicated repeatedly in the smallest interactions and expectations. What we see is the intimacy and sensitivity of a home-based, quasi-familial relationship, suffused with the power of some of the most pervasive and enduring social forces (gender, class and ethnicity). It is unlikely that this will be a simple thing to negotiate, and unsurprising that the mundane details of who does which tasks, how and when matters.

Dishing the dirt: au pairs and cleaning

There is something particularly intimate about dealing with other people's dirt. Yet, while it is clearly a mark of an intensely personal relationship, it is also the case that expecting someone else to deal with your dirt can be an extremely effective way to demonstrate remoteness and disdain. Closeness to or distance from dirt has been a structuring force of social relations and a marker of inequality for centuries. The distribution of 'dirty work' between people indicates their standing in the household and the world at large (see Chapter 2). The au pairs we interviewed explained that while their work could be divided into childcare (including cooking for children, helping with homework and all-day care of infants) and cleaning, there was a great variation in how much childcare versus how much cleaning could be asked for. Every au pair we spoke to preferred childcare and its associated tasks to cleaning work. However, there was a huge range in terms of expectation and understanding of what constituted a reasonable amount of cleaning and childcare. Some hosts had modest demands that involved very little or no cleaning at all and some required the au pair to clean for hours every day, often in addition to childcare, shopping and cooking. In this section we explore the effects of the content of au pairs' work on their experiences, their relationships to hosts and their sense of being 'an equal' within the household.

Cleaning – who should do it, for how long, to what standard and which parts of the house were and were not the responsibility of the au pair – emerged as a fraught area in almost every interview we conducted with au pairs. The notional equality between au pairs and their hosts was often sorely tested by the cleaning requirements many hosts imposed on au pairs. A common complaint by au pairs was that in their own homes they had begun to contribute to household tasks – including cleaning, cooking, help with younger siblings etc. – when they were younger than some of the children in their care. They also noted that they were happy to do their share of keeping communal areas and their own spaces tidy, but that they resented what they felt was the servitude inherent in becoming the cleaner for the entire household and a general dog's body. That is, they were happy to clean if other household members also did their share but they resented being the only person in the house (paid cleaner aside) who did the dirty work. After all, it is difficult to demand that someone cleans up after you while at the same time imagining that they feel they are being treated as your equal.

Oskar said of the cleaning demands made on him:

> It's just a job and they want work and work and work. It's never enough what you do ... They always say 'light housework', but light housework means you have to do everything basically.

The use, without definition, of the phrase 'light housework' to describe au pairs' duties has long been a source of tension. Búriková and Miller (2010) explicitly call for a definition of 'light housework' in the list of recommendations resulting from their research with hosts and au pairs, and BAPAA now provides guidance as to what housework tasks should and should not be expected of au pairs (see Introduction and BAPAA 2017 for details).

Oskar explained that he would be more likely to feel 'part of the family' if there were some reciprocity from the family. He said:

> There was a French girl [I met] and she found a really good family and the mum cleaned the bedroom of the girl, which is really fair, that's really fair.

Oskar explained that he thought it was fair for the 'mum' to clean the room of the au pair because that would indicate that the mother was treating the au pair as a 'big sister' to her actual children. Oskar felt that it was fair for the au pair to do some housework and childcare in exchange for being hosted, but that this should be in the context of the rest of the household also pitching in. If the 'mum' of the household cleaned the bedrooms of the children, she should also clean the bedroom of the au pair, according to Oskar's logic, as this would suggest the au pair was on equal terms with the other junior members of the household. Needless to say, we did not come across any instances where the mother or father of the household cleaned the au pair's bedroom and very few examples of household tasks being shared equally among the household, including but not limited to the au pair. Instead, the majority of au pairs interviewed felt that the term 'light housework' – which was commonly used in au pair wanted ads – was often a euphemism for 'do everything'.

The absence of a precise – or even a loose – definition of 'light housework' and the non-existence of a reliable breakdown of what a reasonable proportion of the au pair's time that would be spent on cleaning versus that to be spent on childcare and on their own pursuits came up time and time again in interviews as a principal source of dissatisfaction and frustration (cf. Búriková 2015). Sasha explained her experience of the negotiation between au pairs and hosts in relation to time, saying:

> I spoke with them on the internet [when arranging the placement], they said to me – I will have 80 per cent look after children and 20 per cent cleaning the house. It was about 70 per cent cleaning the house and 30 per cent look after children … clean all the house, everything; doing washing, ironing, hoovering, almost everything. They had a cleaner, but the cleaner came just once a week, I think, so the rest of the week I had to clean the house. I worked from 8am until 5pm or 5.30pm. Clean the house all morning and look after the children in the afternoons.

The heavy cleaning schedule was a common reason au pairs gave for why they wanted to leave the host family and this was the reason Sasha gave. She said:

> I tried to speak with my host mum and I told her I'm not happy to do all the cleaning and she said me, OK, but she needs somebody who will clean the house. So I told her, OK, so maybe you don't need au pair, you need just a cleaner.

Sasha was an articulate, confident interviewee who was clear that when she signed up to be an au pair this did not mean she had signed up to be the family's live-in cleaner. She explained forcefully why being asked to clean the house every morning did not sit well with her understanding of au pairing as involving equality between herself and the family. She said:

> I'm not happy with them because I told her I can't eat with you, I can't go, for example, go to the trips with you and I don't feel like a part of the family.

Sasha had a plan of action in response to her discomfort – and this discomfort carried over into a suspicion on her part that the very nature of au pairing was flawed because of the difficulty of reconciling cleaning and performing housework and childcare while living in someone's home with equality. Her response was to request references from the family, which she used to support applications for live-out nanny positions.

Freya, 29, from Romania, was among the large number of au pairs we interviewed who found herself in a situation that she perceived to be exploitative. However, unlike Sasha, she did not feel able to stand up to her host mother. Freya described her placement as involving at least 60 hours a week of work. She said that after rising early and helping the children get ready for school, she was required to do housework all morning. She was allowed an hour's break at 1pm before setting off to pick children up from school. She then worked until 8.30 in the evening. Freya said of her experience:

> No, I didn't feel like a part of the family. I remember one evening when some of the girl's colleagues came on a visit with their parents, everybody was in the living room eating pizza but no one invited me to join them. I was so hungry because I had to look after seven kids then and I was so hungry because I had to do so hard work. After that, the host mother asked me to wash the big plates after they were eating pizza. I didn't feel that good, I was very unhappy. I felt the humiliation in that part.

Similarly, Ursula, 23, from Hungary, also discussed her response to the demands of her hosts in terms of experiencing 'humiliation', saying of her host mother:

> Sometimes I felt that she humiliates me and I didn't want to stay there anymore. Sometimes I need to mop the floor with my hands [i.e. on hands and knees] for example.

The humiliation that is felt as a result of being asked to do an unfair amount of cleaning work or to do it in a particularly arduous way, is something that recurs in studies of paid domestic work from around the world (see for example Anderson 2000; Lutz 2011; Marchetti 2014). Anderson (2000) argues that personalistic power is exercised over domestic workers when employers demand that work is done in very specific or unnecessary ways; this form of power is particularly available to employers of live-in domestic workers. As one of Anderson's interviewees, a domestic worker from Ghana working in Athens, says, 'You wouldn't tell your fellow human to do something you would not be happy to do' (2000 p140). In other words, the very act of asking someone to do something that you would not be happy to do yourself is to signal to them that you do not really think of them as a 'fellow human'.

The au pair experiences referred to above revolved around who should do the cleaning in the house and for how long and how the house was cleaned. Dirt, and who has to deal with it, matters in terms of creating and indicating status, particularly within the context of the home (Cox et al. 2011). In a situation such as au pairing, when there is a difference in nationality, between those foregoing cleaning and those taking it up, this distribution of work is also freighted with many centuries of history of racism in the distribution of domestic work, and who is seen as appropriate to do cleaning tasks (Anderson 2000). Allocating cleaning work to someone not only reflects their location in hierarchies of gender, class and ethnicity, it also (re)produces those hierarchies; in contemporary Britain, young people from poorer European countries are increasingly coded as the appropriate people to do the dirty work. The reactions of these au pairs to demands that they do all the cleaning in the house, or that they do it in particular ways – on hands and knees for example – reveal how important the organisation of 'dirty work' is to social relations. As they show, being 'part of the family' and being the family's cleaner were experienced as incompatible. The low status of cleaning work easily transferred itself to the au pair.

Other au pairs interviewed, in addition to questioning why they should be the only household members to clean, also objected to the standard of cleanliness or order imposed by the hosts. For some au pairs, this was a question of different standards families had as to what constitutes an acceptably tidy house. Others felt that the parent (usually the mother) asking them to do the cleaning was neurotic or manipulative. Cleaning standards, like almost everything that goes on behind the closed doors of the private home, are personal. We know very little about what other people think about cleaning and perhaps less about what they do. This means it is very difficult for anyone involved in negotiating cleaning work to know what is 'normal' or reasonable. In addition, cleanliness carries a (rather complicated) moral significance, whereby imputations that someone is too clean or not clean enough have connotations far beyond simple assessments of the state of the bathroom, or the regularity with which the hoover should be used. For example, Johanna, 19, from Finland, said of her placement:

> I think I did expect that I'd do some cleaning at least, but not this much. No, not this much because my family, we are clean in my own family, we are clean, but we are not too clean. So we kind of want to somehow show that the place is lived in, so that there is some living, habiting. But then this house is quite different … this is a really clean house so you have to make sure it's clean.

Lise, 24, from the Czech Republic, felt that the host mother she was living with was imposing unrealistic demands about the level of cleanliness in the house. She said:

> I was almost like a slave. I had to do mostly housework every day around seven, eight hours. It was quite hard … The host mum, she was really perfect – perfectionist. Everything had to be very clean. When she saw just one hair I had to hoover, even the stairs, underneath everything. It was crazy.

In other cases of discord in relation to standards or lack of agreement about who should do what, it was the au pair who objected to the mess in the house. Sonia was 20 years old and from the Czech Republic. She explained that she did not regard herself as obsessive about cleanliness but there were limits. She said of the house she went to:

> Two kids or three kids sleep in one bed; that's not good. And [the] kitchen is not clean … for me very important. I don't like big mess everywhere. For example, when I come in washing machine doesn't work for two weeks … it was stressful, I was very, very bad.

As the comments illustrate, au pairs are able to judge their hosts and find them wanting. That judgement might be that they are mean and demanding, just simply dirty or psychologically unbalanced in their standards. The intimate knowledge that au pairs have of their hosts' habits and standards allows them to make these very personal judgements and this is something which makes hosts extremely uncomfortable (Cox 2006; Hondagneu-Sotelo 2001).

Some of the au pairs we interviewed said they did not want to act as cleaners, full stop. They pointed out that they had no experience of cleaning to the standard their hosts expected and had no interest in developing their cleaning skills to a professional level. Maria, 23, from Bulgaria, like other au pairs we spoke to, explained that she had agreed with a family that she would be their au pair (i.e. provide childcare and general help around the home) as well as being the family's cleaner, but for extra pay. She said:

> Of course, it will be good for me to clean if you pay me. They told me that they will pay me £250 per week. It is very good. Of course, I can clean everything. Anyway, they are paying a cleaner. They can give this money to me.

Maria made clear the distinction that other au pairs we spoke to also discussed – i.e. between 'light cleaning/housework' and cleaning up in the manner that would be expected of any adult member of a household and being a professional cleaner. She said:

> They call light cleaning – vacuuming, dusting, keeping the rooms tidy; but to clean the toilets, to clean the windows – it is not light cleaning. Because I live there, I want to be clean for me too. It is not only for the family.

In contrast to the au pairs we interviewed in Britain, who often decried the amount of cleaning they were asked to do, Elisabeth Stubberud (2015b) found that the au pairs she spoke to in Norway all described the work as 'not much'. After probing deeper, she concluded that this claim was not related to the volume of work the au pairs were doing – which was, in some cases at least, extensive – but rather it was a way to distance themselves from the low status of domestic work and being a 'domestic worker' rather than an au pair. Instead of internalising the humiliation that might result from being expected by their host families to do low status tasks, they rejected the idea of themselves as domestic workers by emphasising their role in childcare and minimising the importance of the cleaning work they carried out.

While the au pairs we met did not appear to employ the same technique to manage their feelings about cleaning work, it was clear from our interviews that many felt that being expected to do too much cleaning, rather than childcare, threatened their status as 'au pair' and implicitly marked their standing within the family.

Paying for others to clean in a domestic space is problematic at the best of times. This is because even if a household paid a professional cleaning agency, so that the person cleaning was paid at least the UK minimum wage, and ensured the person cleaning was paid for holidays and sick days, and pension contributions were made and so on, it remains the case that the transaction involves the householder institutionalising in the labour market the belief that their own time is more valuable than that of the person doing the cleaning (Uhde 2016). This reinforces and perpetuates structural inequalities based on gender, class and ethnicity across society. When cleaning was shifted from being the responsibility of the mother of the house (and it was usually the mother who assumed primary responsibility for cleaning and childcare), on to first a cleaner (who was very often a migrant woman) and then on to an au pair, who was not even paid a wage but paid pocket money, it contributed to a further devaluing of this very real work so that it became an increasingly invisible, undervalued and under-rewarded aspect of domestic life that was done without recognition, usually by a woman (or in some cases a male au pair) who was poorer and younger than the host parents. The au pairs we interviewed had direct experience of the humiliation and resentment involved in the unresolved work of cleaning being shifted on to their shoulders and it contributed to the widespread resentment we encountered about the way in which the work of au pairing is organised.

Who's holding the baby? The fraught terrain of childcare

The care of children in the domestic space emerged as a fraught area for many au pairs we interviewed, as well as for hosts (see Chapter 7). Au pairs are – by definition – young, inexperienced, in a new culture and learning a new language. Different places have different childcare cultures (Vincent et al. 2004; McDowell et al. 2006) and all parents, individuals and families have preferences and eccentricities in the way they go about raising their children and keeping house. Childcare preferences are personal and nuanced and the au pairs we interviewed discussed the difficulty inherent in conforming closely enough to providing highly personalised care for children in line with parental expectations, while not becoming so close to the children that parents felt threatened and jealous (a theme which emerges repeatedly in the literature on paid domestic workers, see for example Hondagneu-Sotelo 2001; Parreñas 2000). Many of the au pairs we interviewed identified their relationship with the children they looked after as the best thing about au pairing (along with 'London' as discussed in Chapter 4) and while the au pairs we met were not in the situation of many of the domestic workers discussed in the Global Care Chains literature (see Chapter 3), who had migrated to care for other people's children while leaving their own behind, we did meet au pairs for whom the bond they had with the children they cared for was a rare light of emotional warmth in an otherwise lonely world.

Au pairs also pointed to children's resentment at their parents' absences and to what they (both children's views as reported by au pairs and the views of au pairs themselves) felt was parental neglect not only in terms of day-to-day care for children but also with regard to children's emotional wellbeing. In terms of cultures of childcare – and associated childcare practices – subjects that came up frequently included what happened at meal times, different expectations in respect to children's contributing to housework, cooking etc., discipline, and the amount of attention and affection children required to thrive.

A number of au pairs we interviewed had been hired to provide household help, shopping and cooking etc. for households in which teenagers lived. It was striking in a number of cases that the au pair was herself not much older than the teenager or teenagers in her care. Reactions of the au pairs we interviewed to the expectation that they should help 'care for' their fellow teenagers ranged from bemusement to scorn. Anita, 24, from Romania, had been hired to be an au pair for two teenagers, aged 18 and 16. Anita said:

> Well, when it involves cooking, I have to cook for them because they don't really know how to cook. Just put it in a toaster, they can cook it … I started cooking when I was I think eight. I think it depends on education and the family social position. The richer you are, I think the more comfortable you are … I don't think – I don't blame anyone for this, it's probably how people think.

This disparity in what is expected of young people can be told in ethnic/national terms too. As an interviewee of Helma Lutz (2011 p55) explained to her, 'as women in Poland, as young girls, we're still prepared for housework. That's the mentality there, every woman must be able to do that'. The inequalities in income which mean that some teenagers are caring for others, operate at a national as well as a household scale.

Anita was paid £150 a week for cooking, cleaning and being a general dog's body for this family. She dismissed out of hand the notion that she was doing this 'as an equal', though, saying:

> Really, in this family that I'm in right now, I don't mind doing the cleaning and the cooking, it's really nice. I really enjoy it even though I'm not treated equal because there's no such thing as being equal, but even though sometimes it's really demanding and I feel overwhelmed.

Anita explained that while she knew she wasn't an equal member of the family – she was there to work for them – at least the transaction was clear. She cooked, cleaned and ran errands and in return she was paid, had a room and a degree of autonomy when she wasn't wanted by the family. She didn't labour the point that she had first become an au pair when not much older than the oldest teenager she was cooking and cleaning for, but she expressed her bemusement in terms of differences stemming from social class and national cultures. Her view was that these teenagers were from a family wealthy enough to pay other people to cook and clean so that they didn't have to. Her aim was to improve her financial position so she no longer needed a live-in position and no longer had to serve other people.

Edina, 21, from the Czech Republic, was less phlegmatic about the ways in which relative wealth and expectations of children might shape character. She said

> It's mainly because they have [an] au pair. In my country we have to do everything [for ourselves]. My kids from current family, they put everything on the floor. They are sitting and watching you, how you tidy up around them … They're very lazy, extremely.

Children learning to 'let the au pair do it' was a frequent complaint among the young men and women we interviewed. A common view to emerge from interviews was that this was not particularly good for the children, but au pairs also felt that the children's parents could have and should have been effective in setting boundaries around behaviour for their children. Beatrice, 25, and also from the Czech Republic, explained that she felt the three children in her care were 'pushing boundaries' in their behaviour towards her (and toward the mother) and that the parents should have addressed this by being firmer about what was and what was not acceptable behaviour. She said:

> She [one of the children in her care] was so difficult that she was crying or lying on the floor and just stick to her mother. It was like the most stressful moment. I was trying to do something about it to give her some toys or some snacks or whatever. Nothing was working. Then I realised she's pushing her mother's boundaries, or boundaries of everyone, and sometimes the children were treating me like a servant. They were sitting around a table and one was, like, 'I want water', so I bring water. Then the middle girl, 'I want water', so I bring water. Not this cup, so another cup. It was like a round.

Beatrice attempted to discuss discipline and boundary setting with the mother of the children, including an account of culturally specific differences in approaches to childcare that existed between the UK and other countries. Beatrice was clear that she was trying to talk to the mother as one adult to another about childcare cultures. She said:

> I was trying to speak with the mother openly and I told her, sometimes you maybe need to put like either strict borders or some – it wasn't even my idea because I was trying to speak with other people at my home and we were just stupidly talking and they told me I think you are either strict or you really sometimes hit the children.
> Now she was scared that I would hit their children! But I just didn't mean that. I was just trying to talk about what to do with children. So it was like this misunderstanding. But she was so hysterical that she talked with all the ladies around the village. So I think there must be rumours about me, the horrible Czech au pair ... she scared me so much, she told me you could be even arrested. I was like, what?

Misunderstandings between the au pair and the parent about what was meant, what was said and what was done were common occurrences, according to the au pairs we interviewed. Parents' fears that the au pair would be violent or cruel to children were widely reported by au pairs and au pairs' fears that they would be accused of such behaviour came up repeatedly in our interviews. When one adds into this emotive and volatile mix, trying to negotiate across a linguistic divide, the potential for misunderstanding is increased.

Freya spoke for many of her fellow au pairs when she gave an account of a typically fractious evening with young children and the mother's response. She said:

> I had to wash their hair [the two girls in her care] three times a week and the girls were so tired she didn't want … was screaming a lot before I had to wash them. The host father went to pick the host mother from the workplace. After I finished washing the older one, she told me she was hungry but I thought the younger one would not be ready for the dinner.
>
> The host mother returned after that and I couldn't give her to eat because the host father used to prepare them the dinner and she didn't tell me what to give them to eat. It was only about 15 minutes to wait until the whole family came at home. After that I was so glad that I finished bathing the younger one and the host mother screamed at me while I was eating, why didn't you give her to eat? It wasn't my intention not to give her to eat but I thought the girl has to be ready for the dinner, the other one. I felt misunderstood.

Freya's experience, that of Beatrice outlined further up and the experiences of many other au pairs we have encountered reflected a contradiction at the heart of the au pair–host arrangement. Au pairs are by definition young, inexperienced men and women who are in many cases still very close to childhood themselves. They are not supposed to have any experience or training in formal childcare and the au pair scheme at its inception was not a scheme to solve the expensive problem of how to arrange childcare for infants and babies for working parents. Yet many parents left their babies, infants, toddlers, fractious, demanding young children and grumpy teenagers with au pairs for hours or even days at a time. It seems inevitable that tensions and difficulties would arise, but this inevitable tension seemed often to be compounded by parental guilt and paranoia about the youth and inexperience of the au pairs. It was the parents' decision to leave these inexperienced young people in charge of their children but then au pairs were blamed for deficits or misunderstandings around care! In many cases it seemed to be parental guilt or anxiety that was being projected on to the au pair rather than any actual shortcoming in the au pair's behaviour toward children (cf. Macdonald 2010 on the projection of mothers' guilt onto nannies in the USA).

The ways in which a number of au pairs we interviewed became the butt of parental frustration and anger about how children were being disciplined or not in their absence ties in with a broader theme about parental absence and neglect that emerged in our interviews. Some of the au pairs we interviewed were hired to work alongside parents – e.g. walking one child to school while a parent (usually the mother) looked after an infant sibling at home. However, more commonly au pairs were providing sole care for one or multiple children as well as being *de facto* housekeepers. Christina, 27, from Latvia, had been hired by a couple to care for their two children. Christina said she worked long days during the week but also on weekends as the parents frequently went out in the evenings and then shut themselves in their bedroom long into the morning, meaning the children came looking for Christina. When asked if she felt she was being asked to assume extra childcare because of the parents' busy lifestyle, Christina said:

> I don't think they're particularly busy. I think they're not mature enough, that's my opinion. It sometimes happens, it doesn't matter that you're maybe 40 but you're just not mature. They quite party a lot and then they can spend all Saturday morning sleeping in bed. So I think when you become parents, especially after 30, I think you have to have thought about it before.

Other au pairs we interviewed talked about finding themselves *in loco parentis* and worrying about their capacity to provide the kind of emotional support they felt the children in their care required. Edina was an au pair to four children. She said of her experience:

> The children are ... for example, the youngest one calls me mummy because her mummy is never at home. So I'm the only parent for them and I am 20 years old and I have four children! Yes, it's not what I expected really, it's too hard. Because sometimes it just happens like this that they don't have time for the children.
> They don't need me because they just treat me like somebody ... because they are really a difficult age actually. [Two of the girls] are only 11 and 9 but they are really grown up. They are really tall, they grow up really fast so they're mentally ... they should be older than they really are. So it's a bit difficult for them because they can't understand what is going on to their bodies and everything and so they need somebody who is adult.

Edina clearly cared that the children she was looking after received attention and advice that was appropriate but saw herself, at 20 years old, as simply not being the right person for such a difficult job.

None of the au pairs we interviewed had formal childcare qualifications yet many had been required to assume sole care of babies and infants, often in the context of being an au pair for a family of multiple siblings of different ages. Au pairs we spoke to who had care of babies were required to manage feeding, as well as sleep, baths, nappies etc. Au pairs were often expected to manage the care of babies and infants while, for example, helping an older sibling with homework and/or cleaning and cooking meals. Some au pairs we interviewed took all this in their stride, but many did not. There was frequent disquiet on the part of au pairs about whether it was appropriate – or even safe – for parents to leave inexperienced young people from a different country with their infants for hours, days or, in rare cases, weeks at a time. In addition to the practical difficulties of performing the childcare and domestic work required, au pairs experienced the emotional fallout of carrying the weight of the pressure on many of these families. As Oskar said:

> They have no Plan B, most of these families. You know, so they rely totally on you.

It is certainly the case that it is difficult for many families to reconcile the pressure of work outside the home with the demands of childcare and domestic responsibilities. Shifting the pressure and responsibility for babies and young children on to an au pair, though, has simply meant that the expense and difficulty of organising appropriate childcare can continue to go unresolved through public policy channels in the UK. It also leaves children vulnerable to sub-standard care by bored or resentful teenagers and creates the perfect storm of tensions about how childcare is performed.

Intimacy and space in the house

Many of the people we spoke to appreciated that they would struggle to afford to live in the UK – in London in particular – if they had to pay for their own accommodation, as well as paying council tax, and for food, bills etc. Nevertheless, many still felt that being constantly on call for the family they were living with and having to share their living space with people who were effectively their employers was a largely negative experience. Many au pairs also spoke of their perception that other than having on-tap childcare and a live-in cleaner/cook/butler, parents and children also resented sharing the space with a stranger and they only tolerated the arrangement because they needed the childcare/domestic help and an au pair represented value for money.

The home is not treated like a traditional workplace. This is both because of its intimate nature – that it exists in distinction to work – and because a live-in worker, like an au pair, cannot leave at the end of the working day. This means that working in someone else's home is suffused with practical and emotional difficulties for both hosts and au pairs. The biggest practical difficulty that au pairs told us about was that they could not limit the time that they work.

For example, Edina, quoted above, said that her concern about being the right person to provide the day-to-day care and emotional support for four children was compounded by the long hours she worked due, she argued, to the parents' attitudes to au pairs compared with their attitude to paid employees such as nannies. Edina said:

> I am supposed to finish my work every day at half past six but most of the time they are late. Most of the families don't respect your time when you are an au pair. This is the worst side of being an au pair because when you're a nanny they respect your time because they have to pay you for every single hour, every single minute. But with an au pair they don't respect your time, you finish – and you can be tired, you don't want to see the children any more, they don't respect that.

Edina nominated the single worst thing about being an au pair as being the lack of respect given to an au pair's time and her life outside the immediate demands of the family she was staying with. Edina felt that because she lived with them, the family took her presence in the home for granted, to a quite extreme degree, as she explained:

> She [the host mother] was in Germany and she didn't tell me. OK, she doesn't have to ask me about the permission, but just tell me. You are a mother. Yes, they just left me for example during the holidays. The father took three children and went to Holland and she left to New York and they left me with one child for one week. She didn't tell me that she was going to New York. I was alone with one child here. So they are not responsible.

This example of taking an au pair's time for granted is unusual, but it is also a logical extension of assuming the au pair will 'be there' with nothing else to do. Many of the au pairs we interviewed experienced the same things but in a less extreme way. Maria, for example, said:

> When I finish work at seven o'clock, every single minute she [the host mother] came in my room. I don't know why. I needed privacy! For example, I finished job; I'm going on Skype and talking with my family, with my friends. Every five minutes she is here – Maria, can you come upstairs? I have to show you something. OK, I am coming upstairs. What is the problem? She told me, can you make orange from these oranges tomorrow? OK, you can tell me this tomorrow? I'm not working; I'm free now.

As this suggests, a key issue for many au pairs that emerged from interviews is what they are and are not supposed to do on weekends and evenings. Are they only on duty – i.e. looking after children, cleaning, picking up after people – for a set number of hours or are they supposed to be permanently on duty? This question might sound apocryphal but it was a very real concern for many of the au pairs we spoke to and was raised by au pairs interviewed by Búriková and Miller (2010) as a key point of confusion and dissatisfaction. The au pairs we talked to described the way in which their duties were presented to them – for example, cleaning up the breakfast table, sorting out laundry, sweeping floors etc. However, if they were only supposed to be working, say, 25 hours per week, for the hours they were not on duty, could they leave the breakfast dishes on the table and washing in the machine? As Sabina, 22, from Romania, put it:

> It's a bit difficult for me, because in my days off, I am not sure that I am supposed to put the toys in their place every time, or I can just behave like I'm in my own home? I think it will never go that far so that I feel that comfortable, like in my own house.

The framing of au pairing as a form of quasi-family membership, makes this question nearly impossible to answer. Some family members are never off duty, would always be responsible for picking up the toys, or putting the washing in the washing machine, but some would not. Is an au pair meant to resemble a Stepford wife – always eager to clean and wait on others – or is she meant to be like a real member of a real family?

For other au pairs, their place in the household was made very clear to them in that when their services were required they were permitted to use the kitchen and other household areas but when they were not required – for example on weekends – they were told to keep out of communal areas and to stay out of sight of the family. This was explained by host families on the grounds that the host family needed some privacy. But au pairs tended to experience this as being very oppressive. Christina, for example, said:

> They think if they pay you, they own you, something like this. So there will be no respect in time wise, but you have the rules and in many things like my au pair friends, they even ask her not to come on Sunday and Saturday in the kitchen. Because they want to have just family breakfast, I think it's quite rude or if you want to try to make sure she's having her some things to make tea or something like this … Yeah not come down or when she was ill not to go out of room and for me it's scary, it's really like Middle Ages, you know?

In these situations, control of the space within the house is used to produce a particular (distant) relationship between the au pair and host. However, what is interesting in Christina's response to this treatment is that rather than it producing a relationship closer to traditional employment, she felt 'owned' by this level of distance and disdain, like a serf in the Middle Ages.

There is also the question of how space in the house was used and whether au pairs were able to protect their personal possessions and their physical privacy. Sonia explained that she had joined a host family that she described as messy and rather chaotic. She explained that she found the lack of privacy afforded to her very oppressive. She said:

> When I opened the door I start crying, really start crying because I have got room, small. I said, that's OK, I have a small room no problem. But there is one bed, that's good; one bathroom … but wardrobe was full of stuff of the family. So all my staying in this family I have got my clothes in my luggage because there is no place for this. When I want close door from my room, door doesn't work. I never closed my door. I say, OK don't be scary come into bathroom. When I come it was one bathroom for seven people. The door for the bathroom doesn't work too.

Zuzanna Búriková (2006) has written powerfully on the au pair's room and the way it can be treated as a semi-public space by the host family.

This includes invasion by children even during time off, space being used for storage by the family (even of unwanted gifts from former au pairs), restrictive rules about the extent to which the space can be personalised, and its use as a guest bedroom if needed, sometimes without the au pair's permission. While a room is cited by both au pairs and hosts as a significant aspect of the au pair's remuneration, the terms on which an au pair has a room in her hosts' house is often quite different from that of a lodger. Unclear boundaries, ambivalent and contradictory notions of family membership and differing expectations from host and au pair, all make the negotiation of space difficult and necessary.

In addition to au pairs discussing their concerns about privacy and space in the house, food, eating, sharing meal times – or not – and use of the kitchen were all frequent areas of difficulty for au pairs. These issues have been raised in past studies of au pairs (Cox 2006; Búriková and Miller 2010), paid domestic workers (Anderson 2000) and for marriage migrants – another group who move to live within another family (Kim 2008), and they were no less important for our participants. For some, the issue was whether their presence was or was not welcome at family meal times. Whether or not the au pair regularly dined with the adults of the house was often a sign of the extent to which the au pair was treated as a live-in servant or a useful guest. But for many au pairs, the very existence of the common British evening meal arrangement in households with young children – that is, children being fed at around 5pm to 6pm and then being dispatched to bed while adults eat later – produced reactions ranging from horror to amusement at the poor quality of the food British families fed their children.

A primary concern that came up multiple times was that there was different food for the family than there was for the au pair, and this was perceived as insulting and humiliating, as well as meaning au pairs often went hungry or spent their own money buying extra food to fill up on. By way of illustration, Sonia said:

> If I need, for example – I say, can you buy for me muesli, they say OK, she buys muesli after two weeks. But if kids want something, for example Nutella in breakfast, they say there isn't no more, she pick up – she go in for shop at the moment. If I need something, no she never do this. Or I drink some juices she say, you drink this juice? I say, yes. She say, no, this is for kids, this is really expensive. If you want some juice you can tell me and I buy for you some cheap juice, not this for kids. Ah, I'm only some cleaner woman.

Maria had a similar experience in respect to food available in the household in which she was staying as an au pair. She said:

> Anyway, she didn't buy me food. There was no food for me for two weeks. I only had to eat rice and potatoes, because she bought a lot of things for her, for her daughter, for her husband. When she came back from shopping, she told me, this is not for you; this is not for you; this is not for you. It was very – she was very rough.

Anderson (2000) reports multiple instances of paid domestic workers being given food that was insufficient or inappropriate, and one case of a live-in domestic worker who was given no food at all and had to beg for some from a neighbour. Domestic workers were expected to eat food they did not like, to eat leftovers from their employers' plates, food that was out of date or that would otherwise be intended for the dog. In these instances, as in the situation quoted by Maria above, food is being used to structure and signal the distance of the relationship between the au pair and host family and the (low) status of the au pair or domestic worker within the household (see also Barbosa 2007; Cox 2006; Marchetti 2014; Ray and Qayum 2009 amongst many others). The organisation of food and other aspects of eating, such as whether au pairs eat with the rest of the family and who does the washing up, are effective sites for this because they happen multiple times every day and cannot be avoided. While an au pair may decide to avoid a possible confrontation, and disappointment, over requesting a lock for her bedroom door, she cannot avoid discovering whether her host family will be generous and caring in the way they organise meals. Food is also a potent carrier of meanings about purity and pollution (Douglas 2002 [1966]), it can be used to signal who is clean and who is dirty, who belongs and who does not. Inequality in the distribution, handling and eating of food is socially and culturally powerful and deeply felt.

Food is also an important element of local and national cultures, something that has to be learnt about and adapted to as part of the migration process. Being an au pair in someone else's home means having very little control over mealtimes and the food consumed and this left some of the au pairs we spoke to feeling disorientated, ill or uncomfortable with changes to their bodies such as weight gain or loss (cf. Búriková and Miller 2010). Some au pairs we interviewed had difficulty adjusting to the less-developed food culture in the UK compared with their home countries and the degree to which some

British families relied on convenience foods. The disrupted eating that many au pairs reported was in some cases due to stress and feelings of dislocation. Lise, for instance, said:

> I tried to feel comfortable but – I understand why but sometimes I felt really in stress and I couldn't sleep. I had nightmares. Sometimes I really couldn't eat like normal – as normal as home because at home I always ate a lot, but not in London. It was different. Maybe it wasn't only just their mistake but they were nice people but I have never seen an au pair who is very happy, who is not in stress, who can really sleep and eat well because always it's even family can be very nice you are not home, you don't feel as comfortable as home. It's not the same.

For others, the family did not provide enough food that the au pair was familiar with or found appetising, or did not provide enough or any food at all or because the meal times and eating habits of the family were so unfamiliar. Isabel, from Spain, for example, said:

> Yeah, it's very different ... when I arrived, I had for lunch one sandwich and a very big Ribena and in Spain you have a proper lunch and a light dinner, and, oh no ... I started eating all the time because I was hungry and you can do that because then you have a lot of dinner, so, yeah.

Many of the au pairs we spoke to came from rural areas and/or countries where low incomes and a strong food culture mean that people cook from scratch every day using meat, vegetables, bulk carbohydrates etc., and meals are an important way in which the day is punctuated, as well as being social occasions for the whole family. Christina spoke for many of her fellow au pairs when she said:

> Food here is problem ... they're not eating like me. Yeah, in the beginning I was really starving all the time because they're mostly buying vegetables and I'm not eating vegetables. I need meat every day or something heavy. Yeah the food is quite ... she's always on diet, he has some problems with ulcer so I don't know, if they're saving money. But there's never bread in the house, at least.

The living-in aspect of au pairing means that food often has to be negotiated and that is a sore spot for both au pairs and their hosts (Cox 2006). It was apparent in our interviews that food was tricky in part because of cultural differences in eating patterns and expectations (as well as because of personal preferences). Cultural differences in food practices and expectations need to be negotiated but are often difficult to articulate or express because assumptions about 'right' or 'normal' ways to eat are deeply held. Coping with changes in food-related behaviours has also been identified as one of the biggest transitional difficulties that marriage migrants face (Kim and Lee 2016). Lee (2016) describes a research project to produce a text book for marriage migrants on food culture in Korea (this included recipes and information about holidays as well as information on symbolic foods, shopping and Korean table manners). Improving understanding about Korean food culture helped migrants to communicate, increased their daily life satisfaction and helped them adapt to Korean society more broadly. Food and food practices are clearly important in the intimate spaces of migration. In a context such as au pairing or live-in domestic work, where the cultures meeting are not simply different, but can also be positioned unequally, practices around food can become yet another arena in which au pairs feel their status is produced and signalled to them.

Living-in also underpins concerns from hosts and au pairs about the possible implications of physical proximity. For most au pairs, if they lived out or only ever saw their hosts when engaging around their work, female au pairs might have very little to do with host dads. However, living-in means that au pairs are present and in contact with dads even if those dads take no part in the organisation of household work. As mentioned in Chapter 5, a common theme on websites such as Mumsnet for 'mums' posting about hosting an au pair involved posts about feelings of jealously and resentment at the youth, beauty, freedom and perceived availability of the au pairs in their homes (see also Chapter 7). Many of these posts revolved around a perception that au pairs were 'flaunting it' in the face of 'mums' who felt that their own age and exhaustion compared unfavourably with the charms of a youthful au pair. A further theme displayed a pronounced paranoia on the part of 'mum' posters that the man of the house would be or was being tempted by the charms of the au pair. For au pairs, such worries could create an unpleasant atmosphere and might even lead to au pairs being sacked (see discussion in Chapter 5, see also Cox 2007), but the greater worry was the unwanted attention of men in the homes where they worked.

None of the au pairs we interviewed reported any romantic or sexual interest in any of the mothers or fathers of the households in which they were staying, but some did report that they perceived some feelings of jealously or possessiveness on the part of the mother. Anita was one who had had this experience before she came to the UK. She said:

> The lady was paranoid and because she had another au pair who
> got married to her husband, now ex-husband, she was paranoid
> with everyone and she couldn't keep au pair because she was always
> paranoid. Paranoid with her new husband and that was very stressful;
> it was two weeks of stress. I wasn't free at all. I didn't have to do a
> lot of stuff because they had a cleaning lady and she was doing the
> cooking, I don't know why I was there to be honest. Home all the
> time. But it was the stress and tension.

The fact that au pairs, based on our research, had no interest in flirting or sexual relations with their host was no bar in some instances to the hosts imposing themselves upon them. Marta, 21, from the Czech Republic, reported her experience of sexual harassment:

> They were quite sympathetic, everything goes well ... but first day
> when I arrived to the airport the [host dad] picked me up. We were
> walking on the road and he, all the time, he tries to hug me, kiss me. It
> was first day when I came. Quite strange, I was a bit surprised. Then I
> said, well maybe he is open mind or – yeah. The kids were very good,
> very nice but problem was with the [host dad] because then, like, one
> week later, he tries to touch me more. He watched me then he asked
> me if I ever had a black man in the bed. So then I wanted to tell my
> host mum I want to finish but when I wanted to tell her, he was like,
> don't tell her anything or I'm going to kill you.

We came across other similar reports of sexual harassment of au pairs by members of the host family. However, it was notable that no au pairs referred to it or apparently perceived it as being sexual harassment in the workplace. This was one consequence of the fact that au pairing was not understood as work or an employment relationship. This meant that far from understanding that they had rights, and that these rights included not being harassed or propositioned in their workplaces, the au pairs that we interviewed did not even discuss these incidents as amounting to wrong doings on the part of their hosts. It was more frequently reported as an awkward situation that they themselves had got themselves into and, if anything, the au pairs appeared to blame themselves for these encounters – or at least feel it was their responsibility for having got into a situation of physical proximity with the men in question. This was also the case with au pairs who experienced physical violence. Anita, for example, said:

> They had a baby, six months, the mum just left the baby with me suddenly and the baby kept on crying all the time. I had to be there because they were working in a restaurant from morning 11 until one at night and had to be with the baby there all the time for two weeks. My head was spinning, she was crying all the time. The dad said I was beating her up and he actually was violent with me and he took me at 4am, he took me to the highway and he said he was going to leave me on the highway in the middle of the night.

Anita was not alone in being accosted by her host or hosts, and other au pairs we spoke to had, for example, been physically ejected by host families in the middle of the night and locked in and out of the home in which they were staying. Again, though, not one au pair we interviewed had considered contacting the police or even perceived that they had been assaulted or that their treatment at the hands of hosts was illegal. Again, the fact that they did not consider themselves to be employed meant they experienced altercations and difficult situations – including being dropped by a motorway in the middle of the night – as their own fault. It was the personalisation of what were in fact deeply uneven relationships in terms of power that conspired to ensure au pairs saw these experiences as personal encounters – and, as such, too trivial or personal to take to the police or other authority figures.

As well as negotiating the physical intimacy of hosts, au pairs also had to navigate their way through the complex hierarchies of class, gender and ethnicity/nationality as they arranged themselves in the household. As we argued in Chapter 2, when domestic work is paid for, inequalities that are traditionally organised on gender lines move to become structured by class and race/ethnic distinctions. And, because performing low-status work, particularly work that is dirty, creates status as well as reflecting it, au pairs were often confronted by the need to come to terms with new positions in social hierarchies, quite different to those they had had in their home countries. Their new social status was produced and signalled to them through the small-scale interactions of daily life within their host's home.

Social class was important in the relationship between the au pair and the host with some au pairs resistant to the tasks they were being asked to do – and the accompanying hierarchical relationship being imposed by the host – on the grounds that they felt themselves to be the social equals if not of a higher social class than their hosts. For example, Maria explained her resistance to the way in which she felt her host was attempting to subjugate her using her membership of a one of the less wealthy EU member states as a way of asserting class superiority. Maria said:

> She told me, 'Oh, from Bulgaria, you came here; you're very dirty, you're so ...'. No! Excuse me, I am a student; I have a diploma. Maybe I'm smarter than you. Okay, it wasn't my luck that I was born in Bulgaria; I'm not born in England. But I am not as stupid as you think. I have travelled around the whole of Europe. My parents are not so poor like you think. My house is three times bigger than yours in Bulgaria. That's true.

Maria's response to her host's racism and feeling of cultural superiority neatly encapsulates the disparity in wealth between East and West Europe and the attempt by hosts to use this disparity to assert a distance between themselves and au pairs from poorer states. In earlier centuries in the UK, this gap would have existed in explicitly class terms in that upper- and middle-class women avoided 'seeing' servant women in their midst by virtue of their class. In the twenty-first century this attempt to negotiate the difficulty of one person requiring another to perform services for them in the domestic space was negotiated by the difference of ethnic, cultural, geographic and economic otherness of migrants. As Maria's response made clear, though, this attempt to subjugate could be resisted by a variety of means – including by the migrant worker in question rejecting the idea that the relative poverty of their country of origin meant they should be grateful for a berth in a wealthier state.

Other au pairs we interviewed questioned the social class difference they felt they were supposed to perceive between themselves and their hosts in terms of relative levels of formal education and/or maturity and life experience. Christina, who was from Latvia, felt that her host family had less respect for her than they would have for someone from a wealthier state. Christina used the example of attitudes to Italian people and Polish people to make her point, saying:

> I think they would be more sensitive to Polish au pair than to Italian ... it's not like 100 years ago with black people, you know in America.

If you're black it is no respect, it's kind of like this, I see it like this. But this – I don't know.

Christina continued, saying that she thought 'very intelligent people will respect everybody'. However, she did not think the family she was staying with were either intelligent or respectful. She explained that she clashed with the family because she did not feel that she shared values with them. She said:

> I was babysitting in the evening, so they went to a restaurant. In the morning I noticed on the table there was like beautiful silver things for pepper and salt, like really beautiful. I said, 'oh wow it's new'. She said, 'oh yeah, we stole it from restaurant last night'. For me it was disgusting because he is 43 and she is 37 and they told me – the kids were eating breakfast. I don't know I would expect it from young people, experiment or want to be wild, but when she, woman, mother, doing this I think it's kind of …

When asked to elaborate on why she did not get on with the host family, she explained that she felt that they were not very well educated and that this compounded their immaturity. All in all, her assessment of the way in which the hosts were raising their children and the way they conducted themselves in the world was not positive, particularly when she compared the way the couple were raising their children with the way in which she herself had been raised. Thus, even though Christina did not want to return to Latvia and she loved the cultural life available in London, she very much rejected the idea that her status was more lowly than that of her hosts. She aspired to being a photographer and spent her leisure time going to exhibitions, reading books about photography etc. She regarded her upbringing and her cultural interests as meaning she felt she had different and more refined tastes and a higher moral code than her employers did.

Living-in is a key feature of the au pair experience, an arrangement which offers the possibility of support and friendly relationships, but one which also contains a number of risks. It is the fact that au pairs are expected to live in their hosts' homes which allows the narrative of family membership and equality to loom so large in what might otherwise quite clearly be an employment relationship. Living-in also means that the relationship is negotiated in intimate moments and spaces, spaces where we have little experience of encountering strangers and making a complex relationship work.

Conclusion

The au pairs we met were sensitive to the many subtle ways in which status was made and communicated within their relationship with their hosts, from the allocation of cleaning versus childcare tasks, the content of meals, the size of a room. The notion of equality was ever present in au pairs' consideration of their experiences but more elusive in those experiences themselves. The fact that they were aware that au pairing was meant to be a relationship between equals made the slights they felt in their daily interactions much more galling than they would otherwise have been.

While we have illustrated here the intimate ground on which au pairs and hosts negotiate equality, these negotiations are not in any simple way isolated and individual, even though the individuals involved are often isolated. Rather they are located within broader social hierarchies of gender, class and ethnicity, that allocate power to the two parties differently and which mean that seemingly small or unimportant actions are carriers of significant meanings.

In the next chapter we hear from hosts who are also trying to sail these stormy waters and not necessarily finding it any easier. The awkwardness of au pair hosting is framed within the competing demands of paid work and childcare, unhelpful partners and demanding children.

7 | GOOD WORKERS? GOOD PARENTS? GOOD HOSTS?

Why would a family invite a young person that they did not know to come and live with them in their home? The majority of hosts of au pairs we interviewed were very clear that they found living with teenagers or young adults from a foreign country at times trying and exasperating. But in answer to the question posed above, hosts went on to explain that the advantages of hosting an au pair – including flexible hours of childcare that could be made to fit around complex and ever-changing work patterns – provided a good reason to overcome the awkwardness and hassle of being a host. Cost was also an important factor, although some interviewees said that even if they could have afforded a live-in or live-out nanny, they would still have chosen to host an au pair instead because what they needed was actually 'another wife' who would help with mundane tasks such as waiting in for tradespeople, grocery shopping, cleaning and ironing, as well as performing childcare during the day and babysitting at night. An au pair was regarded as a more biddable 'extra wife' than a professional nanny or housekeeper would be.

This chapter draws on our interviews with hosts of au pairs to learn more about why flexibility when it came to childcare was so important, and examines the financial incentives and household gender politics that drive the demand for au pairs in the UK. We also consider how hosting an au pair fits with notions of what constitutes being a 'good' parent, with reference to the prevailing UK childcare culture in which preference is given to in-home care and in terms of the added extras au pairs brought by facilitating access for children to extra curricula activities such as sport, music, drama etc. Finally, we investigate what it was like for hosts to share their home with a young stranger and outline the impressions hosts have formed of au pairs from a range of different countries. Despite the vital role au pairs played in the households and close bonds that were sometimes forged with children, we also learned about tensions. It is important to note when considering how the hosts we interviewed talked about their arrangements that this was a self-selected sample and it is unlikely that people would agree to be interviewed if they thought of themselves as 'bad' hosts. This meant that people interviewed typically regarded themselves as generous and fair, which was reflected in the consensus that as a host you have responsibilities to your au pair beyond the bare minimum of pocket money, room and board.

What is the problem that hosts are trying to solve?

All of the hosts we interviewed had decided to host an au pair so that the parent (in the case of lone parent families) or both parents could engage in paid work outside the home. The decision had been made in the context of the perception among those interviewed that they had four main alternatives: public or private nursery for younger children or after school clubs for older; childminder; nanny; au pair. One host had had a grandparent acting as an unpaid childminder/helper but this arrangement had fallen through. Parents worked in a range of industries, including print media and broadcasting, film and theatre, academia, Pilates training, PR and law. Four of the 15 hosts we interviewed were single parents and the remainder co-habited with a partner of the opposite sex. What was notable was the extent to which people we interviewed worked odd and/or long hours that were difficult to reconcile with school hours or with standard nursery or childminder provision. This might be because one parent's job required that they travel abroad frequently, leaving the other parent needing additional childcare support for short but intense bursts. For others, it was because they worked shift patterns, meaning they were sometimes required to do night shifts and sometimes their hours conflicted with the school run. Others again had to be at work early in the morning and/or returned late in the evening, meaning they needed someone else to deliver children to school or nursery, pick them up in the afternoon and feed and bathe them in the evening.

They key problem that hosts were trying to solve was the difficulties they encountered holding down jobs that required long and/or unpredictable hours that clashed with their children's timetables. For most of those we interviewed it was neither financially feasible nor desirable for one parent to be the breadwinner and another a stay-at-home parent. But neither was it possible for both parents (or one parent in the case of single-parent families) to work without having extensive and flexible childcare in place. Parents we interviewed had usually explored a number of options before deciding to host an au pair and had concluded that live-in childcare by someone who could (a) care for children around parents' work hours, (b) be charged with a range of other household tasks and (c) be paid 'pocket money' rather than a wage was the most viable solution to the problem of how to reconcile paid work with family and domestic responsibilities. Below we explore in more detail the issues of family finances, the need for flexibility from the childcare provider and concepts of what constitutes good parenting and, by extension, an adequate form of childcare.

Jo and Arthur lived in Elephant and Castle in London with their two children. They were interviewed separately and both nominated the pressure on their family finances as being a key reason for choosing to host an au pair. Jo said:

> We wouldn't have had the money for a nanny, or even wouldn't have had the money for a nanny share because we're not ... probably our income is about £50,000 in total.

Jo's partner, Arthur, also said the reason for hosting an au pair was driven by the family finances. He said:

> I hate it ... I just find them a huge intrusion. I didn't want one [an au pair], but she [Jo] showed me the economics. We have a house that's big enough to support an extra person.

Arthur continued by explaining that having an au pair was an important part of the package of domestic assistance and time-saving buy-ins he and his partner had put in place to allow them both to work in jobs in the cultural industries that required flexible hours and didn't pay high wages. He explained that in addition to having an au pair living with them, they had made a range of other time- and labour-saving provisions, saying:

> We've returned to the 1930s in terms of having staff in our house. We have a cleaner. We have Ocado delivery. We don't even go to the shops to buy our own groceries ... and I couldn't conceive of having it any other way and because the time I would need to take to do those activities would be time I don't get to spend with my children on Saturday or Sunday or in an evening or time I can't – I mean, my life is full really.

This account of the way in which even relatively cash-strapped middle-class households were able to afford in-home childcare, as well as other household services such as cleaning and food delivery, aptly illustrates the way in which income inequalities in cities such as London have underpinned the growth of domestic services (Cox 2006). Hosting au pairs has expanded so that as well as upper-, upper-middle- and middle-class dual-income households, a range of households with more precarious financial arrangements (including part-time workers, freelance workers and single parents) could afford to host an au pair (see Ozyegin and Hondagneu-Sotelo 2008). Arthur's comment also references new parenting styles, whereby he prioritises time with his children on a Saturday, Sunday or in the evening over doing domestic tasks himself. This is in keeping with Kilkey et al.'s (2013) findings about the reasons given for employing handyman labour in the home. Contemporary modes of fathering emphasise the time fathers spend with children, rather than time spent provisioning in the home. The result is that time spent parenting is multiplied rather than shared, increasing the logic of paying for additional help.

Eleanor was another host who identified family finances as a key reason for hosting an au pair. She had two children aged nine and three and said of her experience juggling childcare and paid work:

> I'm one of those mums who hasn't been able to work for a good eight years because of childcare expense ... none of the salaries I was offered cover the cost of childcare and train and I really think that childcare's very, very expensive and very overrated as well, meaning formal nurseries and stuff.

Eleanor explained that it was only when she and her family moved into a larger house that she had been able to think about returning to work. She said:

> The moment when we moved into a bigger house when we could actually bring an au pair in, we did. I lived in a flat before ... I still haven't got a full-time job. I'm working part time, but it pays off, really. It's cheaper and cost is not just the only thing but it's actually also the flexibility.

Similarly, Lucy explained that she had tried a number of different arrangements and had settled on an au pair because of the cost and flexibility:

For a year I had a girl that would come to my house and it was very expensive. At one point, I think I was paying £1,000 a month. Unsustainable, you're just getting more and more in debt. [not] getting out of it. Then after that we had a nursery was slightly less than that. Maybe £800 ... an expensive nursery, then we go slightly cheaper. As he got older he got cheaper and we had a very lovely Montessori nursery just before he went off to school. At that point that Montessori nursery finished at four and we had childcare like a girl that would come and pick him up. If I had to work late it was tricky but it was okay, we managed.

These explanations highlight not only the relative cost of an au pair as important, and flexibility which we turn to below, but also the fact that au pairs are in part paid with housing wealth rather than cash. This means that the calculations of the cost and value of an au pair are different for different households depending on the size of their house. If a family happens to have a spare room, and wants to buy a larger house regardless of the need for housing an au pair, then that aspect of the cost of an au pair is assumed within other calculations.

Flexibility emerged as a recurrent reason interviewees gave for choosing to host an au pair as a way of solving the 'problem' of childcare. Jobs that required peoples' presence early morning, late/afternoon and weekends were particularly difficult for people with children. For example, Jo worked as a Pilates instructor and many of her sessions were scheduled for slots before or after typical working hours or on weekends. She said of this:

A lot of my work needs flexible hours and having the extra room meant that I could make a choice of having childcare for my four-year-old or when my ten-year-old was at school ... I also didn't want to have the feeling of what happened if something happened and I had to rush back from work. So it gave – so it was also in the respect of childcare hours it was more relaxing, it was less stressful.

Similarly, Siri was a single parent with one child. She said her shift work patterns, including night shifts, meant that she needed a particular form of childcare that could fit around her ever-changing schedule.

The reason I need an au pair is that I'm a shift worker. So I can't move the actual days. I can't move the days I work; either I can work them or not work them but the hours are very prescribed.

And Stephanie said:

> Well my hours never – I don't work very long hours for the firm but
> the provision, if you live in London it takes so long to get anywhere,
> the provision with using child minders and nurseries just isn't enough
> in my experience.

Workers in the UK have been expected to put in some of the longest
and most flexible hours in Europe (Alakeson 2011; Stewart 2011) but
many have still received relatively low pay in relation to housing and
living costs, particularly in cities such as London, Brighton, Oxford
and Cambridge. In addition to the fact that employing an au pair was
cheaper than nursery, childminder or nanny care (see details in Chapter
3), parents also discussed their long commutes and their desire for
more freedom and less stress in terms of the need to rush from work to
a nursery or childminder at the end of the day – and this has also driven
demand for au pairs. Just as Jo explained that it was more relaxing and
less stressful knowing there was someone at home to look after her
children while she was at work, Eleanor said:

> You don't worry whether you're late on a train, you don't worry
> whether you're going to have drinks after work. You don't worry
> about the odd evening – they can jump in and things like that. So the
> flexibility is amazing.

However, the very flexibility from hiring an au pair that hosts
depended upon and enjoyed emerged as principal reason for
dissatisfaction on the part of au pairs we interviewed (as we explored in
the previous chapter). This was because while hosts appreciated having
someone who was at home if they were late on a train or invited for
post-work drinks, the au pairs we spoke to resented the assumption
that they should drop everything if the host required it. This tension
was apparent in a 'blow up' between hosts and au pair described by
Arthur. He said:

> She [the au pair] refused to do anything outside the arranged – oh,
> actually she didn't even do the hours that had been arranged ... Okay,
> I had a sick child. I needed to drive my son into Covent Garden. I
> have a daughter who's lying flat on the carpet with her face down.
> She's got some sort of cold and fever. I say to this woman, I say
> – she's up anyway, so I haven't gone to get her up. I said, 'Would it be

possible for you just to delay going out by 25 minutes so I don't have to put a sick child in the car?' She screamed at me. She screamed, 'I haven't seen my friend for five years. He's coming over.' I was, like, 'Well, okay, I've got the message'.

Arthur explained that the au pair had previously been with a Swedish family who had required her to be on duty 24 hours a day and that he thought that the au pair's insistence on ring fencing her non-working time was perhaps a reaction to that. But he also made it clear that he expected the au pairs staying with them to, if necessary, change their own plans in order to meet the needs of his family. Jo added in respect to this au pair that she understood the issues at play, saying:

> I felt that actually we were in service to her. We were in service to her! Because we were very concerned not to exploit anyone; we don't want to be in a position where we're exploiting a very odd situation where they're working but not working because it's pocket money. So that's a really difficult scenario because actually they are working because they're looking after your child and that's childcare and that's work. So unless there's a cultural exchange and unless everything is very personal then it's exploitation.

Arthur and Jo were clearly trying hard to abide by the idea central to the notion of au pairing that the young person in question should be treated as a guest of sorts. At the same time, though, Arthur had said he 'hated' having an au pair in his house as he found it intrusive – so there were clearly pragmatic reasons to do with the family's childcare needs that were in conflict with the idealistic notion of a cultural exchange experience. The family may well have felt impatient with the au pair for ring fencing her time off and resisting their request that she be 'flexible' when they needed her. But it is telling that so many of the au pairs we interviewed talked about situations such as this, in which the hosts displayed the very unequal power relationships in the home – i.e. that the au pair's time was not really her own even when she was off duty because she lived in the host/employer's home. The demands that British working patterns make on employed parents can be easily transferred to au pairs unless great care is taken not to take advantage of their presence, but this requires a high degree of forbearance on the part of hosts, who are themselves often stressed and overworked.

We interviewed male and female host parents in the course of our research and a very important theme to emerge was the gendered imbalance in responsibility for organising one's work around childcare. This imbalance meant an au pair could be both a solution to practical problems and to friction between parents. Many of the stories we heard from hosts as well as from au pairs suggested that after a couple had children, the male parent continued to work full time, often with increasing hours and travel as he grew in seniority. The female partner, meanwhile, commonly withdrew from the workforce altogether immediately after having a child/children and then negotiated her partial or compromised return to the workforce within the hours of childcare contributed by an au pair (Holloway and Pimlott-Wilson 2016). Ellie, who lived in central London with her male partner and three children, gave a straightforward account of the way in which having an au pair reinforced gendered inequality in division of labour in her home. She said:

> When the au pair came, I did initially think this isn't actually a great help for me, it's just a great help for [male partner] because it means the pressure for him is off, whereas I'm still in the same position; I have three children with one person helping me, it's just that it's a different person now. So it helps inasmuch as I'm not by myself ... but the main help is for him because he doesn't have to come back. So he did do it [help with children], but then he has a good job, it's well paid, he's earning the money, so therefore we have some money to throw at a problem and that's what we did; just threw some money at the problem rather than fighting.

Ellie was articulating what many of our interviewees also discussed: that having an au pair freed up the mother of the family, either by allowing her to work or helping her at high-pressure times such as dinner, bath, bed but that the father of the house's non-responsibility for doing equal childcare remained unchallenged. The role of the au pair as stepping in to replace or assist the mother was often represented by the fact that the mother was responsible for finding and paying an au pair. Arthur and Jo both explained that having an au pair had been Jo's idea and that the main purpose of the au pair was to give Jo some time off childcare to work and to make her life as principal carer of the two children easier. Meanwhile, Arthur's role as principal breadwinner was largely unaffected by having an au pair. Jo said:

> It was like having a second wife. It was like having two wives. I'd come home and she'd say you look tired, do you want me to cook, you don't like cooking.

Arthur, meanwhile, described his remove from the hiring and paying of the au pairs:

> The kids are at school. I don't really understand why we need one [an au pair] not considering Jo's point of view that she might not want it after seven years of being home at a certain time to pick the kids up from school. She might want that to stop now. I'm not getting involved with the selection process. If you [Jo] want to do it, you go ahead and do it ... Once you've found her, I will be supportive, but you've got to do it ... and so Jo would pay the au pairs. That was all their own arrangement

A number of studies have found that households with less equal gendered divisions of labour (largely those where the woman is expected to do all domestic tasks) are more likely to opt to employ paid domestic workers (Gregson and Lowe 1994; Ehrenreich 2003; Cox 2006; Lutz 2008) and, as argued in Chapter 2, it is the broader gendering of responsibility for reproductive labour which underpins demand for domestic workers by lowering the status of this work (see also Anderson 2000). Arthur and Jo's practice of keeping the housework and childcare 'between women' (Rollins 1985) is not uncommon. Hiring an au pair may ease the burden on both male and female hosts, but it rarely challenges the gendered division of reproductive labour, and may in fact cement it, as the work of childcare and housework becomes more invisible to fathers in au pair-hosting households.

Along with costs, flexibility and gender roles, another reason for hosting an au pair was that the type of childcare au pairs provided was in line with what hosts thought constituted 'good' parenting. As discussed in Chapter 3, ideas about parenting have been constructed within cultural, social and political contexts and what is seen as good for a child in one local, national or historical situation might be abhorrent in another. In the UK, it has been widely held that home-based care by a parent or trusted individual was better for a child's development than care in an institution such as a nursery (Gregson and Lowe 1994). The UK childcare culture can be categorised as being somewhere between a Nordic model of childcare and a Southern European model (Williams and Gavanas 2008). The Nordic social care regime, with high involvement of women in paid work and state commitment to public care for both children and older people, sat at one end of this scale. The 'Southern European family care regime', with few public services and much lower rates of mothers' employment, sat at the other. In between there was the UK, along with Germany and the Netherlands where, as far as young children were concerned, their care outside of school was deemed to be the responsibility of the family, whether or not their mothers worked (Anttonen and Sipilä 1996; Williams and Gavanas 2008). In the UK, then, parents have often not accepted nursery care as a standard and acceptable solution to combining work and family commitments, nor have they in many cases been able to rely on networks of family. Instead, hosts discussed a preference for paid 'mother-substitutes' for babies (and a number had employed qualified nannies before au pairs) and/or a combination of this care with nursery, pre-school then school hours as children grew older.

Stacey expressed this in a way which took for granted women's responsibilities for childcare, a preference for 'mother-like' care and an acknowledgement that many women want to work outside the home. She said:

> It depends on the parent, doesn't it? If you're the kind of woman that needs to go out to work to be fulfilled, and that makes you a better mother when you are at home, then I think it's a very good scheme, because it helps you do that. But I think genuinely speaking for the children, there's nobody better than having their parents there.

Laura had also tried a range of childcare options, but expressed her preference for an au pair in terms of consistency and warmth, as well as fitting with work patterns and a local childcare culture which endorsed the use of au pairs:

> [My son] was at a Montessori and because the Montessori finished at 4:00, not at 6:00 – which is what most nurseries finish at – but we really liked the Montessori – we needed somebody to be there from 4:00. We started – initially he was going back to all different people's houses and I was sort of going, picking him up late at night. He was only three or four years old and it just felt really wrong to be dragging him home at sort of six or seven o'clock at night. So we decided to – we just liked the idea of him coming home to his own house even though he might then have his friends back or whatever but he's coming back to an environment he knows. So – and I liked the idea of sort of having the house warm and lit in the evenings for him and when I come home. I just wanted that consistency really. So that was the reason and then lots of our friends have got au pairs so we just carried on really.

In Chapter 3 we discussed the increasing importance of 'enrichment activities' for middle-class children, and it was clear that au pairs could also help with these, as Lucy explained:

> [The au pair] takes him to school and picks him up. Then he has a couple of music lessons a week. Then he has a [play day] a week. Sometimes he has a monthly sports thing but not this term. He has scouts for Friday so he has always an activity that he has to be taken to and collected. This food, homework and music practice, those are the basic things. She also, in her own time, does the family ironing and I make sure there's never too much but it's enough. Because one child is such an easy-peasy job.

Being able to facilitate such activities is important in providing a certain type of childhood and also as a way of investing in a child's future. It is part of the 'competitive' and intensive parenting that is increasingly expected (Holloway and Pimlott Wilson 2014; Lee et al. 2014; Macdonald 2010). Childcare strategies that involve 'competitive care' (Tronto 2006) mitigate against investment in group childcare and feed demand for private, in-home forms of care.

For all our host interviewees, taking on an au pair was a way of balancing the demands of work, particularly demands for flexibility, with finding a form of childcare that was acceptable, perhaps with the added advantage of gaining a 'second wife'. Achieving this was possible because of the availability and affordable, easily accessed in-home care in the shape of an au pair. It is possible to see how the supply of highly flexible, unregulated, au pair labour influenced demand, which then contributed to reaffirming particular local childcare cultures which favour in-home and 'mother-like' care (Williams and Gavanas 2008). This is significant from a broader policy perspective because if forms of in-home commoditised childcare were not as cheap as they commonly were in London, particularly compared with nurseries – and it were not easy and socially acceptable to employ someone – it might well have been the case that rather than rejecting collective forms of care and accepting long hours of work, parents would have had more incentive to rethink their perceptions about what is a reasonable working day or commute time, what made different forms of care suitable or unsuitable for children, and what variables influenced the suitability or quality of care. That is, the availability of an alternative – the low cost of which made it accessible to an increasing range of families

– allowed hosts to avoid recognising that childcare might alternatively be regarded as a 'central public responsibility and that it is wrong to force families to try to solve the problem of childcare on their own' (Tronto 2002 p48).

Hierarchies at home

The hosts we interviewed were all trying to find a way to negotiate the tricky ground of the au pair–host relationship. They had multiple demands on their time and wanted to avoid exploitation of their au pair, but were not always clear what the boundaries of the au pair role could and should be. Many found the relationship uncomfortable, intrusive, as Arthur mentioned above, or just hard work, and could feel like they had suddenly become the parent of a grumpy teenager. As we have argued throughout this book, however it is imagined, the home is not a space that is in any way naturally equal or free from power relations. However, we found that negotiating new hierarchies at home was rarely a welcome task. In this section we look at how hosts saw their role in relation to au pairs by examining how they conceptualised being a 'good' host (often in relation to other 'bad' hosts), how they constructed au pairs by using national stereotypes and how they related to au pairs as additional children. Despite the framing of the au pair scheme in terms of family membership and the usefulness of a 'big sister' to care for younger children, few hosts were happy when their au pair did need them to be a parent.

All the hosts we interviewed wanted to be 'good' hosts. They did not always enjoy the extra effort this might take, but they wanted to avoid exploiting their au pairs and they were clearly appalled at some of the stories they heard about mistreatment. Being a good host was one way to negotiate the awkwardness of having an au pair living in the house, and the new power dynamics that this brought with it. The hosts we met understood the power imbalance between themselves and their au pairs and for most this made them uncomfortable – thinking of themselves as 'good' hosts was one way to deal with this discomfort. As there is so little clear guidance for hosts as to what may or may not be part of the 'au pair deal', the hosts we met often discussed their practice in relation to what they had heard of other hosts doing. Sometimes this was through agencies, online fora or 'school gate' conversations, but it could also be stories which were passed on by au pairs. For example, Laura said:

I think a lot of them feel quite exploited. You get this a lot when you interview them. [name] the German girl, had been somewhere else and been miserable. [their current au pair] had been miserable ... I think being made to do a lot of cleaning and being isolated are things that make them unhappy. But we have a cleaner, so [current au pair] doesn't have to do that. I know she finds it difficult to live on what we pay her. She babysits all over the neighbourhood and she had a job as a waitress for a while. She has to pay her fees [she was studying for a business qualification] and transport and everything. She's 26. She wants to get a job as soon as she can. But I don't know whether she will be able to as her English isn't really very good.

Reflecting on the way she treated au pairs compared to their previous hosts, Laura nominated isolation and excessive housework as being linked to unhappiness but she did not include low pay. This allowed her to construct 'her' au pair as relatively fortunate, thereby negating the specific effects of the low pay she offered for the care of her child. Laura's comment about the effects of the au pair's low pay on her au pair's lifestyle were interesting in that they illustrated a broader contradiction of au pairing as it has been practised in the UK. That is, while it was clear that hosts understood themselves to be responsible for ensuring good conditions for their au pairs, they did not question the payment of pocket money rather than a wage or, to any great extent, the level of the pocket money being paid. This, and the fact that au pairs were not covered by UK minimum wage legislation, meant that hosts were able to discuss the hours an au pair was required to work, the tasks the au pair did and the amount of 'pocket money' paid as being dependent upon their own generosity. Again, this allowed employers to consider themselves generous when they paid more than the lowest recommend rate of pocket money (which was c.£65 at the start of our research) or did not insist on au pairs acting as cleaners as well as childcare workers. This was the case even though employers understood that the pocket money paid was insufficient to live on and far lower than they would have paid for other forms of childcare on the market.

Another effect of hosts gathering information informally was that they reflected on their own practices in relation to the worst 'horror stories' they heard from au pairs. This had the effect of increasing hosts' empathy with au pairs. For example, June stated:

It's just a human thing. I wouldn't have someone in my house and abuse the fact because – and I've seen it and heard the tales. People just doing all hours and being asked to do everything and being full-time cleaner and just – you do hear of people going 'well, it's great because I only pay her 70 quid a week'. It's like, really, you would actually – you're happily doing that to another person are you, to another human being?

Lucy used similar language about being 'human' when telling us of an au pair she had met online who was sharing a room with the two children she was caring for and of another who had been left alone looking after two children when their parents split up and one parent went to France and one to America. She said:

Surely this is not legal? People get away with things like that and I find that absurd as a mother, as a parent. You realise that not everybody does that. If you're going to have your baby sleeping in the same room as your [au pair] – absolutely fundamental should be that the au pair has a separate room. It's unacceptable that the au pair should sleep with children. Because it's their life. They're coming in with their little life and your life. You're just denying their humanity actually if you're just going to say oh you're just there for the children all the time. You're sleeping with the children. I'm sure this family actually did not have the space for this girl to be there. I know it makes it harder for certain family structures but we're not – she wasn't brought up to share a room this girl, with anybody, with babies. You're denying who she is and you're inviting her to [be there] under false – so they lied to her and she'd got on and off the plane and she was here in this mad situation. That's absurd. It's kind of revolting and shameful actually. Because they're young, keen and lovely and the babies are gorgeous, they're very exploitable. This was a Spanish girl who's done an MA. She was no idiot but it took her the whole time to get herself out of that situation and not feel guilty by doing so. Who's there for her in that time? No one. I'm not sure if there should be any heavy duty legislation but it seems to me that what I consider basic common human values are not shared.

June and Lucy were both indignant at the behaviour of other au pair hosts – their comments touch on how quickly a live-in relationship can move from being a bit poorly paid, through exploitation to denial of personhood. Reflecting on stories such as this convinced the hosts we spoke to that they were 'good' hosts, because they knew they were not engaging in the most outrageous forms of exploitation. The downside is that in the absence of similar stories of excellent hosts in common circulation, there was not the same tendency for hosts to compare themselves to others who were more generous or inclusive.

This form of reflection and discussion about what it meant to be a good host also highlighted how personalised the au pair situation is. As Lucy comments 'Who is there for her in that time? No one'. Au pairs are almost entirely reliant on the generosity (or not) of their hosts to provide them with decent conditions. For hosts, this can be a practical burden as well as a psychological one and we turn now to one of the ways in which being a good host could be most burdensome when an au pair acted their age.

Hosting an au pair to provide flexible childcare and housekeeping is affordable because au pairs are not considered to be workers, they do not get the protections of workers and are not entitled to National Minimum Wage. The reason given for them not being considered workers is that they are 'part of the family'. However, when au pairs did behave like part of the family, particularly when they behaved like teenagers, it was rarely welcomed by their hosts and negotiating the quasi-familial relationship could be trying:

Facilitator: Do you have an au pair at the moment?

Interviewee: Yes. She's asleep in her bedroom because she's out till four o'clock every opportunity.

The hosts we interviewed tried to be tolerant of their au pairs' youth and how hard it might be for them to adapt to a new life in a new country. Stacey perhaps summed up the situation best:

It is a big ask to ask a 19-year-old to be Mum … They haven't finished sorting their own problems out, let alone – although the problems are different. I would say on the whole it did work and it got us through the phase that we needed to get through, but it wasn't without trauma

Stephanie gave an insight into what some of these problems might be and how they can play out in an au pair–host relationship:

She was very shy and she was 17 when she joined me. What I hadn't thought about really was that they're children and you end up having another child in the house. She was very, very, very shy. She wouldn't eat. I had real problems getting her to eat. She was obsessed with British Punk and the Sex Pistols and the Ramones from the US as well. She came, I think, from quite a strict family but coming to London – and I think grew up somewhere quite remote in Germany – was quite mind-blowing for her, I think. Also because I wasn't her parent, although I felt quite protective towards her, I encouraged those sides of her. So I bought her an original Sex Pistols photo on eBay and she was quite – I thought that was nice but she found it a bit – I don't know, she said, 'Oh my God, my parents, my parents they'd never have allowed this'. She was thrilled but there was all sorts of odd issues there.

June also described the conflict she felt between being and not being responsible for her au pair when she behaved like an irresponsible young person. She said:

> This was the thing that really annoyed me, was that she would go, 'okay well I'm going out on Saturday night and I'll be back on Sunday morning' and then on Tuesday morning she would turn up. I would have had no idea in that time where she was or who she was with. That's always one of my rules is it's fine I don't mind what you do but if you say you're going to come home and then you decide to stay over just text me and say I'll be back on Sunday evening or Monday morning … You could be having a great time and that's wonderful, you could also be under someone's patio by then. I don't want to be the one ringing up your mum. I mean I have all these kind of mental fantasies ringing up your mother going, 'I'm terribly sorry I had no idea where she was, I didn't report her missing for three days because we never really knew where she was'. So that was the tough one for me because I – just like I don't want to be a teenager's mother but at the same time my – I'm responsible for their safety and their wellbeing while they're with me.

Búriková and Miller's (2010) detailed ethnographic work with Slovak au pairs and their hosts in London is useful in decoding some of these 'odd issues' that au pairs and hosts might bring to their relationship. One point that they make is that for many au pairs their time au pairing is a *rite de passage*, or a time 'out of time'. That is, it is a period when these young people want to stretch their wings, push boundaries and specifically do things that they would not have done at home. The other important point they make, which is borne out in our research, as outlined above, is that, whatever the rules or framing of au pair arrangements might be,

in practice ... most host families are quite ready to acknowledge
that they choose an au pair, over other forms of childcare and house
cleaning, largely because it is what they can afford ... So the initial
decision to have an au pair is very rarely going to be a positive choice
based on some value or ideal, let alone that of the pseudo-family.
(Búriková and Miller 2010 p33)

This means you have the contrary situation whereby hosts need au pairs
to be young people who behave more responsibly than the average person
their age, at a time when those au pairs might actually want to behave,
at least sometimes, quite irresponsibly, and hosts very rarely want to
step in and take the role of parents to them. How this is negotiated is
an important aspect of how power relations manifest in au pair-hosting
homes. The language and location of a quasi-familial relationship are
available but these are not always welcomed by either side.

As well as the power within quasi-parent–child relations, another
hierarchy that characterised host–au pair relationships had to do with
ethnic, or more specifically in our research, national, differences and
stereotypes. For the most part (but not exclusively) au pairing is a
relationship between a host and an au pair of different nationalities.
This means that national 'character' is almost always readily available
as a way for hosts to understand and organise their relationships
with au pairs. As we argued in Chapters 1 and 2, the history of the
employment of paid domestic workers in British homes is a history of
the identification of acceptable white 'others' to take on that work. The
au pair hosts we met were no different to previous generations in their
preferences for who should work in their homes. They used nationality
as a key characteristic in choosing au pairs and in evaluating their au
pairs' behaviour.

The first way in which this was manifest was in recruitment
processes and preferences. We saw in the analysis of Gumtree.com
advertisements that au pairs hosts often specified the nationality of the
person they were looking for. Amongst our interviewees, preferences for
au pairs of particular nationalities, all of them European, were also in
evidence. Some hosts framed this in terms of their own nationality – for
example Italian and French hosts wanting another person to speak that
language at home, or another host who specifically wanted German-
speaking au pairs because it was a language that they did not speak
themselves. However, it was also common for hosts to just decide that
they 'liked' or 'did not like' au pairs from particular countries. Lucy

(who was herself Italian) made a comment that was typical of the sorts of things hosts said on this topic, revealing both how quickly hosts use national characteristics to judge an au pair, and also the idea of a 'cultural barrier' which mitigates against the hiring of au pairs from a culture that was 'too different' from her own:

> Then I had a, for a very short time, I had somebody for a few weeks from Estonia and that was another strange experience because she was [unclear]. The language problem was enormous but also there's a cultural barrier that is much bigger. I think that might be the problem I've got – I know lots of Romanian[s], I think with that particular girl was quite hard and I wouldn't have had her stay on, really. Then I got a Spanish girl, we reacted so strongly to the previous Italian girl, we decided no Italians anymore.

Poppy made a similar comment, while simultaneously highlighting the illogic of this approach and showing how personal preferences interact with policy changes:

> [B]ecause my first Spanish au pair was a disaster, I'm kind of a bit nervous about Spaniards, which is daft really because I speak Spanish, which is why I went for a Spaniard first time around, because I thought if there were language problems it would be fine because I speak Spanish. No, and similarly I've had friends who have had a nightmare with French au pairs, but we've had brilliant French au pairs, so I think it's just someone's personality. Obviously, I need them to have right to work in this country so we had one Turkish au pair who was brilliant but then the law changed so we don't have Turkish au pairs anymore.

This sort of thinking was typical in that for many hosts, a bad or good experience with one au pair of a particular nationality could lead to actively rejecting or seeking out au pairs of that nationality for many years in the future. For example, June said:

> Because we always found – I think, yeah, went back to the Polish girl who worked incredibly hard and that was why we carried on having the Eastern European girls, because their work ethic is extraordinary.

Hiring patterns that were informed by preconceptions about national stereotypes could then lead to the development of concentrations of au pairs forming in particular areas. This happens because people from particular countries gain reputations as being 'suited' to particular posts, employers hire replacement workers through a personal recommendation, and a system of passing jobs between family members and acquaintances develops (Cox 2006). A process of ethnic sifting within markets for in-home care and domestic labour is also found in a variety of national state contexts (see, for example, Lutz 2008 on Germany; Parreñas 2001 on Rome and Los Angeles; Hondagneu-Sotelo 2001 on Los Angeles; Pratt 1999a and 1999b, and Stiell and England 1997 on Canada). Williams and Gavanas (2008), Cox (2006), and Gregson and Lowe (1994) all found that in the UK this process of ethnic sifting translated into people from Australia and New Zealand being concentrated in formal nanny employment, workers from the Global South in domestic service positions and Eastern Europeans in au pair positions. At the time of our research this pattern was supplemented by the movement of Eastern European women into nanny posts – many of whom had previously been au pairs (Busch 2011; 2013) and of women from Spain into au pair posts.

An examination of how hosts negotiate the hierarchies within their homes reveals some of the problems at the heart of au pairing and the ways in which structural inequalities shape day to day life. The hosts we spoke to all wanted to be good, fair, non-exploitative hosts but they were doing this in a situation where there was little guidance or information. Hosts were aware how easy it was for au pairs to be exploited but knew little about what the very best host behaviour would be. The vernacular available for these negotiations, family membership, was not always well suited to the situation at hand and both hosts and au pairs could feel trapped by the expectations of family-like relations. Hosts seemed to find it easier to rely on national stereotypes, both positive and negative, to understand their au pairs and they used these to guide their hiring decisions. Ultimately, the large-scale inequalities of things such as the differing health of the British and Spanish economies were ever present in the day to day lives of hosts and au pairs.

Conclusion

Hosting an au pair was a way for families to get childcare for the hours they needed, at a price they could afford, in a form that was acceptable to them. It was a way for them to be both good workers and good parents, but it left them with the issue of how to be good hosts. The difficulty of combining paid work and childcare was palpable amongst the hosts we spoke to. In particular the difference in hours provided in group settings (nurseries, after school clubs) and the non-standard hours which parents worked was striking. Hosts chose au pairs because they could close this gap in a way they could afford, au pairs were affordable both because of their low 'pocket money' wage, and because part of their remuneration was met through property wealth. In addition au pairs did not confine themselves to just providing childcare. By 'being there' to do housework, wait for deliveries and step in when plans changed, they took stress off parents and made their lives substantially easier. Hosts' use of au pairs to care for children and perform associated domestic work in many cases represented an individual coping strategy engaged in by parents in the absence of comprehensive state provision of appropriate and affordable childcare that matched the requirements of people who worked. This meant there was less impetus on the part of parents – who may also be voters – to press politicians and policy makers to make changes to the way childcare was provided and subsidised in the UK so that it better reflected the incomes and work practices of all social groups. Instead, a low-paid, largely invisible, group of au pairs in effect subsidised lack of government investment in childcare by working for very low wages.

The low pay which au pairs received had to be compensated for, not only with room and board, but also with, as Jo described it, 'a very odd situation'. Hosts had to find a way of living with someone who was meant to be treated 'as an equal' and a 'member of the family', but who quite clearly was not. Both the construction of the au pair ideal, and its location within the space of the private home, make a relationship of 'employer–employee' unwelcome in many host families (even if some hosts felt that's what it was). The result is that the unequal power between au pairs and hosts manifests in other ways and has to be negotiated through the register of parent and child or national differences. One outcome of this is the perpetuation of ethnic/national hierarchies within paid domestic labour, where European women (particularly women from Eastern Europe and now from Spain) are coded as appropriate people to be au pairs. At the time we were researching, when there was a booming 'buyers' market' for au pairs, the existence of preferences such as these amongst hosts was significant as hosts only needed to consider au pairs of the nationality they most favoured. Britain's long history of favouring white 'others' for work in the intimate space of home continues.

CONCLUSION

Recently I was with my friend as she hung washing in the garden. She struggled to fit the au pair's thong on the peg. 'Really?' I said, pinging it between my fingers. 'Oh yes', she said, 'it's what all the 19-year-olds wear'. She hung the pants out in order of size: first the au pair's, then her small daughter's, then her own, a robust style of women's pants that shops now call 'boy shorts', as if posterior coverage was not feminine, but instead the preserve of Christopher Robin (imagine M&S doing a range of 'Girly Knickers' for men). Last came her husband's voluminous boxers. We joked that pant size correlated with household status. (Rumbelow 2015 n.p.)

The very notion of au pairing is predicated on the idea that what au pairs do is not employment or work, because au pairs are described by policy and popular discourse as being *equal* members of the family, yet we found in analysis of advertisements for au pairs, discussions with au pairs, hosts and experts working in the sector, that equality was a long way from being the norm. Rather, the context within which au pairing happens and the structural forces which shape it mean that jokes about au pairs' low status within their hosts' households will be made for some time to come.

Summary: why is au pairing unequal?

In this book we have set out the historical context and structural inequalities which frame au pairing and the lived experiences of au pairs and hosts in the UK during a period of deregulation. We have shown how it has been possible for au pairs to exist as a group of 'non-workers' without rights because the work that they do is not regarded as work. In this conclusion we summarise our arguments and findings thematically, drawing together the threads which run through the chapters of the book. We look at why the history of au pairing and broader patterns of paid domestic employment matter to the nature of au pairing today; why housework matters – the invisibility and low status of domestic work shapes au pairing in myriad ways; why government policies on childcare, migration and working hours matter; and why the organisation of paid work outside the home matters to the status and experience of au pairs.

In the early chapters of the book we set out a relatively detailed history of au pairing and of other forms of paid domestic labour to which au pairing is related (nannies, governesses, maids of all work). Paid domestic work is organised differently in different places, and in relaying this history we argued that paid domestic labour in the UK (and England in particular) has been characterised by two key features which still shape au pairing today: a history of forms of paid domestic work which blur the employee/family member distinction, and a preference for white domestic workers. This history provides the antecedents to au pairing today and it lays the ground for the current situation in a number of ways.

First, this history shapes the types of jobs that are available and imaginable within British homes. The idea of an au pair – a young woman who is not exactly a servant – is not a cultural disruption. There is a long precedent for the employment of domestic workers whose status is blurred and this blurring is available to British families as a way to ease discomfort about the idea of employing a 'servant' or having a stranger in the house. Second, this history shapes who does these jobs. As we showed in the empirical chapters, there is a process of 'race'/ ethnic/national 'sorting' which happens when au pairs are recruited. This sorting begins with government migration policy, which restricts the availability of au pair posts to people from majority white countries (EEA member states, and those which offer Tier 5 Working Holiday Maker reciprocal arrangements, most significantly, Australia and New Zealand). This was a choice on the part of the British government, other countries offer au pair visas to people from anywhere in the world and recruit the majority of their au pairs from outside Europe. However, in the UK the cultural preference for white domestic workers was easily combined with the history of au pairing as an arrangement between European states, to make the current situation (where au pairs are assumed to be EEA nationals) seem both 'natural' and acceptable.

We argued that the work au pairs do is invisible because of the type of tasks they carry out – childcare and housework. To understand this denial of what can be arduous, physical labour, we highlighted the relationship between housework, the gendering of responsibility for this work, and how 'work' has been understood since the industrial revolution and the concomitant physical and financial separation of home and work became common for men. Housework, particularly dealing with dirt, is work of such low status that it is not recognised as work at all, and its low status is transferred onto anyone involved with it. In addition, because housework has historically been done (in the majority of households at least) for free by family members, there is also an association between doing housework and belonging in a family.

It is difficult to overstate how important the social status of housework is to the organisation of au pairing and the experiences of au pairs and hosts. The deep roots of the misrecognition of reproductive labour – deep not only in historical terms but also in their significance in the reordering of daily life – mean that assumptions about the 'right' way to organise domestic labour, and who should do that labour, are also deeply held. The low status of this work means that people who can avoid it, do. This creates gendered inequalities within households and drives demand for paid domestic workers. It also means that au pairs and hosts share an intimate space and negotiate their relationship in the context of this inequality. We showed how au pairs feel about the content of their work and how being given cleaning, rather than childcare tasks, spoke to them of their low status. As Elisabeth Stubberud (2015b p132) comments 'it is difficult for someone to be an equal in a family when she is given the most denigrated work to do'.

Even when housework and childcare are done for pay, the coding of these tasks as something other than 'work' sticks and it is relatively easy for anyone who does this work to slip from the category 'worker' and be absorbed into a category of quasi-family membership. It is the content of the work that au pairs do which means that their labours are not recognised as 'real' work. Joan Tronto (2002 p37) has written, 'The institutional setting of the household is a different setting than the market. Because domestic service takes place inside a private home it is often not regarded as employment at all'. Previously Michael Walzer (1983 p52) had written: 'The principles that rule in the household are those of kinship and love. They establish the underlying pattern of mutuality and obligation, or authority and obedience. The servants have no proper place in that pattern but they have to be assimilated into it' (see also Anderson 2000).

One way in which au pairs are assimilated into these patterns is through the framing of au pairing in terms of family membership and cultural exchange, framings which would not be possible in other settings. The concept of cultural exchange saturates au pairing – in policy, in agency publicity, in au pairs' ambitions and sometimes even in discussions of the things hosts and au pairs most enjoy about the relationship. However, the idea of cultural exchange is built on contradictory beliefs about the home and family and the work that happens in the home. When someone on a student visa works part time in a shop or bar, they are recognised as a worker for that portion of their time. Serving customers or stacking shelves is not called 'cultural exchange' because the person doing it is on a student visa. Yet, for au pairs, the idea of cultural exchange is used to deny the work that they do and this is due to the way they are imagined to belong within family relations of reciprocity, rather than remuneration.

The confusion about the relationship between hosts and au pairs came out when they told us about negotiating the space of the home. While hosts might feel 'invaded' by the presence of an au pair and make rules that the au pair must make herself scarce when she is not working, au pairs described the day to day calculations they were making about when to eat, when to go out, when to use the bathroom. The most mundane activities were a minefield in this intimate but power-laden relationship. This is hardly surprising; the home is a unique space which is based on inequality resulting from the gendered responsibility for reproductive work, but it is also excellent at disguising unequal relations.

These assumptions about reproductive work, who does it and where it should be done, underpin government policy in diverse areas including migration, child and elder care provision, housing and planning and they affect social and cultural expectations. This means that in Britain, families with young children have to negotiate the demands of two competing groups of social expectations, that all adults should work (at least part time) and that families are, for the most part, privately responsible for providing for their childcare needs.

We look in detail at recommendations for policy related to au pairs below, but here we want to highlight how broad the range of policies is which influence au pairing. First, there are policies which influence the supply of au pairs – migration regimes which allow some people in and keep others out, or which let people in only under certain conditions to do certain forms of work. When we were doing our research, nationals of Bulgaria and Romania (the A2) were allowed into Britain as au pairs but not freely allowed to undertake many other forms of work. Before

EU enlargement the same was true of Eastern European 'A8' nationals. These policies create flows which then gain their own momentum – as we described in Chapter 7, people of particular nationalities become identified as appropriate to particular roles and so patterns of migration into particular forms of work remain even after rules change. In an unregulated sector, such as au pairing, the informal relationships, preferences and prejudices which characterise hiring practices are particularly important.

Second there are policies which underpin demand for au pairs. Governments can choose to invest, or not, in making parents' lives easier. In the UK, limited, expensive group childcare makes au pairs a logical option for families who are not wealthy. Long working hours and expectations of flexibility are also underpinned by government policy. The UK has, for many years, adopted relatively limited restrictions on working hours compared to our European neighbours, and policy on things such as parental leave lags behind many other nations. All of these, and other policies, on things such as housing and transport, are part of a regime – a group of policies and cultural expectations – which have left responsibility for childcare largely in the hands of families rather than supporting them collectively.

Last, and closely related to the points above, our research has shown how much the organisation of paid work outside the home matters to the organisation of au pairing (and all other reproductive labour) inside the home. In Chapter 3 we set out data on average working hours and patterns in the UK, and we could trace the effects of these patterns through our empirical chapters – in the demand for long average working hours for au pairs in the advertisements we analysed, in the experiences of au pairs of being expected to be always available at the drop of a hat to cover for hosts caught at work, and in the discussions of our host interviewees about their overwhelming need for flexibility. The demands put on hosts in their work outside the home transfer directly onto au pairs and are an important element of the demand for au pairs and of au pairs' experiences. Hosts praised the flexibility that au pairs offered, flexibility which enabled them to meet their responsibilities in their paid work without the worries that they might have if their children were in time-limited group care or if they were paying a childminder or nanny by the hour. Yet for au pairs, this flexibility could be a burden and demands that they always put their own interests second to those of their hosts indicated to them just how unequal they were. The availability of au pairs to carry out childcare and housework in a way that supports increasingly irregular and unpredictable working patterns means that there is less pressure on parents and their employers to question the need for such working patterns. Rather than reassessing the demands of paid work outside the home, parents look for cheap, flexible in-home care so that they can meet these demands.

Au pairing is not a simple relationship between an individual host and an au pair. It is a complicated activity influenced by a long history and diverse contemporary trends. It is only possible to understand the odd framing of au pairing and the nature of au pair–host relationships by situating contemporary practice within these broader trends. The influences which shape au pairing also underpin inequality between hosts and au pairs, making its construction even more contradictory and confusing. In the following section we focus on what might be done to the regulation of au pairing in Britain to improve the scheme, but argue that any real transformation of au pairs' status is unlikely in the context we have explored.

Recommendations

We are writing at an uncertain time – with Brexit negotiations taking place, it is unclear what will happen to au pairs in the UK, if and when freedom of movement for EEA nationals ends. The negotiations could provide an excellent opportunity for the government to attend to the au pair sector, to reform it and improve the experiences of au pairs. Whatever the outcome of negotiations it is necessary for the UK government to engage with what au pairing has become and what it ought to be. We have shown and we argue here that the sector is urgently in need of regulatory attention and reform.

We have examined how au pairing is constructed in policy and industry discourses and how it is experienced on the ground to reveal what au pairing *is* in contemporary Britain, but, if it is to work better and to offer fewer opportunities for exploitation and abuse, what *should* it be?

First, if a country is going to have 'au pairs' then au pairing has to be regulated. The current government position of allowing the institution to exist but doing nothing to ensure its proper organisation is absolutely wrong. It has created a race to the bottom and recast much work that ought to be done by experienced, trained nannies into the realm of au pairing. A government should not exclude a group of people from one type of legislative protections (National Minimum Wage, working hours directives) without providing them with equal or better protection through another means. At the very least, the UK government needs to reintroduce clear, firm guidance on what an au pair is (rather than a list of things that can be picked from). These should at minimum reflect the conditions given under the old au pair visa; it would be even better if they reflected the new guidance from BAPAA (2017). Such conditions should be widely disseminated and a clear route to redress should be available for au pairs forced to work in conditions that fall outside them.

Second, we are aware that even when the au pair visa existed there was still substantial abuse of au pairs and confusion about what they could and could not do. Therefore, much more should be done to improve on this minimum standard and to make sure the spirit of au pairing is stuck to in practice. Búriková and Miller (2010) end their book, which examined au pairing while the visa was still in place, with a number of very specific recommendations that are now needed more than ever:

1 Legislation should provide greater clarity about au pairs' rights. Including their rights during their time off, for example that they have the right, but not the duty, to be in the house when they are not working and that any additional work they do (over and above 25 hours plus two evenings of babysitting as was specified in the visa) should be paid at at least NMW rates. The meaning of 'light housework' should be specified and other provisions, such as a separate bedroom with a door that locks must be required.
2 Au pair agencies should be registered and regulated and held to at least the minimum standards of BAPAA.
3 Information about au pairs' rights should be made widely available in the appropriate languages.
4 There needs to be some kind of route to redress. Búriková and Miller (2010) suggest an ombudsman at national and EU level to support this.

We would add to these suggestions recommendations from Lene Løvdal (2015) which were developed by a non-governmental organisation (NGO) working with au pairs in Norway. She argues for five steps to protect au pairs:

- First, au pairs cannot obtain even the most basic rights and access to justice before their legal position as workers is recognised and clarified, and they gain access to workers' rights such as normal wages, paid overtime, and effective protection against unlawful dismissal. No matter the type of residence permit, work must be considered as work, including domestic work and care work.

- Second, there must be effective and accessible remedies when things go wrong. Au pairs are in a weak position relative to their hosts and they need to have real access to redress in ways which do not make them homeless or out of status for immigration purposes.

- Third, the UN and ILO conventions regarding migrant workers and domestic workers must be ratified and implemented. Indirect and structural discrimination must be properly addressed. The Convention on the Elimination of All Kinds of Discrimination Against Women (CEDAW) should be applied on this particular issue, especially its article 5(a) on stereotypes; article 11 on workers' rights and the CEDAW committee's general recommendation no. 26 on women migrant workers.

- Fourth, the state must ensure that au pairs and other migrant domestic workers know about their basic rights and where to get help should they need it. At the very least, all au pairs – whether they need visas or not – should receive information about key rights and where to get help. This information must be given in a way that is truly understandable for the au pair.

- Finally, measures taken must be thoroughly evaluated – and governments must act on the recommendations of the evaluation. The need for domestic help is legitimate, but who should pay for host families' careers and spare time? Should it be poor women from other countries?

Last, we believe that our analysis of au pairing raises some much broader questions about social trends and inequalities and how these should be addressed. The five steps listed above would go a great way towards protecting au pairs from the worst abuses they face and would improve conditions and protections for all by ensuring they were treated as workers. In order to protect au pairs from more subtle forms of denigration and to improve their pay and conditions further, more far-reaching changes in attitudes towards reproductive labour are needed. Au pairing only exists (as a form of 'non-work' framed as cultural exchange) because women's traditional reproductive tasks are not recognised as work and young migrants are imagined as available and suitable to carry out low-status and low-paid work. Hosts hire au pairs because the demands of the workplace are not in any way matched by social support, such as flexible nursery provision or other appropriate state-provided collective forms of reproduction. All of this is problematic and the root causes of the low status of reproductive labour and demand for highly flexible forms of privatised childcare need to be addressed.

The context of the growth of au pairing, and of attempts by hosts to ensure a supply of cheap and flexible childcare labour, is the paucity of state-funded childcare and other forms of support for families, combined with increasing working hours particularly for parents of young children. From the UK to Australia, the burden of the withering of the welfare state and the intensification of demands from employers is transferred through working families to the shoulders of au pairs and other care workers. In a number of countries, states have responded to new working patterns and the difficulties of combining home and work by facilitating au pair employment (and in some places other forms of domestic work), for example by offering hosts tax breaks and most importantly by refusing to regulate au pairing in the interests of au pairs and so protect them from exploitation and over work, as has happened in the UK. A better solution than just making cheap, unregulated childcare labour available would be to address the looming crisis of childcare costs and working hours and the effects of the unequal distribution of reproductive labour – a burden which falls on women and can prove a trigger to taking on a paid domestic worker. Our research suggested that the way in which UK policymakers in 2008 removed state responsibility for managing the activities of au pairs, was the result of inattention and oversight rather than deliberate intent. However, this very oversight is indicative of the extent to which caring for children, cooking, cleaning, shopping and general household upkeep were devalued forms of work. It is this neglect of care and housework which has produced a situation where a very large number of au pairs are working in the UK without any real protections or any great prospect of real equality.

REFERENCES

4Children (2015) 'High childcare costs mean one in five parents are considering reducing hours or giving up work altogether in 2015'. Press release, 4Children [Online], 8 January 2015. Available at: www.4children.org.uk/News/Detail/High-childcare-costs-mean-one-in-five-parents-are-considering-reducing-hours-or-giving-up-work-altogether-in-2015 [Accessed 11 August 2015].

Aguilar Pérez, M. (2015) 'The cosmopolitan dilemma: Fantasy, work and the experiences of Mexican au pairs in the USA'. *In:* Cox, R. (Ed.) *Au Pairs' Lives in Global Context: Sisters or Servants?* Basingstoke: Palgrave Macmillan, pp203–218.

Aitken, S. (2016) *The Awkward Spaces of Fathering.* London and New York: Routledge.

Alakeson, V. (2011). 'Childcare: Failing to meet the needs of working parents'. UCL DERA [Online]. Available at: http://dera.ioe.ac.uk/id/eprint/28302 [Accessed 22 December 2017].

Ally, S. (2013) '"Just one small cap is enough!": Servants, detergents, and their prosthetic significance'. *African Studies* 72, pp321–352.

Anderson, B. (2000) *Doing the Dirty Work: The Global Politics of Domestic Labour.* London: Zed Books.

Anderson, B. (2009) 'What's in a name? Immigration controls and subjectivities: the case of au pair and domestic worker visa holders in the UK'. *Subjectivity* 29(1), pp407–424.

Anderson, B. (2010) 'Migration, immigration controls and the fashioning of precarious workers'. *Work, Employment & Society* 24(2), pp300–317.

Anderson, B. (2014) 'Nations, migration and domestic labour: The case of the UK'. *Women's Studies International Forum* [Online] 46, pp5–12. Available at: doi:10.1016/j.wsif.2014.01.005 [Accessed 19 December 2017].

Anderson, B., Ruhs, M., Rogaly, B. and Spencer, S. (2006) 'Fair enough? Central and East European migrants in low-wage employment in the UK'. COMPAS, Oxford. Available at: www.compas.ox.ac.uk/2006/pr-2006-changing_status_fair_enough/ [Accessed 11 June 2018].

Anttonen, A. and Sipilä, J. (1996) 'European social care services: Is it possible to identify models?' *Journal of European Social Policy* 6(2), pp87–100.

Bakan, A. and Stasiulis D.K. (1995) 'Making the match: Domestic placement agencies and the racialization of women's household work'. *Signs* 20(2), pp303–335.

Baldassar, L. and Merla, L. (2014) 'Introduction: Transnational family caregiving through the lens of circulation'. *In:* Baldassar, L. and Merla, L. (Eds), *Transnational Families, Migration and the Circulation of Care: Understanding Mobility and Absence in Family Life.* London: Routledge, pp3–24.

BAPAA (2017) 'What is an au pair?' Available at: http://bapaa.org.uk/host-families/what-is-an-au-pair/ [Accessed 18 January 2018].

Barbagallo, C. (2016) *The Political Economy of Reproduction: Motherhood, Work and the Home in Neoliberal Britain.* Unpublished PhD Thesis, University of East London. Available at: http://roar.uel.ac.uk/5177/1/Camille%20Barbagallo%20PhD%20Thesis%202016.pdf [Accessed 13 April 2018].

Barbosa, L. (2007) 'Domestic workers and pollution in Brazil'. *In:* Campkin, B. and Cox, R. (Eds), *Dirt: New Geographies of Cleanliness and Contamination*. London: I.B. Tauris, pp25–33.

Berg, L. (2015) 'Hiding in plain sight: Au pairs in Australia'. *In:* Cox, R. (Ed.), *Au Pairs' Lives in Global Context: Sisters or Servants?* Basingstoke: Palgrave Macmillan, pp187–202.

Bikova, M. (2010) 'The snake in the grass of gender equality: Au pairing in women-friendly Norway'. *In:* Widding-Isaksen, L. (Ed.), *Global Care Work: Gender and Migration in Nordic Societies*. Lund: Nordic Academic Press, pp49–68.

Bikova, M. (2015) 'In a minefield of transnational social relations: Filipino au pairs between moral obligations and personal ambitions'. *In:* Cox, R. (Ed.), *Au Pairs' Lives in Global Context: Sisters or Servants?* Basingstoke: Palgrave Macmillan, pp87–103.

Bonnett, A. (2000) *White Identities: Historical and International Perspectives*. Harlow: Prentice Hall.

Bonnett, A. (2008) 'Whiteness and the West'. *In:* Dwyer, C. and Bressy, C. (Eds), *New Geographies of Race and Racism*. Aldershot: Ashgate, pp17–28.

Boris, E. and Parreñas, R.S. (2010) 'Introduction'. *In:* Boris, E., and Parreñas, R.S. (Eds), *Intimate Labors: Cultures, Technologies, and the Politics of Care*. Stanford, CA: Stanford Social Sciences, pp1–12.

Boserup, E. (1970) *Women's Role in Economic Development*. London: Earthscan.

Boterman, W.R. and Bridge, G. (2015) 'Gender, class and space in the field of parenthood: Comparing middle-class-fraction in Amsterdam and London'. *Transactions of the Institute of British Geographers* 40(2), pp249–261.

Boyer, K., Reimer, S. and Irvine, L. (2013) 'The nursery workspace, emotional labour and contested understandings of commoditised childcare in the contemporary UK'. *Gender, Space and Culture* 14(5), pp517–540.

Búriková, Z. (2006) 'The embarrassment of co-presence: Au pairs and their rooms'. *Home Cultures* 3(2), pp99–122.

Búriková, Z. (2015) '"Good families" and the shadows of servitude: Au pair gossip and norms of au pair employment'. *In:* Cox, R. (Ed.), *Au Pairs' Lives in Global Context: Sisters or Servants?* Basingstoke: Palgrave Macmillan, pp36–52.

Búriková, Z. (2016) EU enlargement and au pairing in the United Kingdom. *Nordic Journal of Migration Research* 6(4), pp207–214.

Búriková, Z. and Miller, D. (2010) *Au Pair*. Cambridge: Polity Press.

Burke, T. (1996) *Lifebouy Men and Lux Women: Commodification, Consumption and Cleanliness in Modern Zimbabwe*. London: Leicester University Press.

Busch, N. (2011) *A Migrant Division of Labour in the Global City? Commoditised In-Home Childcare in London 2004–2010*. PhD Thesis, Birkbeck, University of London.

Busch, N. (2012) 'Deprofessionalisation and informality in the market for commoditised care'. *In:* Sollund, R.A. (Ed.), *Transnational Migration, Gender and Rights*. Advances in Ecopolitics, vol. 10. Bingley: Emerald, pp53–75.

Busch, N. (2013) 'The employment of migrant nannies in the UK: Negotiating social class in an open market for commoditised in-home care'. *Social and Cultural Geography* 14(5), pp541–557.

Busch, N. (2015) 'When work doesn't pay: Outcomes of a deregulated childcare market and au pair policy vacuum in the UK'. *In:* Cox, R. (Ed.), *Au Pairs' Lives in Global Context: Sisters or Servants?* Basingstoke: Palgrave Macmillan, pp53–69.

Calleman, C. (2010) 'Cultural exchange or cheap domestic labour? Constructions of "au pair" in four Nordic countries'. *In*: Isaksen, L.W. (Ed.), *Global Care Work: Gender and Migration in Nordic Societies*. Lund: Nordic Academic Press, pp69–96.

Cameron, G. and Kiss, G.D. (2017) *Holiday Childcare Survey 2017*. Family and Childcare Trust. Available at: www.familyandchildcaretrust.org/holiday-childcare-survey-2017 [Accessed 18 April 2018].

Conradson, D. and Latham, A. (2007) 'The affective possibilities of London: Antipodean transnationals and the overseas experience'. *Mobilities* 2(2), pp231–254.

Coser, L. (1973) 'Servants: The obsolescence of an occupational role'. *Social Forces* 52(1), pp31–40.

Council of Europe (1969) European Agreement on 'Au Pair' Placement and Protocol Thereto. Strasbourg, 24 November 1969 [Online]. Available at: https://rm.coe.int/168007231c [Accessed 11 December 2017].

Cox, R. (1999) 'The role of ethnicity in shaping the domestic employment sector in Britain'. *In*: Momsen, J.H. (Ed.), *Gender, Migration and Domestic Service*. London: Routledge, pp134–147.

Cox, R. (2006) *The Servant Problem: Domestic Employment in a Global Economy*. London: I.B. Tauris.

Cox, R. (2007) 'The au pair body: Sex object, sister or student?' *European Journal of Women's Studies* 14(3), pp281–296.

Cox, R. (2010) 'Hired hubbies and mobile mums: Gendered skills in domestic service'. *Renewal* 18(1–2), pp51–58.

Cox, R. (2011) 'Competitive mothering and delegated care: Class relationships in nanny and au pair employment'. *Studies in the Maternal* 3 (2), no pages.

Cox, R. (2012) 'Gendered Work and Migration Regimes'. *In*: Sollund, R. (Ed.), *Transnational Migration, Gender and Rights*. Advances in Ecopolitics, vol. 10. Bingley: Emerald, pp33–52.

Cox, R. (2015a) 'Introduction'. *In*: Cox, R. (Ed.), *Au Pairs' Lives in Global Context: Sisters or Servants?* Basingstoke: Palgrave Macmillan, pp1–18.

Cox, R. (Ed.) (2015b) *Au Pairs' Lives in Global Context: Sisters or Servants?* Basingstoke: Palgrave Macmillan.

Cox, R. (2015c) 'Conclusion'. *In*: Cox, R. (Ed.), *Au Pairs' Lives in Global Context: Sisters or Servants?* Basingstoke: Palgrave Macmillan, pp239–249.

Cox, R. and Busch, N. (2016a) '"This is the life I want": Au pairs' perceptions of life in a global city'. *Nordic Journal of Migration Research* 6(4), pp234–242.

Cox, R. and Busch, N. (2016b) 'Gendered work and citizenship: Diverse experiences of au pairing in the UK'. *In*: Gullikstad, B., Kristensen, G.K. and Ringrose, P. (Eds), *Paid Migrant Domestic Labour in a Changing Europe: Questions of Gender Equality and Citizenship*. Basingstoke: Palgrave Macmillan, pp101–124.

Cox, R. and Narula, R. (2003) 'Playing happy families: Rules and relationships in au pair employing households in London, England'. *Gender, Place and Culture* 10(4), pp333–344.

Cox, R., George, R., Horne, R.H., Nagle, R., Pisani, E., Ralph, B. and Smith, V. (2011) *Dirt: The Filthy Reality of Everyday Life*. London: Profile Books.

Cuban, S. (2013) *Deskilling Migrant Women in the Global Care Industry*. Basingstoke: Palgrave Macmillan.

Cuban, S. (2017a) '"Any sacrifice is worthwhile doing": Latina au pairs migrating to the United States for opportunities'. *Journal of Immigrant and Refugee Studies* [Online],

January 2017. Available at: doi.org/10.1080/15562948.2016.1263775 [Accessed 19 December 2017].

Cuban, S. (2017b) *Transnational Family Communications: Immigrants and ICTs*. Basingstoke: Palgrave Macmillan.

Dalgas, K. (2016) 'Filipino au pairs on the move'. *Nordic Journal of Migration Research* 6(4), pp199–206.

Davidoff, L. (1995) *Worlds Between: Historical Perspectives on Gender and Class*. Cambridge: Polity Press.

Dearden, L. (2014) 'London is "the most desirable city in the world to work in", study finds'. *The Independent* [Online]. Available at: www.independent.co.uk/news/uk/home-news/london-is-the-most-desirable-city-in-the-world-to-work-in-study-finds-9779868.html [Accessed 22 December 2017].

Delap, L. (2011) *Knowing Their Place: Domestic Service in Twentieth Century Britain*. Oxford: Oxford University Press.

Dorling, D. (2015) 'Income inequality in the UK: Comparisons with five large Western European countries and the USA'. *Applied Geography* 61, pp24–34.

Douglas, M. (2002 [1966]) *Purity and Danger: An Analysis of Concepts of Pollution and Taboo*. London: Routledge & Kegan Paul.

Durin, S. (2015) 'Ethnicity and the au pair experience: Latin American au pairs in Marseille, France'. *In:* Cox, R. (Ed.), *Au Pairs' Lives in Global Context: Sisters or Servants?* Basingstoke: Palgrave Macmillan, pp155–169.

Ehrenreich, B. (2003) 'Maid to order'. *In:* Ehrenreich, B. and Hochschild, A.R. (Eds), *Global Woman: Nannies, Maids and Sex Workers in the New Economy*. London: Granta Books, pp85–103.

Ehrenreich, B. and Hochschild, A.R. (Eds) (2003) *Global Woman: Nannies, Maids and Sex Workers in the New Economy*. London: Granta Books.

Faircloth, C. (2014a) 'Intensive parenting and the expansion of parenting'. *In:* Lee, E., Bristow, J., Faircloth, C. and Macvarish, J. (Eds), *Parenting Culture Studies*. Basingstoke: Palgrave Macmillan, pp25–50.

Faircloth, C. (2014b) 'Intensive fatherhood? The (un)involved dad'. *In:* Lee, E., Bristow, J., Faircloth, C. and Macvarish, J. (Eds), *Parenting Culture Studies*. Basingstoke: Palgrave Macmillan, pp184–199.

Family and Childcare Trust (2015) *Childcare for London Parents with Atypical Work Patterns: What Are the Problems and How Should We Fix Them*. [Online]. Available at: www.familyandchildcaretrust.org/file/1687/download?token=iM8QwUOo [Accessed 21 December 2017].

Federici, S. (2012) *Revolution at Point Zero: Housework, Reproduction and Feminist Struggle*. Oakland, CA: PM Press.

Fox, J.E., Moroşanu, L. and Szilassy, E. (2012) 'The racialization of the new European migration to the UK'. *Sociology* [Online] 46(4), pp680–695. Available at: doi:10.1177/0038038511425558 [Accessed 21 December 2017].

Gambles, R. (2010) 'Going public? Articulations of the personal and political on Mumsnet.com'. *In:* Mahony, N., Newman, J. and Barnet, C. (Eds), *Rethinking the Public: Innovations in Research Theory and Politics*. Bristol: Policy Press, pp29–42.

Geserick, C. (2015) '"She doesn't think it will work out": Why au pairs in the USA leave their host family early'. *In:* Cox, R. (Ed.), *Au Pairs' Lives in Global Context: Sisters or Servants?* Basingstoke: Palgrave Macmillan, pp219–234.

Geserick, C. (2016) 'America is the dream of so many things'. *Nordic Journal of Migration Research* 6(4), pp243–251.

Glenn, E.N. (2010) *Forced to Care: Coercion and Caregiving in America*. Cambridge, MA, and London: Harvard University Press.

Good Schools Guide (2018) 'What type of boarding – full, weekly or flexi?' [Online]. Available at: www.goodschoolsguide.co.uk/choosing-a-school/independent-schools/what-type-of-boarding-full-weekly-or-flexi [Accessed 18 April 2018].

gov.uk (2015) *Help Paying for Childcare*. [Online]. Available at: www.gov.uk/help-with-childcare-costs/free-childcare-and-education-for-2-to-4-year-olds [Accessed 11 August 2015].

Gregson, N. and Lowe, M. (1994) *Servicing the Middle Classes: Class, Gender and Waged Domestic Labour in Contemporary Britain*. London: Routledge.

Guevarra, A.R. (2014) 'Supermaids: The racial branding of global Filipino care labour'. *In:* Anderson, B. and Shutes, I. (Eds), *Migration and Care Labour: Theory, Policy and Politics*. Basingstoke: Palgrave Macmillan, pp130–150.

Gullikstad, B. and Annfelt, T. (2016) 'The au pair scheme as "cultural exchange": Effects of Norwegian au pair policy on gender equality and citizenship'. *In:* Gullikstad, B., Korsnes, K. and Ringrose, P. (Eds), *Paid Migrant Domestic Labour in a Changing Europe*. London: Palgrave Macmillan, pp55–78.

Gullikstad, B., Kristensen, G.K. and Ringrose, P. (2016) 'Paid migrant domestic labour, gender equality, and citizenship in a changing Europe: An introduction'. *In:* Gullikstad, B., Korsnes, K. and Ringrose, P. (Eds), *Paid Migrant Domestic Labour in a Changing Europe*. Basingstoke: Palgrave Macmillan, pp1–29.

Hall, C. (1995 [1973]) 'The history of the housewife'. *In:* Malos, E. (Ed.), *The Politics of Housework*. Cheltenham: New Clarion Press, pp34–58.

Harding, C. and Cottell, J. (2018) *Childcare Survey 2018*. Family and Childcare Trust. [Online]. Available at: www.familyandchildcaretrust.org/childcare-survey-2018 [Accessed 18 April 2018].

Haskins, V. and Lowrie, C. (Eds) (2015) *Colonization and Domestic Service: Historical and Contemporary Perspectives*. London: Routledge.

Hayden, D. (1981) *The Grand Domestic Revolution: The History of Feminist Designs for American Homes, Neighbourhoods and Cities*. Cambridge, MA: MIT Press.

Hays, S. (1996) *The Cultural Contradictions of Motherhood*. New Haven, CT, and London: Yale University Press.

Hecht, J. (1954) *Continental and Colonial Servants in Eighteenth Century England*. Smith Studies in History, vol. 40. Northampton, MA: Department of History of Smith College.

Hegewisch, A., Liepmann, H., Hayes, J. and Harmann, H. (2010) 'Separate and not equal? Gender segregation in the labor market and the gender wage gap'. Institute for Women's Policy Research Briefing Paper C377 [Online], September 2010. Available at: www.iwpr.org/publications/pubs/separate-and-not-equal-gender-segregation-in-the-labor-market-and-the-gender-wage-gap [Accessed 19 December 2017].

Hess, S. and Puckhaber, A. (2004) '"Big sisters" are better domestic servants?! Comments on the booming au pair business'. *Feminist Review* 77(1), pp65–67.

Higman, B.W. (2002) *Domestic Service in Australia*. Melbourne: Melbourne University Press.

Higman, B.W. (2015) 'An historical perspective: Colonial continuities in the global geography of domestic service'. *In:* Haskins, V.K. and Lowrie, C. (Eds), *Colonization and Domestic Service: Historical and Contemporary Perspectives*. London and New York: Routledge, pp19–37.

Hill, D. (2015) 'London childcare costs are squeezing parents out of work'. *The Guardian* [Online], 8 January 2015. Available at: www.theguardian.com/uk-news/davehillblog/2015/jan/08/london-childcare-costs-are-squeezing-parents-out-of-work [Accessed 11 August 2015].

Hochschild, A.R. (1989) *The Second Shift*. New York: Avon Books.

Hochschild, A.R. (2000) 'Global care chains and emotional surplus value'. *In:* Hutton, W. and Giddens, A. (Eds), *On the Edge: Living with Global Capitalism*. London: Jonathan Cape, pp130–146.

Hochschild, A.R. (2003) 'Love and gold'. *In*: Ehrenreich, B. and Hochschild, A. (Eds), *Global Woman: Nannies, Maids and Sex Workers in the New Economy*. London: Granta Books, pp15–30.

Holden, K. (2013) *Nanny Knows Best: The History of the British Nanny*. Stroud: The History Press.

Holloway, S. and Pimlott-Wilson, H. (2014) 'Enriching children, institutionalizing childhood? Geographies of play, extracurricular activities, and parenting in England'. *Annals of the Association of American Geographers* 104(3), pp613–662.

Holloway, S. and Pimlott-Wilson, H. (2016) 'New economy, neoliberal state and professionalised parenting: Mothers' labour market engagement and state support for social reproduction in class-differentiated Britain'. *Transactions of the Institute of British Geographers* 41(4), pp376–388.

Hondagneu-Sotelo, P. (2001) *Doméstica: Immigrant Workers Cleaning and Caring in the Shadows of Affluence*. Berkeley, CA: University of California Press.

Hughes, K. (1993) *The Victorian Governess*. London: Hambledon Press.

Hutchinson, J. (2014) London named Best City for Culture and Tate Modern lands three prizes at international awards night. *Mail Online* [Online]. Available at: www.dailymail.co.uk/travel/travel_news/article-2789137/london-named-best-city-culture-tate-modern-lands-three-prizes-international-awards-night.html [Accessed 11 June 2018].

Ignatiev, N. (1995) *How the Irish Became White*. London and New York: Routledge.

International Au Pair Association (IAPA) (2014a) 'About International Au Pair Association'. [Online]. Available at: http://iapa.org/about/ [Accessed 4 May 2014].

International Au Pair Association (IAPA) (2014b) 'Objectives'. [Online]. Available at: http://iapa.org/about/objectives/ [Accessed 6 May 2014].

International Labour Organisation (ILO) (2011) *Decent Work for Domestic Workers: Convention 189, Recommendation 201*. International Labour Organisation, Geneva. [Online]. Available at: www.ilo.org/wcmsp5/groups/public/---ed_protect/---protrav/---travail/documents/publication/wcms_168266.pdf [Accessed 14 May 2014].

IRS (2013) 'Au pairs'. [Online]. Available at: www.irs.gov/Individuals/International-Taxpayers/Au-Pairs [Accessed 14 May 2014].

Isaksen, L.W. (Ed.) (2010) *Global Care Work: Gender and Migration in Nordic Societies*. Lund: Nordic Academic Press.

Jarman, J., Blackburn, R.M. and Racko, G. (2012) 'The dimensions of occupational gender segregation in industrial countries'. *Sociology* 46(6), pp1003–1019.

Jarvis, H. (1999) 'The tangled webs we weave: Household strategies to co-ordinate home and work'. *Employment and Society* 13(2), pp225–247.

Jarvis, H. (2005) 'Moving to London time: Household co-ordination and the infrastructure of everyday life'. *Time and Society* 14(1), pp133–154.

Jarvis, H. and Pratt, A. (2006) 'Bringing it all back home: The extensification and "overflowing" of work. The case of San Francisco's new media households'. *Geoforum* 37(3), pp331–339.

Johnson, L. and Lloyd, J. (2004) *Sentenced to Everyday Life: Feminism and the Housewife*. Oxford: Berg.

Jowitt, J. (2014) 'Reality check: What does childcare really cost?' *The Guardian* [Online], 5 March 2014. Available at: www.theguardian.com/news/reality-check/2014/mar/04/children-childcare-cost-of-living-work-mortgage [Accessed 21 December 2017].

Kilkey, M., Perrons, D. and Plomien, A. (2013) *Gender, Migration and Domestic Work: Masculinities, Male Labour and Fathering in the UK and USA*. Basingstoke: Palgrave Macmillan.

Kim, H.-S. (2008) 'International marriage migrant women in Korea'. *Korean Journal of Women Health Nursing* 14(4), pp248–256.

Kim, J.-H. and Lee, M.-H. (2016) Dietary behavior of marriage migrant women according to their nationality in multicultural families. *Korean Journal of Community Nutrition* 21(1), pp53–64.

Kopplin, Z. (2017) 'They think we are slaves: The U.S. au pair program is riddled with problems – and new documents show that the State Department might know more than it is letting on'. *Politico* [Online], 27 March 2017. Available at: www.politico.com/magazine/story/2017/03/au-pair-program-abuse-state-department-214956 [Accessed 11 December 2017].

Lee, E. (2014) 'Experts and parenting culture'. *In:* Lee, E., Bristow, J., Faircloth, C. and Macvarish, J. (Eds), *Parenting Culture Studies*. Basingstoke: Palgrave Macmillan, pp51–75.

Lee, E., Bristow, J., Faircloth, C. and Macvarish, J. (Eds) (2014) *Parenting Culture Studies*. Basingstoke: Palgrave Macmillan.

Lee, J.-S. (2016) 'Development of a Korean food culture education textbook for married female migrants'. *Korean Journal of Community Nutrition* 21(5), pp415–425.

Liarou, E. (2008) 'The cultural politics of identity: Film, television and immigration in post-war Britain, 1951–1967'. Unpublished PhD Thesis, Birkbeck, University of London.

Liarou, E. (2015) '"Pink slave" or "modern young woman"? A history of the au pair in Britain'. *In:* Cox, R. (Ed.), *Au Pairs' Lives in Global Context: Sisters or Servants?* Basingstoke: Palgrave Macmillan, pp19–35.

Lutz, H. (Ed.) (2008) *Migration and Domestic Work: A European Perspective on a Global Theme*. Aldershot: Ashgate.

Lutz, H. (2011) *The New Maids*. London: Zed Books.

Lutz, H. and Palenga-Möllenbeck, E. (2012) 'Care workers, care drain and care chains: Reflections on care, migration and citizenship'. *Social Politics* 19(1), pp15–37.

Løvdal, L. (2015) 'Au pairs in Norway: Experiences from an outreach project'. *In:* Cox, R. (Ed.), *Au Pairs' Lives in Global Context: Sisters or Servants?* Basingstoke: Palgrave Macmillan, pp136–150.

Macdonald, C.L. (2010) *Shadow Mothers: Nannies, Au Pairs, and the Micropolitics of Mothering*. Berkeley, CA: University of California Press.

Madianou, M. and Miller, D. (2011) 'Mobile phone parenting: Reconfiguring relationships between Filipina migrant mothers and their left-behind children'. *New Media & Society* 13(3), pp457–470.

Madianou, M. and Miller, D. (2013) *Migration and New Media: Transnational Families and Polymedia*. Oxon: Routledge.

Manalansan, M.F. (2006) Queer intersections: Sexuality and gender in migration studies. *International Migration Review* 40(1), pp224–249.

Mansell, C. (2018) 'EHS 2018 special: Upstairs, downstairs? Experiences of female servants in England, 1550–1650'. *Economic History Society: The Long Run* [Online], 6 April 2018. Available at: https://ehsthelongrun.net/2018/04/06/upstairs-downstairs-experiences-of-female-servants-in-england-1550-1650/ [Accessed 13 April 2018].

Marchetti, S. (2014) *Black Girls: Migrant Domestic Workers and Colonial Legacies*. Leiden and Boston, MA: Brill.

McClintock, A. (1995) *Imperial Leather: Race, Gender and Sexuality in the Colonial Contest*. New York and Oxford: Routledge.

McDowell, L. (2005) *Hard Labour: The Forgotten Voices of Latvian Migrant Volunteer Workers*. London: UCL Press.

McDowell, L. (2008) 'Thinking through work: Complex inequalities, constructions of difference and trans-national migrants'. *Progress in Human Geography* 32(4), pp491–507.

McDowell, L. (2009) 'Old and new European economic migrants: Whiteness and managed migration policies'. *Journal of Ethnic and Migration Studies* 35(1), pp19–36.

McDowell, L., Ward, K., Perrons, D., Ray, K. and Fagan, C. (2006) 'Place, class and local circuits of reproduction: Exploring the social geography of middle-class childcare in London'. *Urban Studies* 43(12), pp2163–2182.

McIntosh, S. (2013) Hollowing out and the future of the labour market. BIS Research Paper Number 134, Department for Business, Innovation and Skills, London. [Online]. Available at: https://assets.publishing.service.gov.uk/government/uploads/system/uploads/attachment_data/file/250206/bis-13-1213-hollowing-out-and-future-of-the-labour-market.pdf [Accessed 23 July 2018].

Mckay, D. (2007) '"Sending dollars shows feeling": Emotions and economies in Filipino migration'. *Mobilities* 2(2), pp175–194.

Miani, C. and Hoorens, S. (2014) *Parents at Work: Men and Women Participating in the Labour Force*. [Online]. Short Statistical Report, no. 2, Prepared for the European Commission, Directorate-General of Justice and Fundamental Rights, RAND Europe. [Online]. Available at: http://ec.europa.eu/justice/gender-equality/files/documents/140502_gender_equality_workforce_ssr2_en.pdf [Accessed 21 December 2017].

MSE (2015) 'Childcare vouchers: Cut childcare costs by £1,000/ year'. *Money Saving Expert* [Online]. Available at: www.moneysavingexpert.com/family/childcare-vouchers [Accessed 21 December 2017].

Murray-West, R. (2012) 'Wanted: One au pair. Result: 2,000 applications'. *The Telegraph* [Online], 1 October 2012. Available at: www.telegraph.co.uk/lifestyle/9579502/Wanted-one-au-pair.-Result-2000-applications.html [Accessed 20 December 2017].

Nesbitt-Ahmed, Z. (2016) *The Same but Different: The Everyday Lives of Female and Male Domestic Workers in Lagos, Nigeria*. PhD Thesis, London School of Economics and Political Science (LSE).

Newcombe, E. (2004) 'Temporary migration to the UK as an "Au pair": Cultural exchange or reproductive labour?' Sussex Migration Working Paper [Online], no. 21. Available at: www.sussex.ac.uk/migration/documents/mwp21.pdf [Accessed 21 December 2017].

O'Doherty, N. (2012) 'Britain's worst commutes: How workers spend 75 minutes a day getting to and from the office (and for women it's getting worse)'. *The Mail Online* [Online], 13 November 2012. Available at: www.dailymail.co.uk/news/article-2232243/London-commute-Workers-spend-75-minutes-day-getting-work-worse-women.html#ixzz3j5L78zar [Accessed 17 August 2015].

Oakley, A. (1976 [1974]) *Housewife*. London: Pelican Books.

Office for National Statistics (ONS) (2013) *Full Report: Women in the Labour Market*. ONS [Online], 25 September 2013. Available at: www.ons.gov.uk/ons/dcp171776_328352.pdf [Accessed 20 December 2017].

Office for National Statistics (ONS) (2016) 'Women shoulder the responsibility of unpaid work'. ONS [Online], 10 November 2016. Available at: http://visual.ons.gov.uk/the-value-of-your-unpaid-work/ [Accessed 20 December 2017].

Office for National Statistics (ONS) (2017) 'Household disposable income and inequality in the UK: Financial year ending 2016'. ONS [Online]. Available at: www.ons.gov.uk/peoplepopulationandcommunity/ personalandhouseholdfinances/incomeandwealth/bulletins/ householddisposableincomeandinequality/ financialyearending2016 [Accessed 11 December 2017].

Ozyegin, G. and Hondagneu-Sotelo, P. (2008) 'Conclusion: Domestic Work, Migration and New Gender Order in Contemporary Europe'. *In:* Lutz, H. (ed.), *Migration and Domestic Work: A European Perspective on a Global Theme*. Aldershot: Ashgate, pp195–208.

Parfitt, T. (2017) 'Middle class fears as foreign nannies "put off moving to UK" after Brexit vote'. *Express* [Online], 17 July 2017. Available at: www.express.co.uk/news/uk/829638/Brexit-au-pairs-nannies-childcare-European-Union-migration-Theresa-May-Brussels [Accessed 11 December 2017].

Parmar, P. (1982) 'Gender, race and class: Asian women in resistance'. Centre for Contemporary Cultural Studies (CCCS), *The Empire Strikes Back: Race and Racism in 70s Britain*. London: Hutchinson, pp235–274.

Parreñas, R.S. (2000) 'Migrant Filipina domestic workers and the international division of reproductive labor'. *Gender and Society* 14(4), pp560–580.

Parreñas, R.S. (2001) *Servants of Globalization: Women, Migration and Domestic Work*. Stanford, CA: Stanford University Press.

Pederson, S. and Smithson, J. (2013) 'Mothers with attitude: How the Mumsnet parenting forum offers space for new forms of femininity to emerge online'. *Women's Studies International Forum* 38, pp97–106.

Phizacklea, A. (1983) *One Way Ticket: Migration and Female Labour*. London: Routledge.

Pratt, G. (1999a) 'Is this Canada? Domestic workers' experiences in Vancouver BC'. *In:* Momsen, J.H. (Ed.), *Gender Migration and Domestic Service*. London: Routledge, pp23–42.

Pratt, G. (1999b) 'From registered nurse to registered nanny: Discursive geographies of Filipina domestic workers in Vancouver, B.C.'. *Economic Geography* [Online] 75, pp215–236. Available at: www.jstor.org/stable/144575 [Accessed 20 December 2017].

Quijano, A. (2000) 'Coloniality of power, Eurocentrism, and Latin America'. *Napantla: Views from the South* 1(3), pp533–580.

Ray, R. and Qayum, S. (2009) *Cultures of Servitude: Modernity, Domesticity and Class in India*. Stanford, CA: Stanford University Press.

Rohde-Abuba, C. (2016) 'The good girl from Russia can do it all'. *Nordic Journal of Migration Research* 6(4), pp215–223.

Rohde-Abuba, C. and Tkach, O. (2016) 'Finding oneself abroad'. *Nordic Journal of Migration Research* 6(4), pp193–198.

Rollins, J. (1985) *Between Women: Domestics and Their Employers*. Philadelphia, PA: Temple University Press.

Romero, M. (1992) *Maid in the USA*. New York and London: Routledge.

Romero, M., Preston, V. and Giles, W. (2014) 'Care work in a globalizing world'. *In:* Romero, M., Preston, V. and Giles, W. (Eds), *When Care Work Goes Global: Locating the Social Relations of Domestic Work*. Aldershot: Ashgate, pp1–28.

Rosenbaum, S. (2014) 'Domestic disturbances: Immigrant workers, middle-class employers, and the American dream in Los Angeles'. *In:* Romero, M., Preston, V. and Giles, W. (Eds), *When Care Work Goes Global: Locating the Social Relations of Domestic Work*. Aldershot: Ashgate, pp129–138.

Rumbelow, H. (2015) 'From thongs to drawers: The hidden underworld'. *The Times* [Online], 5 June 2015. Available at: www.thetimes.co.uk/article/from-thongs-to-drawers-the-hidden-underworld-oof2ztgfd9j [Accessed 20 December 2017].

Rutter, J. (2015) *Childcare Costs Survey 2015*. Family and Childcare Trust [Online]. Available at: www.familyandchildcaretrust.org/childcare-survey-2015 [Accessed 7 June 2018].

Salami, B. and Nelson, S. (2014) 'The downward occupational mobility of internationally educated nurses to domestic workers'. *Nursing Inquiry* 21, pp153–161.

Sambrook, P. (2002) *The Country House Servant*. Stroud: Sutton Publishing in association with The National Trust.

Sarti, R. (2014) 'Historians, social scientists, servants and domestic workers: Fifty years of research on domestic and care work'. *International Review of Social History* 59, pp279–314.

Scott, J. and Clery, E. (n.d.) 'Gender roles: An incomplete revolution?' Report from the British Attitudes Survey [Online]. Available at: www.bsa.natcen.ac.uk/media/38457/bsa30_gender_roles_final.pdf [Accessed 19 December 2017].

Smith, A. (2015) Part of the family? Experiences of au pairs in Ireland. *In:* Cox R. (Eds), *Au Pairs' Lives in Global Context: Sisters or Servants?* London: Palgrave Macmillan, pp170–184.

Smith, J.L. (2008) 'The silent abuse suffered by nannies and au pairs'. *The Telegraph* [Online], 6 September 2008. Available at: www.telegraph.co.uk/news/uknews/2695891/The-silent-abuse-suffered-by- nannies-and-au-pairs.html [Accessed 11 December 2017].

Souralová, A. (2012) 'Au pair' (Review). *Journal of Ethnic and Migration Studies* 38(6), pp1025–1027.

Steedman, C. (2009) *Labours Lost: Domestic Service and the Making of Modern England*. Cambridge: Cambridge University Press.

Stenum, H. (2010) 'Au pair migration and new inequalities: The transnational production of corruption'. *In:* Isaksen, L.W. (Ed.), *Global Care Work: Gender and Migration in Nordic Societies*. Lund: Nordic Academic Press, pp23–48.

Stewart, H. (2011) 'Who works the longest hours in Europe? Office for National Statistics Datablog'. *The Guardian* [Online], 8 December 2011. Available at: www.theguardian.com/news/datablog/2011/dec/08/europe-working-hours [Accessed 17 August 2015].

Stiell, B. and England, K. (1997) 'Domestic distinctions: Constructing difference among paid domestic workers in Toronto'. *Gender, Place and Culture* 4(3), pp339–359.

Stiell, B. and England, K. (1999) 'Jamaican domestics, Filipina housekeepers and English nannies: Representations of Toronto's foreign domestic workers'. *In:* Momsen, J.H. (Ed.), *Gender, Migration and Domestic Service.* London: Routledge, pp43–61.

Stratford, H. (2015) 'What is a live out au pair?' [Online]. Available at: www. startanaupairagency.co.uk/what-liveout-au-pair.html [Accessed 10 December 2017].

Stubberud, E. (2015a) 'Framing the au pair: Problems of sex, work and motherhood in Norwegian au pair documentaries'. *NORA Nordic Journal of Feminist and Gender Research* 23(2), pp125–139.

Stubberud, E. (2015b) '"It's not much": Affective (boundary) work in the au pair scheme'. *In:* Cox, R. (Ed.), *Au Pairs' Lives in Global Context: Sisters or Servants?* Basingstoke: Palgrave Macmillan, pp121–135.

Tkach, O. (2016) 'Now I know Norway from within'. *Nordic Journal of Migration Research* 6(4), pp224–233.

Tosh, J. (2007 [1999]) *A Man's Place: Masculinity and the Middle Class Home in Victorian England.* New Haven, CT, and London: Yale University Press.

Tronto, J.C. (1993) *Moral Boundaries: A Political Argument for an Ethic of Care.* Hove: Psychology Press.

Tronto, J.C. (2002) 'The "nanny" question in feminism'. *Hypatia* 17(2), pp34–51.

Tronto, J.C. (2006) 'Vicious and virtuous circles of care: When decent caring privileges social irresponsibility'. *In:* Hamington, M. and Miller, D.C. (Eds), *Socializing Care: Feminist Ethics and Public Issues.* Lanham, MD: Rowman & Littlefield.

Tronto, J.C. (2011) 'Caring about care workers: Caring solutions to an issue of global justice'. *In:* Mahon, R. and Robinson, F. (Eds), *The Global Political Economy of Care: Integrating Ethics and Social Politics.* Vancouver: University of British Columbia Press, pp162–177.

Tyner, J.A. (1999) The web-based recruitment of female foreign domestic workers in Asia. *Singapore Journal of Tropical Geography* 20(2), pp193–209.

Uhde, Z. (2016) 'Social bias within the institution of hired domestic care: Global interactions and migration'. *Civitas* [Online] 16(4), pp682–787. Available at: http://revistaseletronicas.pucrs.br/ojs/index.php/civitas/article/view/23051/15241 [Accessed 11 June 2018].

Vincent, C., Ball, S.J. and Kemp, S. (2004) 'The social geography of childcare: Making up a middle-class child'. *British Journal of the Sociology of Education* 25(2), pp229–244.

Walia, H. (2010) 'Transient servitude: Migrant labour in Canada and the apartheid of citizenship'. *Race and Class* 52(1), pp71–84.

Walling, A. (2005) 'Analysis in brief: Families and work'. *Labour Market Trends,* July, pp275–283.

Walter, B. (2001) *Outsiders Inside: Whiteness, Place and Irish Women.* London and New York: Routledge.

Walter, B. (2004) 'Irish domestic servants and English national identity'. *In:* Fauve-Chamaoux, A. (Ed.), *Domestic Service and the Formation of European Identity: Understanding the Globalization of Domestic Work, 16th–21st Centuries.* Bern: Peter Lang, pp471–488.

Walzer, M. (1983) *Spheres of Justice: A Defense of Pluralism and Equity.* New York: Basic Books.

Weaver, M. (2016) 'Polish envoy voices concerns about Brexit xenophobia after Harlow killing'. *The Guardian* [Online], 31 August 2016. Available at: www.theguardian. com/uk-news/2016/aug/31/mp-horror-over-killing-of-polish-man-in-harlow-robert-halfon [Accessed 19 December 2017].

Webster, W. (1998) *Imagining Home: Gender, 'Race', and National Identity, 1945–64.* Hove: Psychology Press.

Williams, F. and Gavanas, A. (2008) 'The intersection of childcare regimes and migration regimes: A three-country study'. *In:* Lutz, H. (Ed.), *Migration and Domestic Work: A European Perspective on a Global Theme.* Aldershot: Ashgate, pp13–28.

Wills, J., May, J., Datta, K., Evans, Y., Herbert, J. and McIlwaine, C. (2009) 'London's migrant division of labour'. *European Urban and Regional Studies* 16(3), pp257–271.

Wygant, D. (2013) 'Why London is the world's most stimulating city'. *The Huffington Post* [Online], 20 January 2013. www.huffingtonpost.com/david-wygant/london-travel-visit_b_2147565.html [Accessed 11 June 2018].

Yeates, N. (2009) *Globalizing Care Economies and Migrant Workers: Explorations in Global Care Chains.* Basingstoke: Palgrave.

Yeates, N. (2012) 'Global care chains: A state-of-the-art review and future directions in care tansnationalization research'. *Global Networks* 12(2), pp135–154.

Yodanis, C. and Lauer, S.R. (1997) 'Foreign visitor, exchange student or family member? A study of au pair policies in the United States, United Kingdom and Australia'. *International Journal of Sociology and Social Policy* 25(9), pp41–64.

Øien, C. (2009) *On Equal Terms? An Evaluation of the Norwegian Au Pair Scheme.* Oslo: Fafo.

INDEX

Note: Page numbers in italic indicate tables.

ZED

Zed is a platform for marginalised voices across the globe.

It is the world's largest publishing collective and a world leading example of alternative, non-hierarchical business practice.

It has no CEO, no MD and no bosses and is owned and managed by its workers who are all on equal pay.

It makes its content available in as many languages as possible.

It publishes content critical of oppressive power structures and regimes.

It publishes content that changes its readers' thinking.

It publishes content that other publishers won't and that the establishment finds threatening.

It has been subject to repeated acts of censorship by states and corporations.

It fights all forms of censorship.

It is financially and ideologically independent of any party, corporation, state or individual.

Its books are shared all over the world.

www.zedbooks.net
@ZedBooks